Montgomery Ward's Mail-Order Homes

A History and Field Guide to Wardway Homes

Dale Patrick Wolicki
Rosemary Thornton

Gentle Beam Publications

Norfolk, Virginia

Requests for permission to reprint can be sent to:

Gentle Beam Publications
P. O. Box 3472
Portsmouth, VA 23701
gentlebeam@hotmail.com

ISBN: 978-0-9715588-6-1

Printed in the United States of America
June 2010, First Edition

Table of Contents

Montgomery Ward's Mail-Order Homes, A History and Field Guide to Wardway Homes

Rosemary Thornton and Dale Wolicki

Introduction by Rose Thornton

A cozy comfortable home, a bower of roses, a patch of delectable vegetables, your own car, a garage to match your home! What man or woman has not dreamed of such a home? Away from high rents and landlords. A safe and happy place to raise children – a cheerful home where the health and happiness of the entire family are raised to new heights of enjoyment. That is the heritage you may now claim. This far away dream is now a close-up reality.

1927 Wardway Homes catalog

A few weeks after *The New York Times* did a feature story on my work with Sears Homes, I received a handwritten letter from a woman in central Kansas. She'd enclosed a picture of a spacious early 1900s home with the caption "Sears House." Many years earlier, she'd been told that her house had come from the Sears Roebuck mail-order catalog. She was writing to ask if I could identify the particular model.

Studying the picture, I knew it wasn't a Sears House, yet it looked familiar. Where had I seen this house? After a few hours it dawned on me: I'd seen this home's identical twin in Grafton, Illinois (a small town in southwestern Illinois). Methodically turning the pages of various mail order catalogs, I came upon the picture of the Montgomery Ward *Farmland*. The model name was well-selected; it looked like the typical Midwestern farm home. I grabbed the phone and called my friend and co-author, Dale Wolicki.

A Montgomery Ward *Farmland* in Grafton, Illinois circa 1918 (photograph by Rose Thornton).

"What do you know about the Farmland?" I asked him without wasting time on cursory greetings. Dale responded by telling me that it was one of the more popular models for Montgomery Ward but it disappeared from the catalogs after World War One.

"They had some really ugly houses in those first catalogs," Dale replied. "The Farmland wasn't a bad-looking house and had lots of space and was affordably priced."

When I related this information to the homeowner, she was surprised but happy. Years later, after giving more than 200 lectures in a dozen states, I would come to learn that this was a very common mistake. About three-fourths of the people who think they live in a Sears mail-order home are wrong. Most often I find that these folks do have a mail-order home, but it's not a home that came from Sears. Folks may remember that it was a kit home and that it was ordered from a catalog and arrived in a boxcar, but the rest of the details get a little fuzzy through the passing decades.

Throughout much of the 20th Century, Sears and Wards were staunch competitors, selling tens of thousands of items in their general merchandise mail order catalogs. Sears survived; Montgomery Ward is gone. In the early 1900s, these two companies also became competitors in the kit home arena. Looking strictly at the numbers, one would say that Sears "won" because they sold about 70,000 kit homes, while Montgomery Ward probably sold fewer than 30,000 of their Wardway Homes.

Despite this relatively small number, the homes sold by Montgomery Ward were an important part of America's kit home story. The people who own these Wardway Homes are enthusiastic and passionate and eager to learn more about the unique history of their home. And that's the reason for this field guide; to create a reference book for people who want to know more about the mail-order homes of Montgomery Ward.

When Dale and I started publishing books and articles on kit homes, there was very little information available, but as interest in this subject increased, people contacted us and shared their stories, their historic documents, blueprints, catalogs and more. It's our hope that this book will spur interest and bring forth new information about Wardway Homes.

A Note about Catalog Illustrations and Floor Plans

Montgomery Ward mail-order home catalogs are difficult to find, more so than the catalogs of their competitors (such as Sears and Aladdin). Fortunately, Dale had the majority of Wardway Home catalogs. As this book was in its final edit he acquired a rare 1911 *Building Plans of Modern Homes* but has yet to find a 1913 *Building Plans of Modern Homes* which is most likely a reprint of the 1912 catalog.

With few exceptions, most of the illustrations and floor plans featured in this guide have been digitally enhanced. After 80 years, many pages were discolored and torn and faded. In many of the early catalogs, the floor plans were so difficult to read that they had to be redrawn. Alterations to the illustrations or floor plan were done only to enhance clarity and they remain true to the original catalog images.

The Authors

Rose Thornton is the author of five books, including *The Houses That Sears Built*, *Finding the Houses That Sears Built* and *California's Kit Homes*.

Rose has traveled to 24 states to give 200 lectures on Sears Homes, from Bungalow Heaven in Los Angeles to The Smithsonian in Washington, DC. She has addressed a wide variety of audiences from architectural preservationists in Boston, St. Louis and Chicago to kit home enthusiasts in small towns across America. She's appeared on PBS (History Detectives), A&E (Biography), CBS (Sunday Morning News) and her book was featured in its own category on Jeopardy.

Her work has been featured in the Wall Street Journal, New York Times, Christian Science Monitor, Washington Post, L. A. Times, Dallas Morning News, Old House Journal, American Bungalow, Blue Ridge Country and about 100 other publications. Twice in the last three years, the story of her unique career was picked up by the AP and in May 2009, she was interviewed for BBC Radio.

Dale Wolicki is a volunteer with the Bay County Historical Society (Bay City, Michigan), promoting the preservation local pre-cut housing companies Aladdin, Lewis-Liberty, and Sterling. He is also an authority on the mail-order homes of Gordon-Van Tine (www.gordonvantime.com) and other smaller housing manufacturers.

Wolicki has contributed to numerous books, newspapers and magazine articles. He is the author of *The Historic Architecture of Bay City, Michigan*, and co-author of *The Sears Book of Barns, a Reprint of the 1919 Catalog* and *California's Kit Homes: a Reprint of the 1925 Pacific Ready Cut Homes Catalog*. His collection of mail-order housing catalogs is a frequent source of reference for researchers, scholars and reporters.

Although he designs the occasional house, Wolicki spends much of his time site planning, project managing and obtaining zoning approvals for client projects, and restoring his 1928 bungalow in Oxford, Michigan. He has a Masters in Architecture from Lawrence Technological University in Southfield, Michigan.

Acknowledgements

Cindy and Roy Cooper, who allowed Dale to photograph their 1912 Farmland in Ewen, Michigan. Mary Rowse, Historian in Chevy Chase, Maryland, and an authority on mail-order homes in the Washington D.C. area. Ken Wheeler, who accompanied Dale on trips to photograph mail-order houses, most notably the summer of 2009 while Dale limped around on a broken foot. Barbara Brownell, Historian in South Bend, Indiana and an authority on mail-order homes in the area. Gail Ringer and his family, who allowed Rose to photograph their 1916 Ohio in Quinter, Kansas. Ersela Jordan, who invited Rose to tour Beckley, West Virginia and its collection of mail-order homes. Rose's husband, Wayne.

And Rebecca Hunter, noted authority on mail-order homes, a frequent companion on trips to find mail-order homes, and our good friend. She provided numerous photographs and documents for this book.

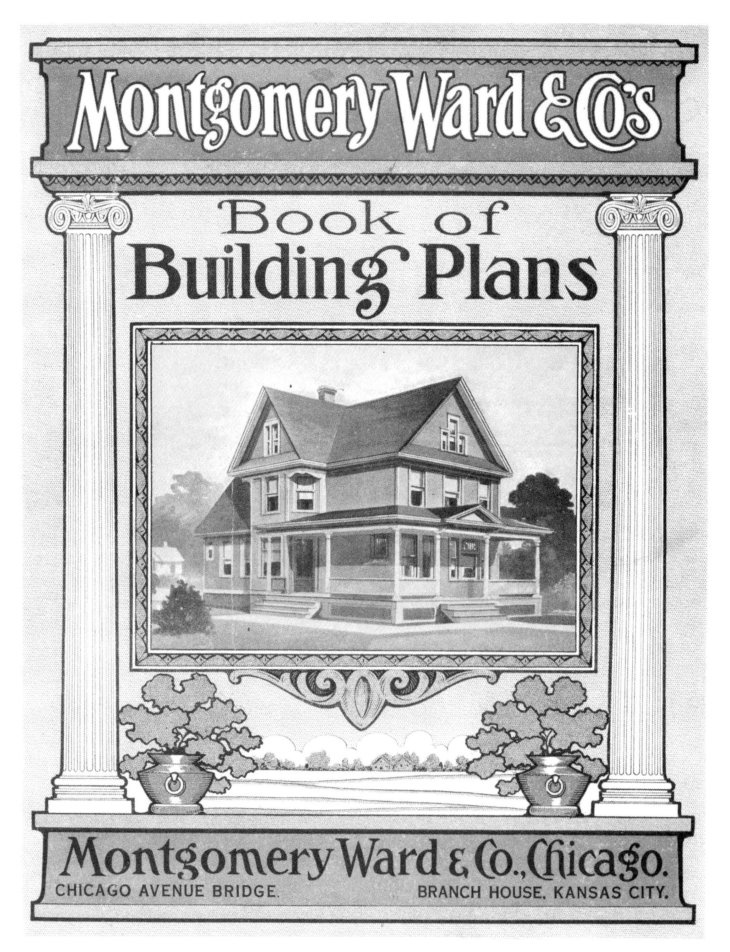

The cover of the 1909 Montgomery Ward *Book of Building Plans*.

The Catalogs

At the turn of the century Sears and Montgomery Ward published several specialty catalogs including building materials. In 1908 Sears started offering house plans, and Montgomery Ward followed in 1909. For one dollar, hopeful homeowners could buy blueprints, together with a detailed inventory listing the building materials that'd be needed to build their own home. An enclosed order form enabled buyers another option: They could order their lumber, hardware, paint, roofing and other building materials from Montgomery Ward.

Ward's first mail-order homes catalog featured 34 pages and 24 houses, as well as a few outbuildings, barns and chicken coops. In characteristic puffery Ward stated, "We have here produced a collection of desirable buildings with the maximum of architectural beauty". The house featured on the cover was Design No. 108, a non-descript, rather dated-looking Victorian home with a wrap-around porch, pedimented entry, Palladian windows, parlor and living room and more than 2,000 square feet of living area.

A blueprint detail circa 1912 for *Model #185*
(Thanks to Rebecca Hunter for this illustration).

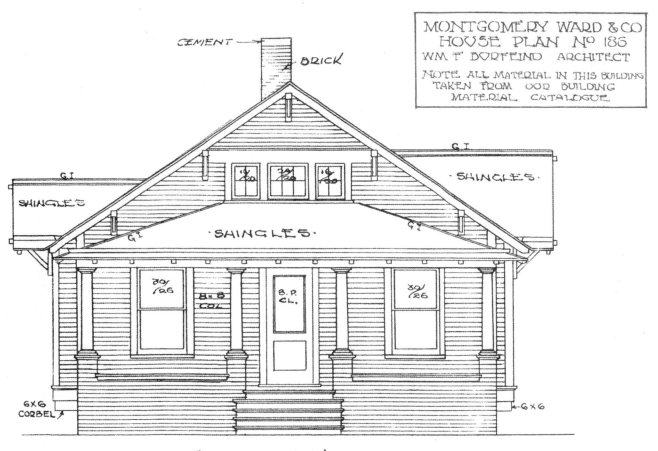

· FRONT · ELEVATION ·

William Radford and House Plan Books

The majority of houses built in the first half of the 20th Century were not pre-cut houses, nor were they designed by architects. Most were built from blueprints purchased through books or magazines. The leader is this field was William Radford of Chicago. A builder by trade, his first book Radford American Homes (1902) featured perspective views and floor plans for 100 houses. Radford's blueprints cost buyers as little as $5, although for an additional fee his architectural staff would modify designs to meet the customers specific needs. Among the customers of Radford were Sears and Montgomery Ward.

Radford's success lead to more of these plan books, including Radford's Ideal Homes (1903), Radford's Bungalow (1908), Radford's Cement Homes (1909), and Radford's Portfolio of Plans (1909). His most influential books, The Steel Square and Its Uses (1907) and Practical Carpentry (1907), were required reading for apprentice carpenters and high school boys taking industrial art courses. His monthly publication (American Builder) provided the building industry with news on residential and commercial construction. Radford retired in the late 1920s, but his books and magazines remained standard reference materials until the Depression.

Other companies that specialized in house plan publications included M.L. Keith of Minneapolis Minnesota (1900-1930), the Architects Small House Service Bureau (1920-1940), C.L. Bowes of Chicago (1910-1925), Garlinghouse of Topeka Kansas (1920-present), Home Builders of Chicago (1925-1940), the Southern Pine Association (1920-1930), and Standard Homes of Washington D.C. (1920-1970).

With some minor cosmetic changes Radford's *Design #2003-B (above)* became Montgomery Ward's *Model #100 (below)* (1909 *Radford's Portfolio of Plans* and 1909 Montgomery Ward *Book of Building Plan*),

The catalog promised that the typical home-buyer would save about one-third the cost with a Montgomery Ward home compared to traditional construction. Accompanying text explained the reason for this savings: "The factory that supplies us is the largest factory in the world. They buy millions of feet of lumber at a time, enough so that the lumber may be thoroughly air dried before being kiln dried. We sell to you at a price which your local dealer can not meet because he would have to pay as much or more to the jobber".

The ad copy that describes these early homes makes for interesting reading. According to the description of Design No. 101, houses of this style always "give the impression that within their walls live a home-loving, prosperous family". Design No. 109 featured a back stairway, which "eliminates the necessity of the farm hands tracking through the front part of the house". Design No. 119 featured four gables and a dormer that would "relieve [the house] of the dry goods box appearance so common with square houses". Another modest home was featured with this comment: "Especially designed for homesteaders, this little cottage was designed for those who do not wish to go to the expense of building a full-sized cottage or house. The principal merit of the building is the cheapness of its construction". Price: $323.

The 1911 *Book of Building Plans* offered the same model houses as 1909 and 1910, but the house featured on the cover was their stylish Arts & Crafts Model #150. The 1912 catalog, renamed *Building Plans of Modern Homes* was expanded to 80 pages with 66 models. Among the new models were two "portable" homes and two portable garages. Frequently described as "panelized" buildings, they consisted of 4' wide and 8' tall prefabricated panels of wall, windows, door or roof and joined using bolts. Ward's contracted with Mershon & Morley of Saginaw, Michigan to produce these panelized buildings.

1914 *Building Plans of Modern Homes* catalog.

History of Aaron Montgomery Ward's Store

In the mid-1800s, Aaron Montgomery Ward was a traveling salesman growing weary of selling his wares from a horse and buggy. He decided that there must be a better way to earn a living, and in 1871, invested his life savings in a new business idea: Direct sales, via mail order. His first business was short-lived, destroyed in the Great Chicago Fire (October 1871) but Ward was back in business by the summer of 1872. His first catalog had only one page and 163 items, most of which were priced under $4. By 1875 the Montgomery Ward catalog was 72 pages. Over the next 20 years, the catalog was improved and enlarged. In 1895, the United States Postmaster reported that the Montgomery Ward was their largest patron. By the turn of the 20th Century, Montgomery Ward & Co. was America's number one retailer. After 50 years of mail-order catalog sales Montgomery Ward opened its first retail store in 1926, following the lead of Sears (who opened its first retail store in 1925). Under the direction of Ward's president George Everett, the retailer opened hundreds of new stores throughout the country.

In 1929, the bottom fell out of the stock market. Within a few months, those hemorrhagic losses had trickled down to the level of retail sales. Throughout 1930 and 1931, Business Week and other financial magazines reported slowing sales and a deflating dollar. Ward's sales dropped 26% in 1930 and 1931 with more than 450 of their 600 retail stores operating in the red. In 1931 and 1932 combined, the retail giant sustained losses of more than $14 million. Montgomery Ward was in dire need of finding someone that could help their company navigate the crisis. According to corporate legend, Chicago business man Sewell Avery, President of US Gypsum, was wooed to Wards during a leisurely Sunday golf game, where he was promised $100,000 in salary plus stock options. November 1931, he officially took his place as chairman of the board, chief executive officer and general manager of Montgomery Ward & Company. A scant two months later, Sewell became company president. Unprofitable departments were closed. He lured top executives away from Sears, negotiated new contracts with cash-strapped suppliers and turned to outside factories to produce products for less money than Ward's own factories.

By the mid-20th Century, competitors such Sears, Penney's, and Macy's, had moved from their downtown locations to the suburbs but Montgomery Ward was slow to follow. Economic historians note this decision as that which brought Ward's demise. In 1976 the cash-strapped retailer was purchased by Mobil Oil but even an influx of cash and new ownership wasn't enough to save the company. In 1985, the hallmark of Ward's business, the mail order catalog, was discontinued. A bankruptcy in 1997 and the closing of 250 stores didn't save Ward. In December 2000, Montgomery Ward announced that their remaining 250 retail stores would permanently close. In 2004, catalog marketer Direct Marketing Services purchased the Montgomery Ward name and launched it as an online retailer *Wards.com.*

Information taken from *The History and Progress of Montgomery Ward and Company* and *The First Hundred Years Are the Toughest*

Renamed *The Book of Homes* the 1915 catalog, and the identical 1916 catalog, featured a color cover with their stylish Model # 200 bungalow perched atop a hill. Although many of the older outdated Radford designs remained, new designs (such as Arts & Crafts homes and bungalows) were introduced. In this catalog, prices were rounded off to the nearest dollar. "For this price" the copy read, "we will furnish all the material to build this home, consisting of all lumber, lath, shingles, finishing lumber, flooring, doors, windows, frames, trim, china closet, medicine cabinet, mantel and grate, hardware, pipe and gutter and painting material. We absolutely guarantee the amount of material we furnish to be sufficient to build the home according to our plans and specifications."

In 1917, the name *Wardway Homes* made its first appearance and the houses were assigned names instead of numbers, and 22 of the 45 designs offered could be ordered with pre-cut lumber. Aladdin Homes had introduced pre-cut mail-order homes in 1906 and as their sales doubled and then tripled, larger companies introduced pre-cut homes. Unlike Sears, who invested heavily in new mills and an architectural staff, Montgomery Ward chose another route. It subcontracted its orders for pre-cut homes to an eastern Iowa lumber mill that offered its own line of mail-order homes, Gordon-VanTine. Founded in 1908, Gordon-VanTine offered catalogs of building materials and house plans much like Sears and Montgomery Ward.

In the spring of 1917 the United States entered World War One. Montgomery Ward continued to receive orders, forwarding them to Gordon-VanTine but restrictions on building materials and a shortage of railroad cars hampered delivery. The 1918 catalog was essentially a revised edition of the previous catalog, the most remarkable difference being a 30% price increase, inflicted by wartime shortages. The Iowa jumped from $981 to $1393, a 42% increase. The Superior went from $973 to $1209, a 24% increase. The Suburban was up from $1393 to $2014, an increase of 44%.

When Did They Introduce Pre-Cut Homes?

Aladdin Homes - 1906
Lewis Homes - 1913
Sterling Homes - 1914
Sears Roebuck Homes - 1915
Gordon-VanTine - 1916
Harris Homes - 1916
Montgomery Ward - 1917
Pacific Homes - 1919
Bennett Homes - 1919

1915 *Book of Homes* catalog.

With the end of World War One, American men and women put their best financial, physical and emotional energies into house, home and family. Magazines and newspapers faithfully and consistently pushed and promoted the government's message that true patriotism could best be shown by investing yourself in the community through home ownership. But there was a problem: a massive housing shortage. Experts estimated that one or two million homes were needed immediately.

In response, the Department of Commerce orchestrated a campaign to promote the construction of homes in both public and private organizations. Many cities established non-profit housing corporations that purchased land and built homes. Companies large and small acquired land to build homes for their employees. General Motors built several neighborhoods of pre-cut homes near their factories in Michigan and Wisconsin. Goodyear Tire & Rubber ordered materials from Sears, and built their own subdivision near their plant in Youngstown, Ohio.

The post-war building boom brought a surge in prices that caused Wardway Homes to stop printing prices in their catalog. Instead they inserted flyers listing model prices for the next thirty or sixty days. "There is not much prospect of a drop in building material prices", noted a price list inserted into the May 1919 catalog. "The advances on lumber, millwork, etc., in the past few years, were largely due to the rising cost of labor. This cost will undoubtedly continue. The resumption of building and the re-opening of the export market (Europe) is bound to create an increased demand, which, of course, will mean still other advances. We advise you therefore, to order early if you expect to build this year".

By 1921, four years of high inflation began to take its toll on the economy. Interest rates soared and customers cut back. Builders and manufacturers, most of whom had purchased significant amounts of building materials on credit, slashed prices. By the summer of 1921 deflation had wiped out post-war increases. "We guarantee that these prices will be the lowest quoted on Wardway Homes during 1921," noted the price insert, "They are the same prices which we quoted in 1918 and we believe a comparison will prove them to be the greatest home values being offered this year."

1918 *Wardway Homes* catalog.

Sometime during 1921, Gordon-VanTine took over Wardway Homes in its entirety, including house design and catalog production. The 1922 *Wardway Homes* catalog showed a marked improvement over earlier catalogs. Uninspired, dated, and tired housing designs were removed and newer designs introduced. Foursquares, bungalows and modest Arts & Crafts homes were offered.

Many of the designs offered by these two companies were identical homes with different names. For instance, The Wardway *Danbury*, an attractive and well-designed bungalow, was the same as the Gordon-VanTine *Model #537*. The *Bellevue*, a spacious Wardway foursquare was identical to the Gordon-VanTine *Model #508*.

Of the 70 models featured in the 1922 Wardway catalog, about half were pulled right from the pages of the Gordon-Van Tine catalog. Even the opening pages extolling the virtues of the pre-cut system were identical to that found in the Gordon-VanTine catalog. The biggest change in the 1922 Wardway Homes catalog was that all the houses were now offered pre-cut, with two or three exceptions.

The 1922 Wardway Homes catalog featured the *Lexington* on its cover.

Home No. 537 and 537B. Material Furnished Either Ready Cut or Not Ready Cut

With some different landscaping Gordon-VanTine's *Model #537* (above) became Montgomery Ward's *Danbury* (left) (1923 Gordon-VanTine and 1923 Montgomery Ward catalogs).

The format established in the 1922 catalog was used through 1928. During this time a few models were dropped and a few added, but the overall layout of the catalog remained unchanged. Newer models tended to be at the front of the catalog. The *Rochelle* and *Beverly* were two-story, three bedroom Colonial homes that would fit perfectly into any subdivision. At $2072 and $2065 they were among the most expensive homes in the 1925 catalog. The smallest and most basic of pre-cut Wardway homes, the *Pullman*, a 20' x 26' four room (no bathroom), one-story, hip roofed box, could still be found at the back of the catalog. At $812 it was the most affordable house in the 1925 Wardway Homes catalog.

The most notable change was in 1927 when Montgomery Ward introduced their mortgage program. "Easiest Payments!" noted a faux sticker on the cover of the catalog. "Our terms are easiest because the low selling prices of our Wardway Homes have reduced every monthly payment to the smallest amount possible on a home designed for permanence. Our Loan Plan - which enables you to use our money at a very low interest rate - saves the average purchaser hundreds of dollars".

In 1929 the catalog was revised yet again, adopting a large 8-1/2" x 11" format that allowed for more detailed descriptions of the houses and benefits of buying a Wardway Home. The 110-page catalog, which featured the new *Cedars* model on the cover, featured 66 models, the majority of which were existing models with new names. Approximately a dozen homes were new models, larger homes designed in the popular Neo-Tudor and Colonial revival style. The back pages of the catalog were dedicated to the selection of bathroom fixtures, interior and exterior doors, paint, hardware, bathroom fixtures, heating systems, woodwork and flooring, and light fixtures.

The 1927 Wardway Homes catalog featured a new cover with the popular *Cambridge* model and a faux sticker reagrding the new mortgage plan.

The 1929 and 1930 *Wardway Homes* catalog.

The 1930 catalog was merely a revision of the earlier catalog and was probably at the printers when the stock market dropped in late 1929. To boost sales Montgomery Ward inserted flyers into the 1930 catalog introducing a new program: Wardway *Certified Contractors* were available to oversee construction, or manage construction of the entire house. With their generous mortgage and certified contractor programs Wardway Home orders increased despite the slump in traditional residential construction during 1930 and 1931.

The most expensive home in the 1931 catalog, which was yet again a revision of the previous catalog, was the *Larchmont*, a fine-looking eight-room, one-and-a-half bath Dutch Colonial with 2,020 square feet, replete with cut-out shutters, flower boxes, laundry chute, and breakfast room (with built-in china hutch). For $60 a month, you could be "the aristocrat of any neighborhood." At the other end of the spectrum was the *Plymouth* ($1278), the *Lawndale* ($1,236) and the *Rosedale* ($998 or $20 a month). The Rosedale was a wee tiny cottage with a mere 520 square feet and two bedrooms that measured only 8 feet by 8 feet. The 1931 catalog described it as "a real bargain...not a flimsy summer cottage but a real, finished, well constructed house that will outlive many other homes built today."

Although Wardway Home sales for the start of 1931 were above 1930 and 1929, by the fall of 1931 sales dropped severely. Montgomery Ward decided to use their leftover 1931 catalogs for the upcoming 1932 building season, inserting updated price sheets that reflected the drop in prices. Wardway Homes closed before any catalogs were mailed out for the spring 1932 building season.

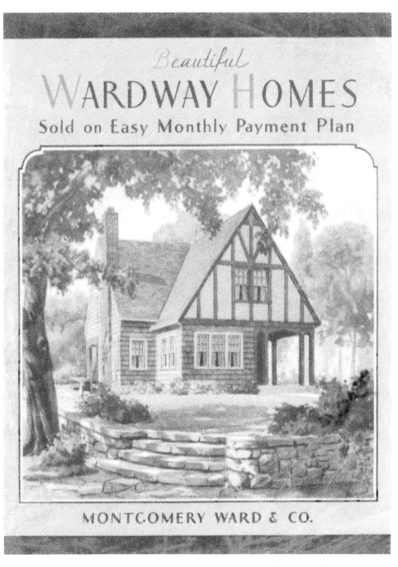

1931 *Wardway Homes* catalog featured the Tudor Revival style *Devonshire* on its cover.

1931 *Wardway Homes* catalog.

Advantages of Pre-cut Homes

In 1927 Wardway estimated that the average two-bedroom home built by traditional methods required about 4,000 cuts with a saw. As most construction sites did not have electrical service, yet alone electrical appliances such as the portable circular saws, all the cuts would have had to be made by hand, a time consuming exhausting process. Joists and wall studs required simple square cuts but rafters and staircases required complex cuts. It was not unusual to find the construction site littered with lumber scraps.

The traditional builder purchased rough lumber from the local lumber yard, and could order millwork, doors and window sash if they did not carry any in stock. The lumber yard would have roofing felt and shingles but anything unusual or special had to be ordered or purchased from the local roofing company. Likewise the local lumber company carried a limited selection or paints and hardware, so anything else had to be ordered or purchased from the local hardware store. It was not unusual for construction of the house to be delayed while waiting on delivery of building materials.

Although the traditional builder might have blueprints he purchased from a plan book publisher such as Radford or Garlinghouse, it was also likely he was working from rough sketches he himself had prepared. Relying on his own judgment, it was not unusual for the finished home to have a less than professional appearance.

All in all, traditional residential construction was uncoordinated and wasteful, creating unnecessary cost and delays that the home builder paid for.

The WARDWAY Ready-Cut System saves about 4000 hand-saw cuts by carpenters. Think of the expensive hours of time this saves you!

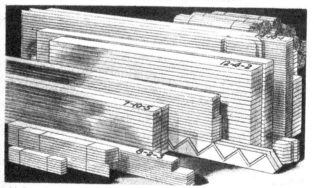

Ten carpenters, sawing as fast as possible, would lose in a race with this automatic cutting machine. Your labor bill is much lower!

Machine Cutting and Accurate Fitting as shown in this picture and the one below, assures greater strength, saves many hours and avoids waste.

1927 *Wardway Homes* catalog.

Wardway Homes referred to their houses as ready-cut, a system they claimed would save the builder thirty to forty percent in costs compared to traditional construction. All designs were standardized to maximize efficiency and reduce waste in materials and labor. Lumber and hardware were purchased in bulk. Wardway employed skilled workers and special machines to cut difficult pieces such as rafters. All lumber was pre-cut to length, guaranteed to fit, ready to nail and labeled for easy assembly. The pre-cut package was shipped with all the materials needed to build to the house (not including masonry or concrete), and referenced to blueprints and an instruction book.

"One Order Brings You Everything!" exclaimed the 1931 Wardway Homes catalog. "At Ward's, in one single order you can get everything you need to complete your home with the exception of masonry materials…. Architectural services, plans and specifications, all lumber and millwork, heating, plumbing, window shades, screens, storm sash, hardware, electric wiring and fixtures; even electric power plant, septic tank, pumps, electric refrigerator, garage, etc., … you do not have to deal with a dozen different concerns and have a dozen different bills of varying amounts and perhaps of unexpectedly large size, all due at about the same time. When you send your single order to Ward's, you deal with one concern only. You know in advance exactly what your complete home will cost."

As in a Skyscraper, Machine-Cut Lengths and Joints Insure Accuracy and Unusual Structural Strength

A WARDWAY Ready-Cut Home is tight-built, solid, strong. You know that joists, studding and rafters will fit with the exactness of the mill-cut steel beams that swing so neatly into place on every skyscraper frame—because machine sawing of every angle and notch insures unfailing accuracy. Your home, built of such precisely fitted joints, will stand the wear of years with far less depreciation than ordinary homes built with hand cut material. Contractors who have erected WARDWAY Homes freely praise the soundness of construction and admit openly the superiority of the WARDWAY Ready-Cut method.

WARDWAY Ready-Cut Homes are so easy to build that thousands do all or part of the work themselves. Every detail of the job is plainly described on easy-to-follow blueprints. Any man who uses tools can do a large part of the work. Every piece of material is marked and numbered for the place where it will be used. The numbers on the material correspond with the numbers on the detailed easy-to-understand building plans we furnish. Every stairway, all pieces for window and door frames, all rafters and joists are cut, marked and bundled—easy to find and easy to nail in place.

1931 Wardway Homes catalog.

The benefits of the pre-cut house were explained in the 1924 Wardway Homes catalog. "One man with the help of the wonderful electrically driven machines in the mill does the work of ten carpenters on the job. That in a nutshell is the secret of the savings of the Wardway system. It has been calculated by experts that an average of 17% of the lumber delivered to erect a house the old way was wasted. An average of three cuts are made in each piece of lumber...if done by hand [this creates] innumerable chances for mistakes. The Wardway Ready-Cut System of exact measurements and scientific cutting eliminates all chance for mistakes".

Any man who could "use tools" was able to erect a Wardway Home and 75% of customers "do all or part of the work themselves", noted the 1929 catalog. Montgomery Ward assured the customer that there'd be no "confusion or hunting for pieces" and later on the same page was this promise: "All small pieces are bundled and marked, such as framing for window and door openings, dormers, sheathing for gables, etc. All large pieces are plainly marked and all pieces which are duplicated (such as studs, joists), are marked alike and are interchangeable".

The instruction booklet, offering guidance on everything from laying out sills to the correct spacing of nails, was surprisingly thin by today's standards. Montgomery Ward expected that at least one member of the construction crew would have experience with residential construction, even if it was the customer's father or uncle. The instruction books were not specific to the individual house designs. The family building a one-story bungalow might be a little confused by the detailed instruction on staircase assembly!

A complete set of instructions also goes with these plans, telling in simple, easily understood terms, just how to go about each step in the process. It is so simple and so thorough that many of our customers with little experience have been able to build their own homes without any difficulty. Your carpenter will find all his questions answered before they arise and you yourself can follow the building and know just what is going on and whether or not it is right all the way through. Many of our customers assure us that this feature of Wardway Homes and instructions alone was worth hundreds of dollars when building (1922 Wardway Homes,).

These Specifications and Instructions are complete in every respect and cover all items required in the construction of this house, recommending the best materials to be used in the building and the correct method of construction and application of same. A good set of specifications is a very important matter, as they in a large measure protect your best interests, and if they are carefully followed will insure the best results obtainable. You should, therefore, be sure that you use the material exactly as directed. There is a piece of material for every part of the building – be sure that you find the right piece before putting it in place. Read the instructions carefully before you start to build. The more carefully you follow them, the more quickly and easily will your building be erected. (1930 Instructions for Erecting Wardway Ready-Cut Home).

1929 Wardway Homes catalog.

Montgomery Ward & Co.~ Please send me
FREE ESTIMATE
of delivered price of the _____ Wardway Home
(Give name of home you like best)

I UNDERSTAND that by obtaining complete information regarding the home I have named above, I shall not be put to any expense nor shall I be obligated in any way whatever.

I also understand that upon receiving this request you will let me know the price of the home named above, freight prepaid; and if I so desire, you will tell me what the amount of each monthly payment would be if I were to buy this home from you on easy payments.

(NOTE: If you desire to buy on our Easy Payment Plan, fill out the reverse side of this sheet in addition to giving the information asked for below.)

The type of construction in which I am interested is . . . . . ☐ Ready-Cut
☐ Not Ready-Cut

I should also like to know your prices on the following "options," as described in your WARDWAY Homes Catalogue for the home named above.

☐ Hot Water Heat	☐ Oak Option	☐ Do you wish us to include a Garage in your estimate?
☐ Steam Heat	☐ Asphalt Shingle Option	
☐ Hot Air Pipe Furnace	☐ Shade Option	Which one? _____
☐ Pipeless Furnace	☐ Screen Option	
☐ "Blackstone" Plumbing Outfit	☐ Storm Sash Option	Size? _____
☐ "La Salle" Plumbing Outfit		
☐ "Sherman" Plumbing Outfit	☐ Knob and Tube } Electric Wiring	I expect to start building about
☐ Laundry Tubs	☐ BX Cable }	(date) _____

Be Sure to Indicate Below the Plan of Payment You Prefer
(For complete explanation of these five plans of payment, see Page 5)

☐ Easy Monthly Payments
If you desire to know what your monthly payments would be on this home, mark "X" in the above space and answer Confidential Questions on back of this blank.

☐ Full Cash With Order

☐ One-fourth Cash, Balance C. O. D.

☐ The "Ninety-Day" Plan

☐ The "Statement of Deposit" Plan

I understand this does not obligate me in any way

Your Name _____

Address _____

Shipping Point
{ If different
from postoffice }
_____

← TEAR OUT ON DOTTED LINE

SEE OTHER SIDE

{ Page 1 }

Inquiry Form inserted in the 1928 *Wardway Homes* catalog.

Building a Wardway Home

A detailed article in the March 1930 *Business Week* provides insight into the process of ordering and building a kit home. In the example, the homeowner hired Sears or Montgomery Ward to act as general contractor:

> When John Jones fills out the Information Blank, telling just what kind of a home he wants, he gets a definite proposition on it. If he accepts this proposition his references are examined. If he is found deserving of long-term credit, a contract is written.

> If the ground on which the house is to be built is 25% or more of the total value when improved, then no down payment is required. Otherwise, Jones must make up the difference in cash. Monthly payments begin four months later. The mail order houses [Ward and Sears] have connections with local real estate men, banks, and building and loan associations, through which reliable appraisals of vacant lots are secured. If Jones, a few years later, desires to pay up balance due, he may take a discount of 1% per year for time yet to run on that portion of the cost which represents materials - as much as 13% if he pays at the end of two years

> Construction now begins. Building time will run from 100 to 150 days. The average time is 90 days. The mail order house acts as a general contractor, subletting jobs to local contractors, many of whom have been erecting ready-cut homes for years. Inspectors, attached to the various sales offices (Ward had 15 sales offices in five states in 1930), visit each job as work progresses. Frequency depends somewhat upon the job and contractor. The average is one inspection a week.

The back cover of the 1931 Wardway Homes catalog featured a blank space onto which the regional office pasted a list of local offices, in this example for eastern Ohio.

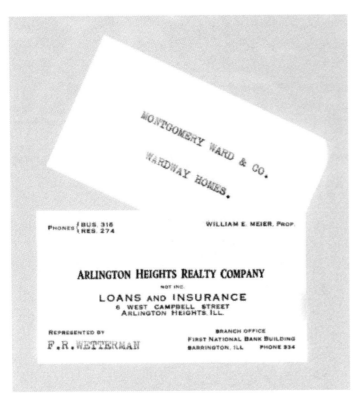

Although the majority of homes were sold through their catalog or store salesrooms, Montgomery Ward allowed independent salesmens such as realtors to sell Wardway Homes, for which they were typically paid a small commission. This card was found tucked inside a 1931 catalog.

Order One House in which to Live and another to Rent

A sidebar on page 43 of the 1919 Wardway Homes catalog promised that you could grow rich if you emptied out your savings account and bought several Wardway Homes. The inset explained that most savings accounts brought in a measly 3 - 4% in interest income, but a go-getter could earn 6% or more by buying and building a Wardway Home and renting it out for $20 per month. Their conclusion was flawed, as it assumed 100% occupancy and left out an important part of the equation: deadbeat tenants.

No attempt is made to interfere with the local contractor's established methods of hiring or using labor. If union labor is available, it is likely to be used. Economies are sought, but not at the workingman's expense. They result from speed in building, which follows naturally when parts are supplied accurately cut to measure and numbered, each for its place, and when workmen move on from one job to another gaining in skill and experience as they go.

While costs vary somewhat according to locality, freight rates, wage scales, it usually holds true that about half the money John Jones pays goes to local contracting and supply houses, 80% of their quota for labor, 20% for materials. Incidentally, work done to the home by the owner himself is counted as cash. The firm supplies a little more than 90% of all materials going into the ready-cut homes.

The article noted that after the two retail giants began offering "easy financing" and construction supervision, sales of homes showed a dramatic increase.

Once the order was received, Montgomery Ward assigned it to a salesman who'd work hard to sell the customer a few upgrades. For an additional $30 or $40, even the smallest home could have beautiful oak floors and trim instead of plain old pine. For a mere $20, storm doors and windows could be added to the order, and surely they'd pay for themselves on the coldest of winter days.

Window shades added only $10 to the cost (and that was half the cost of a local hardware store, Wards promised!). Drywall (as compared to lath and plaster) added $60 to the bottom line, but that money was a true savings, since it expedited the plastering work (and its labor costs). On larger homes the salesman might push for more significant changes such as customizing room sizes, relocating walls, repositioning doors, adding bay windows and porches, and half-baths. It was the rare order that made it past the salesman without an upgrade.

At the same time, the interior design staff mailed the soon-to-be homeowner catalogs showcasing wall paper, rugs, furniture and appliances. Everything the new homeowner could want or need could be purchased from Montgomery Ward, at a price that'd beat the local merchant's best price. The finance department prepared the mortgage documents, which had to be signed by the customer before the order could ship. The architectural department sent a construction handbook, together with the information on preparing the home's foundation, including details on dimensions, water and sewer lines.

Orders requiring cosmetic changes (such as an upgrade to oak floors and trim) were sent directly to the mill; orders requiring structural changes were forwarded to the architectural department at Gordon-VanTine. Taking blueprints, which at the time were actually white lines on a blue background, draftsmen used red or yellow crayons to note the required alterations, adding dimensions and making notes. Structural alterations requiring special attention were sent to mill, while those for trim, windows, doors and other pieces of finished lumber were sent to the cabinetry shop. At these locations the pieces were cut, sanded, finished, labeled with an ink crayon, and a notation made on the blueprint with a description of the part.

When the order was ready to ship, a railroad box car was pulled up to the loading platform. Inside the warehouse, a worker pushed a handcart through the long aisles, loading up lumber, kegs of nails, roofing materials, cans of paint, and other materials. The railroad car was thoughtfully loaded, so that the pieces needed first would end up on top when unloaded at the site. The foundation plate was loaded at the bottom of the rail car, followed by sills, floor joists, flooring, wall studs, top plate, exterior wall sheathing, and ceiling joist or rafters. If there was an upper floor the process was repeated. The miscellaneous hardware, such as kegs of nails, cans of paint, flashing and gutters were piled on top, with doors and windows placed in a corner of the railroad car.

Once the railroad car was closed, locked and on its way, Montgomery Ward sent their customer a telegram, advising them that the order had been shipped and was now the responsibility of the railroad. Delivery by railroads was a constant source of trouble for the pre-cut housing industry. Ideally the order would arrive at the local depot in three to six weeks but most often, the box car appeared at the depot in 8-12 weeks. It was not unusual for railroad cars to sit at transfer yards for several weeks, delayed by local and national priorities in shipping, bad weather and floods, strikes and repair projects. Customers were reminded to deal directly with the railroad, but in cases of an extreme delay, Montgomery Ward would involve itself.

At the local depot, the railroad car was shuffled onto a side track and the customer was sent a notice informing him that his house had arrived. Typically, the customer had 24-48 hours to unload all those pieces and parts, before incurring a penalty. Many people hired a local mover or trucking company to unload the car, check the bill of materials, and deliver the order to the building site. Montgomery Wards was to be notified immediately of any shortages in the order, or damage to the merchandise.

NEW!
15-YEAR LOANS
for HOME BUILDERS
offered by
MONTGOMERY WARD & CO.

Easiest Terms Possible—Bigger Loans
Longer Terms and Smaller Payments

NOW Ward's makes it easier than ever before for you to own that home of your own! Under our amazing new plan all you need is a building lot and a little cash. In fact our new loan plans are so liberal that in some cases no cash whatever is required. Monthly payments are smaller and easier too. Think of it! You pay a little each month—much less than you now pay for rent, while enjoying the many comforts and conveniences that only owning a WARDWAY Home affords—and in a few years your home will be fully paid for.

(1) **NO DOWN PAYMENT**
   We take care of all expenses including cost of arranging loan, continuing and examining title papers, recording fee, mortgage tax, etc. Insurance is all you need to pay for.
(2) **EXTRA CASH SUPPLIED**
   Enough extra cash is also furnished by Ward's to cover the greater part of construction cost, in addition to cost of material specified in Book of Homes.
(3) **LOWEST MONTHLY PAYMENTS**
   Payments less than rent! Only $33.76 a month for a $4000 loan—less than 1 per cent. Interest at 6 per cent on **unpaid balance only** is included in the small payment. All the rest goes to pay off the loan.
(4) **FIFTEEN YEARS TO PAY!**
   After then you will own your home clear—no further payments to anyone. Your rent has bought you your home and paid for it, and you have not been burdened with payments that have been hard to carry.
(5) **LOAN NEVER NEEDS TO BE RENEWED!**
   Ward's new liberal plan saves you all the worry and expense of renewing a mortgage. Never a large sum to pay at any time.

Ward's is not in the banking business. Ward's is simply a great merchant—a big store, selling all kinds of merchandise to ten million customers. Ward's time payment plan is just another service offered at cost to help each customer to enjoy **years sooner** the pleasure of a home of his own. That's why Ward's finance charges are so much less than those usually made by finance companies who must make a profit out of each loan.

Now it's up to you! The door is open! Telephone or call at our nearest office—or fill out and mail the blank on Page 109. Let's get that home right away—NOW! Soon it will be all paid for, out of rent money—and you'll be independent. *Write us today!*

MONTHLY PAYMENTS
REDUCED!
Far Lower Than Present Rent

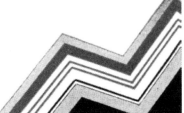

Mortgage Plan Flyer inserted into a 1930 *Wardway Homes* catalog.

Financing Your Wardway Home

Ward is not in the banking business. Ward is simply a great merchant. Ward's time payment plan is just another service offered at cost to help each customer to enjoy years sooner the pleasure of a home of his own.

These words, written on the back page of the 1929 Wardway Homes catalog, had the ring of truth. Many a hopeful soul was enabled to buy a home of their own due to Wards' "time payment plan" and their simple mortgage qualification process.

The world of home mortgages was a very different affair in that day and time. Banks were often owned and operated by local businessmen. Typically, one of the bank's directors was directly involved in the local building and/or real estate industry. These banks often refused to grant mortgages for homes that were manufactured outside their community. To counter this problem, pre-cut home companies established their own mortgage programs.

In 1915, Sterling Homes became the first pre-cut housing company to offer a mortgage program. Sears introduced their mortgage program in 1917 but did not push the program until 1923. Wardway Homes was not so eager to jump into the mortgage business and only did so in late 1926 when sales of Sears Homes surged ahead of Wardway Homes.

The Wardway mortgage application asked about the lot size, its cost and to whom the lot was titled. Like the comparable mortgage application from Sears, the Wardway application asked for the homeowner's age, marital status and occupation. In 1927, Wardway offered 60% mortgages at 6% interest and a minimum monthly payment equal to 1% of the outstanding loan amount. One year later, they were offering 15-year fully-amortized notes and 75% loan-to-value ratio. If the homebuilder owned his own lot, the 75% loan-to-value ratio was immediately satisfied. In other words, he could build a home of his own with no cash out of pocket. The applicant was expected to provide free labor or pay for the construction costs out of pocket.

Although it took a few years to get the mortgage program established, it proved very successful. By 1929 Wardway Homes boasted that 95% of their customers were taking advantage of their easy financing plans.

Aladdin Homes "Cash Only" Policy

Aladdin Homes was the one pre-cut housing company that did not have a mortgage program. It sold its houses for "cash only". Customers placing an order with full payment were typically allowed a small discount on the purchase price of their home, while others were required to provide a deposit of 25% with their order and the balance upon delivery. "This is not meant as a reflection on your financial standing," noted the 1918 catalog, "but it is an invariable rule". The cash-only policy allowed Aladdin to minimize costs in that it did not have to maintain an administrative staff for handling mortgages or pass the cost of bad accounts onto other customers. The "cash only" policy cost Aladdin orders but it helped to avoid having to pursue delinquent homeowners.

When the stock market crashed in October 1929 its immediate impact on the mail-order housing industry was minimal as the building season was over. Although traditional housings starts were down for 1930, sales of pre-cut homes surpassed those of 1929 thanks to the expanded mortgage programs. "Much the same type of plan for home-building and financing announced recently by Sears, Roebuck and Company has been adopted by Montgomery Ward Company", reported *Business Week* in March of 1930. When Wards announced that pre-cut housing sales for the 1931 building season were running 28% ahead of 1930 the *Chicago Daily Tribune* thought the news worthy of an interview with Wardway Homes manager J.A. Webber.

> *The continuous increase in sales of Wardway homes during the last fourteen and one-half months seems to upset the commonly accepted notion that people are not prepared to build at this time. In the early part of 1930 Ward's announced a new loan plan which made available a huge fund for those who intended to build one or two family residences.... The construction of homes made possible by these loans helped to keep thousands of men employed during the last year. (April 5, 1931)*

The sales increases were largely the result of Sears and Montgomery Ward having dropped their credit requirements and offering additional incentives. Robert Betcone, son of David Betcone (a staff architect within the Sears Modern Homes department 1926-1934) explained that salesmen pushed hard for customers to take on heavy mortgages, regardless of their credit or income. Throughout 1930 and 1931 sales climbed but mortgage defaults soared.

On January 22, 1932 Congress established the *Reconstruction Finance Corporation*, an agency that provided loans to the banking and mortgage industry. It was hoped that an infusion of tax dollars into the banks would repair the badly wounded mortgage industry. With this fresh cash, mortgage bankers could offer sweeter deals than their competitors – like Montgomery Ward. Unable to compete for new mortgages, Montgomery Ward eliminated their home mortgage program in 1932.

J.A. & Eva Tolman built this *Trenton* in Georgetown, Kentucky with a Wardway mortgage in 1929 (photograph by Dale Wolicki).

Typical Mortgage Agreement

In the summer of 1929 J.A. Tolman and his wife Eva decided to build a Wardway *Trenton* in Georgetown, Kentucky. Like many customers they purchased the house with a standard Wardway mortgage.

Paragraph 1: Tolmans' and Montgomery-Ward entered into a "Trust Deed" mortgage on July 29, 1929.

Paragraph 2: Specifies that the principal of the mortgage was $5100.00 with an annual interest rate of 6%, payable in 179 monthly installments of $44.74 (This was a 15 year mortgage)

Paragraph 3: Required the lot on which the house would be built was free of debt and pledged as collateral.

Paragraph 4: Provided for a legal description of the lot on which the house would be built.

Paragraph 5: Required the Tolmans maintain the house in good condition during the term of the mortgage and to pay all taxes and assessments against the house and property.

Paragraph 6: Allowed Montgomery-Ward to pay for any back taxes or liens filed against property but unpaid by the Tolmans, adding it and administrative fees to the principal owed.

Paragraph 7: If the Tolmans failed to make monthly payments, taxes, liens or other encumbrances Montgomery-Ward could start foreclosing procedures.

Paragraph 8: Having filed for foreclosure Montgomery-Ward could appoint a Receiver to collect any rents or profits generated by the property. (This paragraph was for property owners and speculative home builders who rented or sold the house on land contract)

Paragraph 9: Specified that foreclosure procedures would follow any and all applicable laws, and that any administrative fees would not be in excess of those allowed by the law.

Paragraph 10: Should the Tolmans transfer title to the property, Montgomery-Wards Trust Deed was the first lien on the tile and the company could demand payment in full immediately. (This paragraph allowed Montgomery-Ward to foreclose on properties sold or transferred by title without their approval).

Paragraph 11: The property could not be sold or transferred until the mortgage had been paid in full.

Paragraph 12: The mortgage was be to used solely for construction of a house on the specified property.

Paragraph 13: Mrs. Tolman released dower rights to the property during the term of the mortgage.

Paragraph 14: Allowed the Tolmans to make additional payments on the mortgage principal.

Paragraph 15: When the mortgage was paid off Montgomery-Ward would file the proper Discharge papers terminating the Trust Deed.

Beautiful

WARDWAY HOMES

Sold on Easy Monthly Payment Plan

MONTGOMERY WARD & CO.

The last *Wardway Homes* catalog in 1931.

The End
of Wardway Homes

In January 1932, in the depths of the Great Depression, Montgomery Ward hired Sewell Avery, President of the United States Gypsum Company, to guide the company out of economic trouble. He was best known for his incredible financial sagacity and his ability to peek around dark economic corners. Within days, Avery slashed Montgomery Ward's workforce and eliminated departments, including Wardway Homes.

Avery decided closing Wardway Homes would allow Montgomery Ward to focus on what that company did best: general merchandise. He recognized Sears Homes had a substantial lead in the pre-cut housing industry and that the Hoover administration's *Reconstruction Finance Corporation* would increase the involvement of the government in the banking industry. With an infusion of federal money, banks could refinance home mortgages at a lower rate, including those held by Montgomery Ward. Without the profitable mortgage program Avery decided it was time to close Wardway Homes.

In April 1933, Fortune Magazine offered their own analysis as to why Wardway Homes did not succeed.

> *Since 1908, Sears, Roebuck has been opening a market for small, compact, low-cost houses and has achieved a complete housing business. It has become the only U. S. organization which acts as a financier, mortgage bank, architect, supplier of materials, contractor and laborer. For a while, Montgomery Ward tried to follow suit, but Sears was on the job first, took the cream of the business...*

Unlike Sears, Montgomery Ward did not hold mortgages. By contrast, they would bundle their mortgages and sell them to a bank. This was before the days of federally funded secondary mortgage behemoths such as Fannie Mae and Freddie Mack. Montgomery Ward exited the mortgage business without significant loss and unlike Sears, they never faced the public relations nightmare of having to evict customers from their homes. Sears foreclosed on $4 million in bad mortgages in 1933 and astounding $11 million in 1934 before they ended their home financing program.

Gordon-Van Tine stepped in quickly to fill outstanding orders of Wardway Homes. Their architectural staff revised the designs of several popular Wardway homes so they could be included in the next Gordon-Van Tine catalog. The records, letters and drawings of both companies were destroyed when Gordon-Van Tine closed in 1947.

The 1932 Montgomery Ward *Building Material* catalog mentioned Wardway Homes, but requests for information were forwarded to Gordon-VanTine

WHEREVER YOU GO!

Montgomery Ward & Co.

WARDWAY HOMES

One of the scores of Wardway Homes in Pontiac, Mich.

See the **NEW WARDWAY HOMES** *Near You!*

A FEW WARDWAY HOMES ON A SINGLE STREET

It will be a pleasure for us to take you to Wardway homes similar to these, built in your vicinity.

Above is a Wardway Home built in Ann Arbor, Mich.

1931 Wardway Homes promotional brouchure.

How to Identify a Wardway Home

In 1931, Ward published a 32-page promotional brochure filled with glowing testimonials from exuberant new homeowners. Several of the beautiful homes featured in this brochure are captioned with the words, "A Wardway Home of Special Design."

In other words, some of the houses in that brochure bear little or no resemblance to the any of the designs shown in the following pages of this field guide. The 1929 Wardway Homes catalog made this generous offer:

Changes can be made in the plans for any of our Wardway Homes…You may find that some alteration will make your home more comfortable, more convenient to meet some individual requirement. We will gladly arrange for any changes you wish.

Wardway Homes promoted a variety of upgrades and optional extras, such as sun porches, sleeping porches, side porches, more windows, bigger windows, doors instead of windows and more. Homeowners could opt for custom entry porches or they could order the Mayflower's ornate porch tacked on to the Larchmont's front entry (or any other combination). Buyers sometimes "puffed" their house by adding a few extra feet to one or both sides. One of the most common changes were steeply pitched roofs, pulled up to create extra space for upstairs bedrooms. It's likely that 30% - 50% of Wardway Homes were customized when built. In those cases, you must find documentation to authenticate your Wardway home.

The Six Simple Signs

1) Marked lumber
2) Paper labels
3) Blueprints and Catalogs
4) Mortgage records
5) Building permits
6) Field guide

A Wardway Cranford in Flint, Michigan that would be difficult to recognize unless you looked for additional information and documentation at the local court house (photography by Dale Wolicki).

1) Marked Lumber: Pre-cut homes were designed for easy assembly by novice builders. The framing members were stamped with hyphenated numbers, such as 14-7-3 or 9-10-3 and these numbers were also referenced on the blueprints. The numbers were usually placed on the wide side of the lumber, near the end. Not all lumber was stamped. In some instances, specific parts such stairway treads were bundled together with metal bands or scrap lath and only the top piece was marked. Blue grease pencil markings on rafters, floor joists, subflooring and other pieces of lumber can also be an indication of a pre-cut home. Sometimes these grease pencil markings mention model number, model name, and customer order number. You'll need a bright light to hunt down these numbers.

Only the top piece is marked on this bundle of interior door trim, discovered in the attic of a Montgomery Ward *Farmland* in Ewen, Michigan (photograph by Dale Wolicki).

The roof rafters in this Rockford, Illinois Wardway Home have identification stamps (near their ends) and grease pencil marks indicating the length of the rafter (photograph by Rebecca Hunter).

A wood scrap found in the attic of a Wardway Home in Flint, Michigan was once part of a shipping crate (photograph by Dale Wolicki).

As an example, Architectural Historian Rebecca Hunter invited us to accompany her on an investigation of a suspected kit home in Illinois. Built in the late 1910s, the owner said that her father had ordered the house from Sears and built it himself. We started in the attic and worked out way down to the basement. Using bright flashlights and three pairs of keen eyes, we grew discouraged when we couldn't find any stamped lumber or identifying marks. Then we turned a corner in that dimly lit basement and found a clue.

The coal room had a rickety old door, hastily fashioned 80 years earlier from scrap lumber. Although the letters were faded and upside down, the stamp was recognizable: *Gordon VanTine, Davenport, Iowa*. The coal-room door had originally been part of a wooden shipping crate.

2) Paper Labels: We've often found paper labels on the back of millwork (baseboard molding, door and window trim) of Wardway Homes. Shipping labels, in and of themselves, are not proof positive that you have a pre-cut home, as it could indicate that the building materials, and nothing more, were ordered from the mail-order companies. Wardway Homes were shipped by rail from the Gordon-Van Tine mills in Davenport, Iowa, Portland, Oregon and Hattiesburg, Mississippi, and the shipping labels will identify these cities.

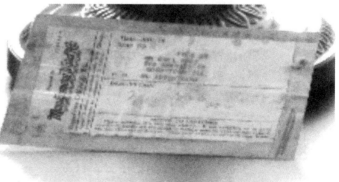

Paper labels found in a Rockford, Illinois Wardway Home. The bottom label is frequently found on the back of interior trim (photograph by Rebecca Hunter).

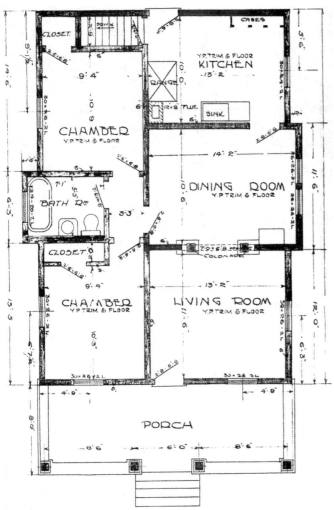

3) Blueprints and Catalogs: Blueprints are a rare find as they were the property of the housing manufacturer, and (hoping to prevent others from using their designs), asked that they be returned when construction was complete. "All plans and blue prints remain the property of Montgomery Ward & Company," noted the 1921 catalog, "and are furnished only for use in the construction of our buildings." Homeowners have told us that they've found blueprints in the attic, or on the bottom shelf of built-in bookcases and in other nooks and crannies.

Occasionally we are shown original catalogs handed down through successive homeowners, a slip of paper indicating the page where their pre-cut home is featured. As catalogs were advertisements they were never meant to be saved, and originals are increasing difficult to find. Online auction sites have depleted the stock of catalogs hidden on bookshelves and in basements. Within the few years several universities have slowly acquired collections of mail-order housing catalogs. Reprints of more popular housing catalogs for Sears Roebuck and Aladdin are available.

A blueprint circa 1912 for *Model #185* (thanks to Rebecca Hunter for this illustration).

THIS INDENTURE made this twenty ninth day of July A.D. 1929 by and between J. A. Tolman and Eva R. Tolman his wife of Anderson, county of Monroe, and state of West Virginia hereinafter referred to as the party of the first part, and Thomas P. Riordan, of 618 West Chicago Avenue, of the city of Chicago, County of Cook and State of Illinois, party of the second part, as Trustee as hereinafter specified.

WITNESSETH:

That, whereas the party of the first part is justly indebted to the legal holder or holders of the one Principal Promissory note hereinafter described in the principal sum of fifty one hundred and no/100 dollars $5100.00) secured to be paid by the one Principal Promissory note of the said party of the first part, bearing even date herewith, made payable to the order of themselves and by them duly endorsed and delivered in and by which said Principal Promissory note, said party of the first part promises to pay the sum of fifty one hundred and no/100 dollars ($5100.00) in one hundred seventy nine (179) installments

A typical Wardway Home mortgage will specify the principal, the monthly payment schedule and the annual interest rate but will not mention Montgomery Ward & Company (collection of Dale Wolicki).

4) Mortgage Records: In late 1926, Ward began offering home mortgages. To track down Wardway Homes through this venue, start at your local courthouse. Locate the mortgage and the *grantee* index that lists who received the mortgage. Many assume the grantee name to look for would be Montgomery Ward but in fact look for Thomas P. Riordan, a Montgomery Ward trustee that approved mortgages. The front of the grantee record will be indexed by last name. The index may direct you to look on pages 72-78 for the name Riordan. In some states, Wardway mortgage documents are called Deed in Trust and are actually listed in the Deed Index.

Once you find the pages with the last name Riordan, start looking for Thomas P. Further to the right of that same line, you'll find the homeowner's name and typically you'll see something like, "book #339, page 198." This means the mortgage document can be found on page 198 of book #339. In that book on that line, you'll see the grantee's name (Thomas P. Riordan) and the grantor's name (Mr. & Mrs. Q. T. Piehause). In a perfect world, the document will state that Mr. & Mrs. Q. T. Piehause live at 489 Elm Street in Belleville, Illinois, but it's not that easy. The mortgage will include a legal description, typically a lot in a plat or subdivision such as "Lot 12, Greenmead Sub". With this description you can determine the address by visiting the Office of Maps & Plats or the City Assessor's Office.

If the legal description is too complex look for a mention of streets, places and directions such as "the north side of Coal House Road, west of the Board of Education property." Sometimes you can find the address on Coal House Road in old directories at your local library or museum but many times you will have to get out of your car and walk along Coal House Road, carefully examining each house to see if it's a kit home.

Looking through the courthouse records you might also find the Mortgage Release which will tell you when the mortgage was paid off. Sometimes, you'll find an Assignment where Montgomery Ward waived their Due on Sale clause and permitted the existing mortgage to be assumed by a new buyer. This was common occurrence during the Great Depression. A sheriff's sale, sheriff's deed, or court order indicates that the original owner may have lost their Wardway Home to foreclosure.

5) Original Building Permits: In Washington, DC, historian Mary Rowse discovered that housing manufacturers such as Sears Roebuck and Gordon-VanTine were sometimes listed as the architect on original building permits. Although most municipalities discarded these documents along ago, it never hurts to ask the building department if they've retained these records.

6) Field Guide: During their 22 years in the mail-order home business, Wardway Homes offered more than 100 designs of homes. This book has been thoughtfully organized in a way that'll make finding each design within its pages simple and direct. Start by familiarizing yourself with the designs and housing styles in this book. Look at their rooflines, the window arrangement, the pitch of the roof and other distinctive features. Then hop in the car and drive around your community and see if you can find a few.

Above all, the process should be fun. We've been doing this for many years and it's often challenging and usually enlightening and always a pure delight.

We hope this book – and the accompanying delight of finding these heretofore undiscovered architectural treasures – brings you as much joy as it's brought us.

The Competitors

Montgomery Ward was one of many pre-cut housing companies doing business in the early 20th Century. Through the intervening decades, the term "Sears House" has become the vernacular term for any pre-cut house. About three-fourths of the time people who think they have a Sears Home are wrong. Often we find that they do have a kit home, but it's a kit home from one of these other companies. For this reason, we've included some information on these other companies.

Sears Roebuck and Co.,

In 1908, an ad appeared on page 594 of the Sears Roebuck catalog which said "Let us be your architect, without cost to you." Interested customers were invited to request a new specialty catalog, *Book of Modern Homes and Building Plans*. This catalog contained 44 pages and 22 house designs. Would be homeowners pored over the pages of this catalog and when they found a house that fit their lifestyle, their budget and their lot, they put a $1 "good faith deposit" in an envelope and sent it to Sears Roebuck. By return mail, Sears sent a complete set of blueprints and an inventory of the building materials they'd need to construct the house, all of which could be ordered from Sears.

In 1915, Sears Homes evolved into true "pre-cut homes" with all the building materials needed for construction. Shipped by boxcar, each kit contained about 30,000 pieces. Framing members were numbered to facilitate construction. Blueprints were drawn with the novice homebuilder in mind, listing each numbered member and its precise placement. An instruction manual came with the kit. Sears promised that "a man of average abilities could assemble a Sear's kit home in about 90 days." These kits were made with the finest of materials, including cypress for window trim, clapboard, fascia and soffit, and first-growth, top-grade southern yellow pine for framing members. Compared to conventional construction, homeowners saved about 30% by building their home from a kit. About 50% of the kit homes were built by the homeowner while the balance were professionally built.

Sears offered more than 370 house designs and sold about 70,000 kit homes. Increasingly complex building codes, the Great Depression and federally sponsored mortgage programs were the primary reasons that Sears closed their Modern Homes Department in 1940. Unfortunately, sometime after World War II, all records involving Sears Homes were destroyed during a corporate housecleaning.

"If you have made up mind to break away from the rent paying class this year and join the independent army of home owners, you could not have made a better beginning than by getting this Book of Modern Homes"

- 1913 Sears, Roebuck and Company

A Sears *Newcastle* in Annapolis, Maryland (photograph by Rose Thornton).

A Sears *Alhambra* in Lexington, Virginia (photograph by Rose Thornton).

A Sears *Crescent* in Norfolk, Virginia (photograph by Rose Thornton).

Aladdin Homes

Named for the tale of the mythical genie that built a castle overnight for his master, Aladdin Homes, founded in 1906 by Bay City, Michigan brothers Otto and William Sovereign, was the first company to offer houses whose lumber was pre-cut, marked for assembly and referenced to a blueprint, thus the name pre-cut homes. Aladdin set the standards for the pre-cut housing industry, with advertising and catalog of stylish models, colorful illustrations, and descriptive text.

Unlike other pre-cut housing companies, Aladdin did not have commissioned salesmen or a mortgage program. All houses were sold through catalogs and on a strict cash only policy that allowed Aladdin Homes to operate with minimal staff and free of debt, the resulting savings being passed along to the customer.

Initially Aladdin contracted its orders out to local and regional lumber companies but eventually established mills in Michigan, North Carolina, Mississippi and Oregon, shipping twenty-five hundred homes a year. During the Depression, sales dropped to a few hundred homes but rebounded when Montgomery Ward and Sears exited the housing industry.

During World War Two Aladdin manufactured military barracks, emergency housing and shipping crates. Post-war restrictions on prices and building materials kept the Aladdin mills closed until 1947. Throughout the 1950s the company shipped more than two thousand Ranch and Colonial homes a year. The increasing popularity of mobile and prefabricated homes brought a sharp drop in sales during the 1960s and 1970s.

Aladdin Homes closed in 1981 having shipped approximately 100,000 homes throughout the United States, Canada and England. The records for Aladdin Homes are located at the Clarke Historical Library, Central Michigan University in Mt.Pleasant, Michigan.

"Aladdin service is equal to any demand made of it. No matter what your requirements are - a single home or a complete city - the Aladdin organization is capable of handling it with the greatest dispatch."

- 1919 Aladdin Homes

An Aladdin *Marsden* in Dodge Center, Minnesota (photograph by Dale Wolicki).

The *Pomona* was Aladdin's most popular home. This model built near their Bay City offices was used for advertising and tours by prospective customers (photograph by Dale Wolicki).

An Aladdin *Charleston* built in Bonita Springs, Florida (photograph by Dale Wolicki).

A Lewis *Marlboro* in Portsmouth, Virginia (photograph by Rose Thornton).

Lewis-Liberty Homes

In 1906 Lewis Manufacturing was contracted by the Sovereign brothers to fabricate and ship the first Aladdin Home. With each passing year housing orders doubled, requiring Lewis Manufacturing to expand their facilities. In 1913 orders for the spring building season overwhelmed Lewis Manufacturing and the company refused to make further improvements unless they were given ownership interest in Aladdin Homes. The Sovereign brothers refused and Lewis Manufacturing lost the Aladdin Homes contract. As they still owned the mills, lumber and machinery necessary to produce pre-cut homes, Lewis Manufacturing created Lewis Homes in late 1913.

Within a few years Lewis Homes was Aladdin Homes' largest competitor, shipping approximately fifteen hundred homes annually. When a 1925 fire destroyed the lumberyard, Lewis Manufacturing renamed the pre-cut home company Liberty Homes to distinguish it from their other operations. Although Liberty Homes did not have salesmen on staff, the company had a network of local representatives who sold homes throughout the midwestern and eastern United States.

A Lewis *Malvern*, one of many Lewis Homes built in Chevy Chase, Maryland (photograph by Mary Rowse).

The drop in pre-cut housing sales during the Depression was offset by sales of architectural millwork for prominent residences, banks and office buildings. In 1938 Liberty Homes boosted orders when it introduced a mortgage program approved by the Federal Housing Administration (FHA). During World War Two the mill manufactured military barracks, emergency housing and shipping crates. A 1944 advertising campaign allowed customers to use Liberty Bonds as deposits on Liberty Homes to be shipped once civilian production resumed.

During the 1950s the company shipped thousand of homes throughout the United States but sales dropped as mobile and prefabricated homes replaced pre-cut homes for affordable housing. Lewis Manufacturing closed in 1975 having sold 75,000 houses.

"In dealing with us we save you the time you would waste in dickering with lumber dealers, hardware men and other dealers from whom you would have to buy the many materials for your home."

- *1919 Lewis Homes*

A small simple Liberty *Lafayette* in Montpiler, Ohio (photograph by Dale Wolicki).

Gordon-VanTine

Established in 1907, Gordon-VanTine was a subsidiary of U.N. Roberts, a Davenport Iowa lumber mill. Its first catalogs were devoted to building materials but a catalog of house plans was introduced in 1912. While many suppliers fought the pre-cut housing industry Gordon-VanTine introduced its own line of *Ready-Cut Homes* in 1916.

When Montgomery Ward added pre-cut homes they subcontracted the orders to Gordon-VanTine. At its peak in the late 1920s Gordon-VanTine was shipping 2500 homes a year. The Depression and closing of Wardway Homes dropped annual production to a few hundred homes. Throughout the war orders for temporary housing and shipping crates kept Gordon-VanTine busy.

When World War Two ended, Gordon-VanTine mailed housing catalogs to eager customers but inserted notices that prices or availability could not be guaranteed because of post-war restrictions and regulations. Throughout 1946, Gordon-VanTine's mills sat idle while the federal government allotted building materials and money to speculative politically connected prefabricated housing companies. In 1947 U.N Roberts and Gordon-VanTine were sold to the *Cleveland Wrecking Company*. Although the new owner claimed it would continue to manufacture pre-cut homes, it knew Gordon-VanTine was worth more on the auction block than as a business. In July 1947 it was announced operations at U.N. Roberts and Gordon-VanTine would cease immediately. Within days all lumber, hardware and building materials were sold to the highest bidder.

In their forty years of operation it is estimated Gordon-VanTine manufactured approximately 75,000 plan book and pre-cut houses.

"Our enormous volume of business enables us to give our customers more - in service - to sell them homes which, though costing no more, are worth much more, not only in what they can be sold for when finished, but in comfort, beauty, convenience and satisfaction."

- 1919 Gordon-VanTine

A *Model #534* located only a few blocks away from the Gordon-VanTine factory in Davenport, Iowa (photograph by Dale Wolicki).

An unaltered Gordon-VanTine *Model #540* in Moline, Illinois (photograph by Rebecca Hunter).

A Gordon-VanTine *Model #607* in New Castle, Indiana (photograph by Dale Wolicki).

Pacific Ready Cut Homes

An unaltered Pacific Homes *Model #85* in Monrovia, California (photograph by Rose Thornton & Dale Wolicki).

Pacific Homes *Model #392* in Anaheim, California (photograph by Rose Thornton).

Pacific Homes *Model ##396* in Anaheim, California (photograph by Dale Wolicki and Rose Thornton).

If you're living in a bungalow in southern California, chances are very good that it came from Pacific Ready Cut Homes, a Los Angeles company that sold about 40,000 plan book and pre-cut homes.

Although the lumber company dated back to 1908 it did not did not start manufacturing pre-cut homes until after World War One. From 1918 – 1940, they offered more than 500 designs, ranging from modest four-room worker cottages to spacious two-story bungalows. The company also prided themselves on their one-of-a-kind custom designs and it's likely that this architectural service represented a significant part of their overall sales.

Pacific's 24-acre mill was in Vernon, about 20 miles from the Los Angeles Port. Sales offices were in the Los Angeles area and in large cities throughout California. The company's literature boasted sales to faraway lands such as Alaska, Hawaii, Belgium, England and France.

The story of this uniquely Californian company has a uniquely Californian ending. In 1929, Meyers Butte (son of company president William Butte) convinced his father that they should use their sawmill to create a few surfboards. The first boards produced were made of solid redwood, measured 10 feet long and weighed a hefty 70 pounds. The company chose a simple logo for their surfboards that, according to Eastern philosophies, denoted peace and prosperity, the *swastika*. When Hitler's atrocities became world headlines in 1938, the emblem disappeared from Pacific Homes' surfboards and they adopted a new name - Waikiki Surfboards.

Pacific Homes left the homebuilding business after World War Two and focused exclusively on surfboards.

"With its tremendous financial resources, its 24 acres of manufacturing facilities, its 1000 skilled employees, its staff of expert architects, its armies of construction craftsmen, plus the sincere and abiding determination of its executives to see that your are unconditionally satisfied .... presents you with the finest opportunity you will ever have to realize this ambition of yours to get greatest home value."

-1925 Pacific's Book of Homes

Sterling Homes

When the Sovereign brothers refused to give Lewis Manufacturing an ownership interest in Aladdin Homes, they contracted to send orders to International Mill & Timber, a Bay City lumber company. Unfortunately, IM&T failed to keep up with orders, so the Sovereign brothers purchased a local lumber mill and terminated their agreement with IM&T. Following the lead of Lewis Manufacturing, IM&T introduced their own line of pre-cut homes in 1915, naming them Sterling Homes.

Unlike Aladdin and Lewis, who required cash with all orders, IM&T was the first to offer mortgages with which customers could purchase their home. The company also offered construction services for developers, the largest being one thousand houses built at Flint Michigan for General Motors.

A subsidiary company, the Bay City Ready-Cut House Company, mailed out its first catalog just weeks before the start of World War One. Both companies struggled with wartime restrictions on building materials and railroads. A post-war advertising campaign brought a surge in housing orders but added to a heavy debt. A recession in early 1921 forced International Mill & Timber into bankruptcy.

Bay City lumberman Leopold Kantzler purchased the assets of IM&T and had Sterling Homes back in business with a new focus on cottages and smaller homes. Like other companies, it manufactured temporary housing and military buildings during World War Two. At the peak of the post-war building boom Sterling Homes shipped over 250 homes a month.

Hampered by outdated models and advertising, Sterling Home sales dropped throughout the 1960s. The last catalog was printed in 1971 but was mailed out with updated price lists until 1974 when the company closed having manufactured approximately 45,000 homes.

"We will help you make your dream come true - your dream of a home that is really a home. We will send you a home that will be more cherished as the years pass on. We want to see you own a Sterling System Home which will be a joy through your life, and which will be passed on to your children as a fitting inheritance."

- 1917 Sterling Homes

Frequently described by local historians as a "Sears House", this Bativa, Illinois house is actually a *Vernon* from Sterling Homes (photograph by Rebecca Hunter & Dale Wolicki).

The Michigan Department of Agriculture purchased this Sterling *Senator* to provide housing for the state chicken hatchery in Waterford Township near Pontiac (photograph by Dale Wolicki).

Sterling Homes offered to provide the materials and the labor to build entire subdivisions of Sterling Homes such as this street in Lockport, New York (photograph by Dale Wolicki).

Bennett Homes

This Bennett Home *Birmingham* in Buffalo, New York (photograph by Dale Wolicki).

This *LaSalle* is located only a few blocks from the Bennett Homes factory in North Tonawanda, New York (photograph by Dale Wolicki).

A perfect unaltered *Maralowe* in Tonawanda, New York (photograph by Dale Wolicki).

Although Bennett Lumber dates back to 1902, this North Tonawanda, New York lumber company did not enter the pre-cut housing market until 1919. The first *Bennett Homes* catalog featured Bungalows and Four-square houses, many of which were strikingly similar to the popular models offered by other pre-cut housing companies.

Unlike other housing companies Bennett marketed its homes primarily to the northeastern United States, an area that experienced a significant building boom after World War One. Annual sales were in excess of one thousand until the Depression. By January 1933 sales had dropped and the company was surrendered to its largest creditor. Bennett continued to offer pre-cut homes despite the lingering Depression, although the majority of sales were for building materials related to residential repairs and renovation. Sales climbed when Bennett redesigned its houses to conform to *Federal Housing Administration* guidelines for mortgages.

In early 1940 *Bennett Homes and Lumber* was re-named *Bennett Lumber Company*, a change that reflected the fact that company had eliminated its pre-cut housing operations to avoid union efforts to organize the mill. Bennett returned to the pre-cut housing market in 1954 with a catalog of Ranch and Colonial style homes. Sales remained strong into the 1960's but dropped as mobile and prefabricated homes became increasing popular.

Bennett Lumber closed in late 1960s having manufactured approximately 15,000 homes.

"The best home designs and plans have been produced by Bennett for hundreds to share the profits. A huge modern mill in the heart of the lumber market has been equipped with labor and waste saving machinery so that you can reap the advantage and savings of the Bennett Way in securing a home of fine design, greater convenience, and genuine durability."

- 1935 Bennett Homes

Harris Homes

by Rebecca Hunter

Moses Harris settled in Chicago by 1871, where he entered the feed business, but later expanded into the lumber. In 1893 Harris incorporated the *Chicago House Wrecking Company*, an architectural salvage firm that secured contracts for the demolition of exhibitions such as the 1893 *World Columbian Exhibition*. In 1913, the company name was changed to *Harris Brothers*.

In 1908, the company began offering house plans and building materials through mail-order catalogs. They introduced pre-cut homes in 1916. The price included all framing lumbers, girders, joists, rafters and studding in #1 yellow pine stock; creosoted wall plates; sheathing, lath, roof, and sub-floor of yellow pine; flooring "clear and free from knots"; Washington red cedar shingles; siding in a choice of three woods; cut-to-fit door and window trim; porch material of clear Oregon fir; stairway, doors, windows; interior trim, hardware, building paper, galvanized gutters and downspouts. Available at additional cost were heating and plumbing fixtures, paint, window shades and cabinets. Ninety days was deemed sufficient time to erect any of the Harris designs.

Throughout the 1920s Harris Homes kept busy, shipping building material and pre-cut housing orders but sales slumped during the Depression. The last Harris Homes catalog is the 1931 *Summer Bungalows* catalog. In the 1930's, to attract more repeat business, the company began marketing materials to contractors rather than to individual homeowners.

After World War II, Harris Brothers supplied millwork to Sears Roebuck, Montgomery Ward and many major housing companies. Although the company remained in business for many more years the last Harris Brothers building materials catalog was mailed out in 1958.

Rebecca Hunter, Elgin Illinois, is a noted authority on mail-order homes, particularly those from Sears and Harris.

A Harris Homes *Model #152* in Lockport, New York (photograph by Dale Wolicki).

A very popular Harris Homes *Model #1000* in Elgin, Illinois (photograph by Rebecca Hunter).

This Harris Home *Model #5010* in Louisville, Illinois is an unusual early Bungalow with a Victorian tower (photograph by Rebecca Hunter).

Other Pre-Cut Housing Companies

The success of the large pre-cut housing companies inspired many local lumberyards to enter the manufactured housing industry. Most failed within a few years of their first catalog. Others survived by manufacturing sectional cottages, garages and farm structures. Some of the more notable companies were, Hodgson Homes of Boston, Massachusetts (1892-1980), Artcraft Homes from the Berkshire Lumber Company of Pittsfield Massachusetts (1916-1920), Bossert Homes of Brooklyn New York (1915-1930), Houston Ready-Cut House Company of Houston Texas (1920-1950), Economy Homes of West Chicago (1920-1960), Mershon & Morley of Saginaw Michigan (1905-1930), St.Johns Portable House Company of St.Johns Michigan (1920-1930), Minter Homes of Huntington West Virginia (1920-1940), American Portable House Company of Seattle Washington (1910-1915), Thayer Portable Houses of Keene New Hampshire (1920-1940), Togan-Stiles of Grand Rapids Michigan (1920-1930), Quickbilt Bungalows by Tuxbury Lumber Company of Charleston South Carolina (1916-1920), and Wyckoff Lumber & Manufacturing of Ithaca New York (1905-1910).

The vertical battens along the side wall of this house in St.Johns, Michigan helped to identify it as a panelized structure from the nearby *St.John Portable House Company* (photograph by Dale Wolicki).

Minter Homes supplied the houses for Nitro, West Virginia, a World War One town built around a new nitroglycerine plant (photograph by Dale Wolicki).

Mershon & Morley were one of many portable/panelized housing company that operated at the turn of the twentith century, even before pre-cut houses (collection of Dale Wolicki).

"The experimental stage in the manufacture of Portable Buildings has been passed, and, while there yet remains some things that may be improved, still we have at last produced a high class building that will meet all of the requirements of those desiring a portable building at a nominal expense. Improved machinery and factory facilities have made this possible and practical builders have insured to our customers a substantial, architecturally correct building - one, in fact, that is portable only, inasmuch as it is shipped from the factory in sections, having been assembled by workmen of experience, so that it is complete in every detail and easily erected by non-skilled labor, the building being fully as substantial as a permanent structure and so constructed that no nails are used in its erection, thus insuring portability in every part. These buildings are so constructed that they may be lived in year round, so they are as easily heated as any permanently erected frame structure.

- 1919 Thayer Portable House

Canadian Mail-Order Housing Companies - British Columbia Mill Timber & Trading, Aladdin, Eaton and Halliday

Canada's pre-cut housing industry consisted of four principal manufacturers, *British Columbia Mill Timber & Trading, Eatons, Aladdin, and Halliday.*

British Columbia Mill Timber & Trading, based in Vancouver, was a pioneer in the pre-cut housing industry, operating briefly between 1904 and 1911.

Eatons is best remembered for its catalogs of general merchandise but in 1910 the company introduced mail-order homes that were sold exclusively in the western territories. Contrary to popular belief Eaton Homes were not pre-cut or pre-fabricated. They were plan book homes for which Eatons provided the building materials.

The Canadian Aladdin Company was established in 1914 to avoid violation of America's neutrality in World War One. Aladdin had offices in Toronto and mills scattered throughout Canada until the 1950s. Although Aladdin published a Canadian catalog most of the models were identical to those offered in their American catalog.

Halliday was the largest general merchandise catalog company in Canada and evidence suggests it was their largest manufacturer of pre-cut homes. Halliday issued its first catalog of pre-cut homes in 1919, expecting a surge in residential construction as soldiers returned home from World War One and immigrants settled into central and western Canada. Most of the homes were designed exclusively for the Canadian market but many were copies of American designs from Aladdin and Sears. Halliday Homes can be found throughout Ontario and Quebec, and to a lesser extent throughout western Canada.

For information on mail-order homes in Canada, read *Cataloque Houses, Eatons' and Others,* written by Les Henry, Professor Emeritus at the University of Saskatchewan.

An Aladdin *Victoria* in Cambridge, Ontario, Canada (photograph by Dale Wolicki).

A Halliday Homes *Kenilworth* in Beach o' Pines, Ontario, Canada (photograph by Dale Wolicki).

A Halliday *Hamilton* in Cedar Springs, Ontario, Canada (photograph by Dale Wolicki).

"The Monteroy"—Material Supplied Either Ready-Cut or Not Ready-Cut

An Ever Popular Five-Room Bungalow

THIS one-floor home has all the features which have made the bungalow so popular, and yet is a little more conservative in exterior appearance. A particularly pleasing feature is the dining room extension window with its gable roof breaking up the roof line and adding greatly to exterior appearance and interior comfort. You may screen any or all of the fine porch, making an outdoor living room for summer which will be much appreciated by the entire family.

Inside there is no wasted space, every inch being usable and livable. The front door enters the fine living room, which is lighted by a large window in each outside wall. A cased opening leads into the dining room, throwing the two rooms practically together into one large light room. Observe the careful attention which has been given to wall space in these two rooms. Several different arrangements of furniture are permitted, a fact which will appeal to every housewife.

The kitchen is unusually light, with two windows and the glazed rear door. It is most convenient as well, with our fine pantry case No. 861, illustrated on Page 54, built into the wall. This case includes shelves, drawers, bins, mixing board and plenty of space for all the kitchen utensils and supplies. The door to the cellar steps is adjacent to the door on the rear entry porch, making it convenient to reach from either outside or inside. Space is planned for the ice box on the rear porch, where it is cool and easily accessible from the kitchen and can be iced without the iceman coming into the house.

The sleeping quarters [...]
the dining room. The [...]
any of the three [...]
bedroom has its own [...]
Page 54, is furnished [...]

The basement [...]
frames, etc. The [...]
keeping with its [...]

Size of Home, 24 feet wide by 34 feet long

One Story Front Gable

Kenmore (1917-1931 Ready-Cut)

Similar to Sears *Hampton* and Aladdin *Stanhope*
1917 ($876), 1918 ($1121), 1919 ($1381), 1920 ($1341), 1921 ($1341),
1922 ($1606), 1923 ($1688), 1924 ($1558), 1925 ($1558), 1926 ($1558),
1927 ($1569), 1928 ($1618), 1929 ($1618), 1930 ($1710), 1931 ($1660)

*"The strong appeal which the Kenmore makes to home lovers is due
no less to its charming simplicity of appearance than to its distinctly
practical and cozy interior arrangement. It occupies but little ground
yet provides a surprising amount of floor space - more than enough
for the average family. Not a bit of space is wasted; every inch is
conveniently available for comfortable living. As you enter the living
room from the large front porch, a bedroom with a roomy closet is
found to the left. Straight ahead through French doors of attractive
design is the dining room - a bright, cheery room, radiating hospitality. Large twin windows welcome the sunshine and, in summer, the
cooling breezes. A bedroom of generous size opens off the left of the
dining room. A convenient closet is found in this room. A hall giving
access to a third bedroom and conveniently located bathroom also
opens off the dining room. It would be difficult to build a home more
economical or more convenient than the Kenmore. You have probably
already have noticed the generous size of every one of its six comfortable rooms, the large amount of bedroom space and the roomy porch
for which the whole family will be grateful during the hot months.*

- 1924 Wardway Homes

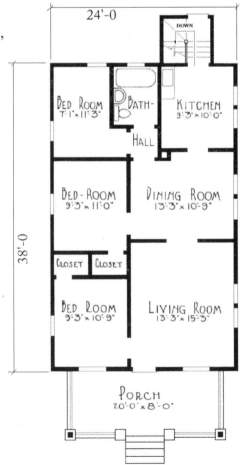

Lawndale (1917-1931 Ready-Cut)

1917 ($548), 1918 ($718), 1919 ($899), 1920 ($873), 1921 ($873), 1922 ($1012), 1923 ($1080), 1924 ($958), 1925 ($958), 1926 ($958), 1927 (A. $1046, B. $1090), 1928 (A. $1078 , B. $1124), 1929 (B. $1196), 1930 (B. $1262), 1931 (B. $1236)

"The Lawndale is one of the most popular five-room homes of the bungalow type. It has a most attractive exterior, with divided light Colonial windows and a bungalow front door to match. The large front porch is a big feature. The shingled side walls, favored by so many buyers, add distinctiveness to the home. This shingled effect has also been carried out in the porch column pedestals in an unusual way. You have two plans from which to choose; the difference being in the arrangement of the kitchen and bathroom and the adding of a basement in Plan B."

- 1927 Wardway Homes

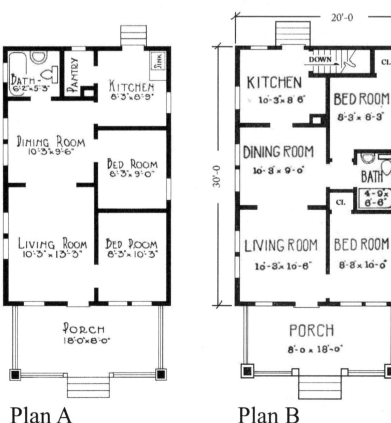

Plan A   Plan B

Venice (1917-1928 Ready-Cut)

Similar to Sears #205/Winona

1917 (A. Not Offered, B.$1093), 1918 (A.$1146, B. $1361), 1919 (A. $1574, B. $1373),
1920 (A. $1471, B. $1334), 1921 (A. $1471, B. $1334), 1922 (A. $1597, B. $1750),
1923 (A. $1626, B. $1867), 1924 (A. $1504, B. $1727), 1925 (A. $1504, B. $1727),
1926 (A. $1504, B. $1727), 1927 (A. $1546, B. $1751), 1928 (A. $1594, B. $1805)

"The massive paneled porch columns and newels of the Venice, the interesting effect obtained by paneling the gables and sidewalls above the belt course over the high grade, slate surfaced roofing, and the cornice brackets, present a unique and harmonious exterior. The front door is handsome, and the upper sash of the front wall windows are divided. The Venice has an interior arrangment which appeals strongly to every housewife. Living Room and Dining Room are practically one, with a cased opening between. Dining Room has an unbroken wall space for buffet or china closet. A large pantry is a feature of the kitchen, providing plenty of room for all equipment and supplies. Convenient locations for range and work-table are provided."

- 1928 Wardway Homes

24'-0"

BED ROOM
10'-3" x 11'-3"

PANTRY
5'-0" x 7'-9"

KITCHEN
8'-9" x 11'-3"

RANGE

STOOP

DOWN

CLOSET

BATH
6'-9" x 5'-6"

HALL

DINING ROOM
12'-3" x 11'-6"

CLOSET

BED ROOM
10'-3" x 11'-3"

LIVING ROOM
12'-3" x 11'-3"

36'-0"

PORCH
24'-0" x 8'-0"

Plan A

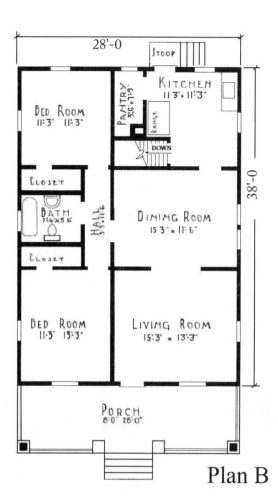

28'-0"

BED ROOM
11'-3" x 11'-3"

PANTRY
3'-6" x 7'-9"

KITCHEN
11'-3" x 11'-3"

RANGE

STOOP

DOWN

CLOSET

BATH
7'-6" x 5'-6"

HALL

DINING ROOM
15'-3" x 11'-6"

CLOSET

BED ROOM
11'-3" x 13'-3"

LIVING ROOM
15'-3" x 13'-3"

38'-0"

PORCH
8'-0" x 28'-0"

Plan B

The Sears *#205/Winona* (above) and Wardway *Venice* are frequently confused (1920 Sears Modern Homes)

Raymond (1918-1931 Ready-Cut)

1918 ($919), 1919 ($1061), 1920 ($1030),
1921 ($1030), 1922 ($1222), 1923 ($1292), 1924 ($1195),
1925 ($1195), 1926 ($1195), 1927 ($1195), 1928 ($1232),
1929 ($1282), 1930 ($1341), 1931 ($1335)

"Unusually skillful designing has overcome, in the Raymond, much of the monotony of appearance found in homes of moderate costs. The strikingly handsome exterior, its gracefully balanced proportions, and the exceptionally pleasing way in which every detail has been arranged, give this Wardway Home the charm and dignity of a home costing more than twice as much, if built without the benefit of Wards' experience.

The price makes a distinct appeal to all who must be careful of expenditures. No extravagance, no waste, nothing but sound common sense and good judgment is found in the exterior or interior design. It is a home economical to build, requires but very little ground space, and is easy to keep warm and comfortable during the cold months. These, added to the beautiful appearance, leave little more for the most critical and discriminating buyer to wish.

- 1924 Wardway Homes

Allerton - Renamed Newton in 1929 (1922-1929 Ready-Cut)
Gordon-Vantine Design

1922 (A. $2249), 1923 (A. $2150), 1924 (A. $1979),
1925 (A.$1995), 1926 (A. $1995), 1927 (A. $2106),
1928 (A.$2171, B.$2423), 1929 (A.$2215, B.$2614)

"You may choose either Plan A, which has a large attic floored over the entire house; or you may order Plan B, which has a finished second floor with two rooms and two closets. Plan B has the identical first floor plan show in A, in addition to its finished upstairs. The Allerton is a conservative, home-like style, certain to remain always in favor. With its wide eaves, broad porch and many windows, the exterior strongly suggests the comfort which the convenient interior arrangement assures. Outside the walls are neatly shingled. The belt course, which also serves as a cap for the windows, the timber brackets supporting the eaves, and the divided upper sash of windows, all give just enough trimming. The living room has four windows and there is a glazed front door. A small hall connects this room, the front two bedrooms, bath and attic stairs. There are twin windows in the dining room and a wide cased opening into the living room. There is a large wash room opening off this room, which connects with the rear porch."

- *1928 Wardway Homes*

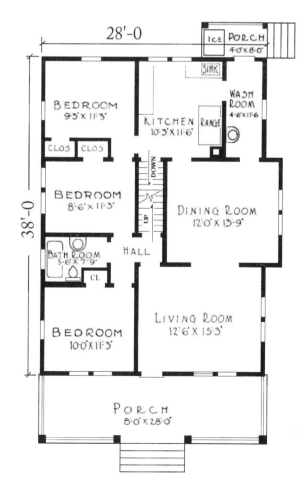

#186 - Renamed Irving in 1917; Monteroy 1922; Warner 1929
(1915-1916 Not Ready-Cut; 1917-1930 Ready-Cut)

Gordon-VanTine Design

1915 ($738 NRC), 1916 ($710 NRC), 1917 ($798),
1918 ($1138), 1919 ($1380), 1920 ($1339), 1921 ($1339),
1922 ($1685), 1923 ($1629, 1924 ($1525), 1925 ($1495),
1926 ($1495), 1927 ($1556), 1928 ($1604), 1929 ($1770),
1930 ($1770)

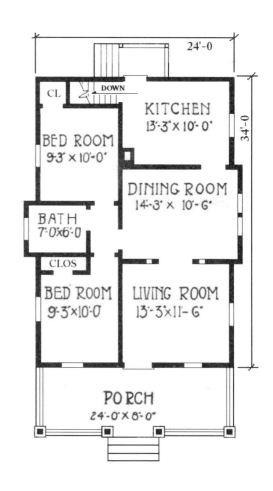

"You have likely noticed the cut of our Irving home in the large 1917 catalogue. Yes, there is a reason for it being there for it is one of our most popular sellers. Can you conceive of a five-room bungalow more artistically designed as to exterior and more conveniently arranged interior? The spacious front porch extends the full width of the house. Entering we find a large living room connected with dining room by our attractive Mission colonnade. The overhanging bay makes the dining room particularly large and well lighted. In the kitchen, plenty of wall space has been provided for stoves, sink and any built-in kitchen fixtures owner may desire."

- 1917 Book of Homes

The *Monteroy* had paired windows in the gable attic but no brackets.

The Wardway *Warner* has clipped gables.

A Wardway *Monteroy* in Woodstock, Illinois (photographs by Rebecca Hunter).

#200 - Renamed Lyola in 1917 (1914-1924 Not Ready-Cut)

1914 ($1100 NRC), 1915 ($1092 NRC), 1916 ($1045 NRC), 1917 ($1248 NRC),
1918 ($1641 NRC), 1919 ($1994 NRC), 1920 ($1936 NRC), 1921 ($1936 NRC),
1922 ($2228 NRC), 1923 ($2455 NRC), 1924 ($2270 NRC)

"This home makes a prompt and lasting appeal to the lover of the bungalow design. The gentle slope of the porch roof with its broad span, the massed columns and solid rail, give a most charming and hospitable first impression. The wide barge board with supporting cornice brackets, the fancy gable sash, the divided upper sash of the windows and the beautiful divided light bevel-plate front door, are details which make the Lyola distinctive in any neighborhood.

The interior is of admirable arrangement. The cheery fireplace at the end of a large living room, with space for bookcases beneath windows on either side, gives a real incentive for gathering around the family hearth. You enter the dining room through a beautiful mission colonnade. The bay window admits a flood of light and affords a very pleasant outlook. Either of the two walls furnishes excellent space for a buffet. Note the large, well lighted pantry off the kitchen - a convenience which cannot be overestimated. Two windows and a glazed rear door give plenty of light and air. The attic and cellar stairs are well located for space saving - one over the other. On the left side of the house are three bedrooms, each with ample closet space, and the bath, large enough to accommodate fixtures without waste space"

- 1923 Wardway Homes

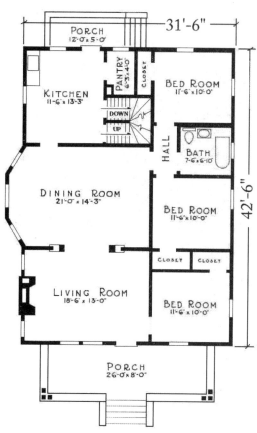

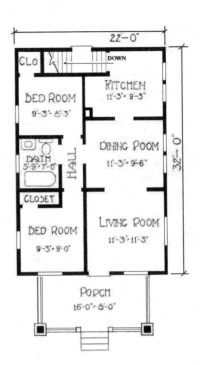

Abbott (1918 Not Ready-Cut)
1918 ($984)

"A design which bears an air of distinction. Its exterior attractiveness is due largely to the spacious porch, exceptionally well adapted and a departure from the styles most commonly in vogue. The floor plan is in keeping with the regular established Wardway 5-room bungalows. Not an inch of waste space; not a needless step exacted, not a modern necessity overlooked. These are Wardway's watchword and distinguishing points of superiority. The floor plan of the Abbott contains them all."

-1918 Wardway Homes

Bayliss (1918-1921 Ready-Cut)
1918 ($1032), 1919 ($1266), 1920 ($1169), 1921 ($1169)

"Do you like a home that is compact and conveniently arranged? Then the Bayliss will please you. Note its broad open porch with low gabled roof. And the attractive bay window off the dining room affording just the place for a cozy seat and pillows. Study the convenient arrangement of the rooms - from the living room, you step directly into the dining room, with the kitchen just beyond. Turning to the left, from the dining room, you find the two bed rooms - connected with each other and with the bathroom by a short handy hall. Could anything be more convenient and practical than this arrangement?"

-1918 Wardway Homes

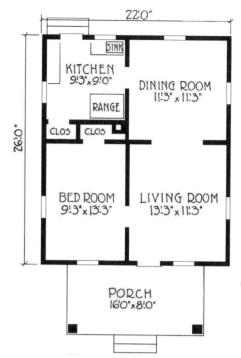

KITCHEN
9'3" x 9'0"

DINING ROOM
11'3" x 11'3"

RANGE

CLOS CLOS

BED ROOM
9'3" x 13'3"

LIVING ROOM
13'3" x 11'3"

22'-0"

26'-0"

PORCH
16'0" x 8'0"

1 Story Front Gable Attached Porch

Avoca (1922-1924 Ready-Cut)
Gordon-VanTine Design
1922 ($1060), 1923 ($1071), 1924 ($1012)

"Wardway architects have been most successful in making inexpensive homes attractive. The Avoca is no exception. Most excellent taste has been shown in the planning and arrangement of this cozy design. The complete harmony of porch and main roof and the proper spacing of windows and doors, combine to give this little home a most attractive appearance. The outside walls are covered with siding to the belt line and clear red cedar shingles from that point to the frieze board."
                                                                          - 1923 Wardway Homes

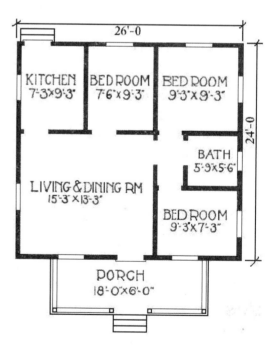

KITCHEN
7'-3" x 9'-3"

BED ROOM
7'-6" x 9'-3"

BED ROOM
9'-3" x 9'-3"

BATH
5'-9" x 5'-6"

LIVING & DINING RM
15'-3" x 13'-3"

BED ROOM
9'-3" x 7'-3"

26'-0"

24'-0"

PORCH
18'-0" x 6'-0"

1 Story Front Gable Attached Porch

Columbia (1917 Ready-Cut)
1917 ($665)

"The Columbia was designed especially for the family that requires several bedrooms and prefers not to build the larger or more expensive home. An examination of its interior will reveal a very pleasantly combined living room and dining room, from which a small hallway leads to two cozy bedrooms with bath between. To the rear of the living room are the kitchen and third bedroom. Notice the abundance of light each room has, the two corner bedrooms each have two full sized windows."
                                                                          - 1917 Wardway Homes

Troy (1922-1926 Not Ready-Cut)

Gordon-VanTine Design
1922 ($1525), 1923 ($1535), 1924 (Not Featured),
1925 ($1435), 1926 ($1435)

"There is a surprising amount of living space in this house. The exterior is simple but in excellent taste. The wide porch serves to set off the home and gives an air of hospitable comfort very much desired. The front door opens directly into the living room. This is connected with the dining room by a wide cased opening which makes these rooms practically one and gives the effect of added space. To the rear of the dining room is the kitchen – very carefully planned to make the work of the housewife easy and pleasant. Our special kitchen case is built right into the wall. This case contains shelves, drawers, bins, mixing board and space for all kitchen utensils and needed supplies. It is a most appreciated feature, as it simplifies and systematizes the work and keeps things out of the way and where they belong. It is furnished at no extra cost. The sink and case are so placed that they are flooded with light from the large twin window. The cellar steps lead down through an extension at the rear of the kitchen, which also makes room for the ice box. This arrangement permits supplies to be taken into the cellar without passing through the kitchen."

- 1923 Wardway Homes

DOWN

KITCHEN
11'3' x 8'6'

RANGE

SINK

BEDROOM
11'3'x 8'6'

CLOS

DINING ROOM
11'3' x 11'6'

BEDROOM
11'3' x 10'8'

CLOS   CLOS

LIVING ROOM
11'3' x 12'0'

BEDROOM
11'3' x 11'0'

34'0'

24'0'

PORCH
20'0' x 8'0'

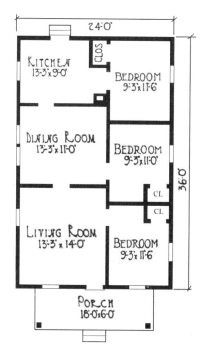

Youngstown Cottage (1922-1927)
1922 ($942), 1923 ($966), 1924 ($875),
1925 ($875), 1926 ($875), 1927 ($832)

"This design is the most pretentious of our workmen's cottages. It provides ample living space for a large family. If all rooms are not needed to house the family, it is always possible to rent one or more, a fact that makes the Youngstown a popular design in any industrial community. Each of the bedrooms has a convenient closet. The large front porch adds greatly to the appearance and comfort of the home. All timbers are Number 1 Yellow Pine of substantial dimensions that give solid construction."

- 1927 Wardway Homes

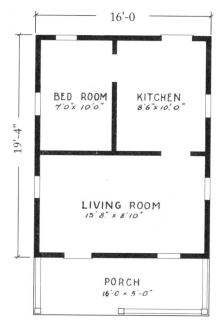

#300 (1912-1916 Not Ready-Cut)
1912 ($206 NRC), 1914 ($218 NRC),
1915 ($240 Panelized), 1916 ($218 Panelized)

"A very neat and tasteful three room house ready to put together and live in the day after it is received. A fair sized bedroom, a kitchen large enough for cooking and eating purposes, and a good sized living room make up a convenient floor layout, while the exterior has a pleasing appearance that is brought out more strikingly when the house is placed in its setting. Ready-Made houses require no tools except a hammer and wrench. They are made in sections, assembled at the factory to see that they fit perfectly. We furnish full directions for setting up, so that you can do the work yourself with the help of a handy man."

- 1915 Book of Homes

1 Story Front Gable
Offset Attached Porch

Laurel (1922-1928 Ready-Cut)

Gordon-VanTine Design
1922 ($2028), 1923 ($1922), 1924 ($1825), 1925 ($1795),
1926 ($2110), 1927 ($1854), 1928 ($1911)

Very similar to Essex but the Essex measures 24' wide by 36'
deep and has a dining room box bay window.

*"In exterior appearance this home preserves the craftsman note
so widely sought in bungalow planning. The wide porch extending beyond the house line adds much to the attractiveness of the
appearance and even more to the living comfort of the home. The
boxed-up rail makes it easy to screen the porch when it serves
as an outdoor living room. The wide, low eaves insure plenty
of shade and keep out all but the hardest of driving rains. The
outside walls are covered with siding, except in the gables above
the belt course, where clear red cedar shingles are used, laid
alternatively two and seven inches to the weather. The divided-
light Plymouth windows and Oakland front door are additional
touches which add to the charm of the exterior appearance."*

- 1924 Wardway Homes

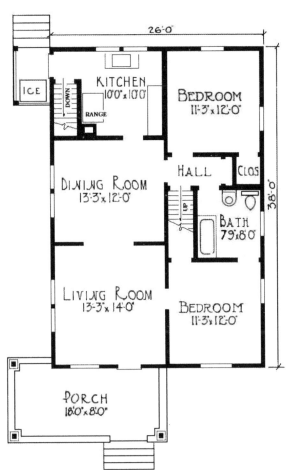

Essex - Renamed Van Dyke in 1929 (1922-1929 Ready-Cut)

Gordon-VanTine Design

1922 ($1635), 1923 ($1585), 1924 ($1447), 1925 ($1452),
1926 ($1452), 1927 ($1506), 1928 ($1553), 1929 ($1674)

"The wide eaves and sharply cut barge boards of the Essex are typical of the much desired genuine California style bungalow. The outside walls, including the porch pillars, are sided. The porch gable and the little space above the belt course of the main gable are shingle - giving an especially pleasing effect. The inset porch imparts a hospitable, inviting appearance to the home, which is also carefully carried out in the interior plan. All in all this is as compact, convenient and charming a little home as you will find in a long day's travel. And the Wardway system of manufacture, wholesale prices and ready-cut construction, place it within easy reach of all who really desire to build and own a home. The Essex is a home you will always enjoy."

- 1928 Wardway Homes

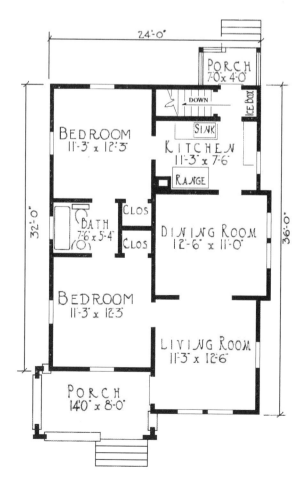

Lorraine - Renamed Gorham 1929 (1925-1929 Ready-Cut)

Gordon-VanTine Design

1925 ($1492), 1926 ($1492), 1927 ($1557), 1928 ($1598), 1929 ($1754)

"The Lorraine is truly a distinctive bungalow. No matter where it is built, its attractive craftsman architecture unfailingly sets it apart as a charming home. The effective combining of the gable-roof porch and the pergola give it an unusually pleasing entrance, which welcomes and attracts all who approach this home."

- 1927 Wardway Homes

The 1929 *Gorham* featured clipped gables and no porch trellis

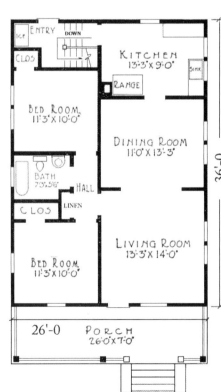

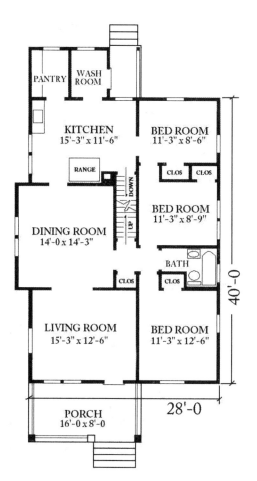

Hinsdale-1st (1926 Ready-Cut)

Gordon-VanTine Design
1926 ($2220)

"The Hinsdale has been designed primarily as a farm home although it is equally as suitable for a suburban or city residence. Farm houses all on one floor are becoming more and more popular each year as they are so convenient and so much easier to care for."

- 1926 Wardway Homes

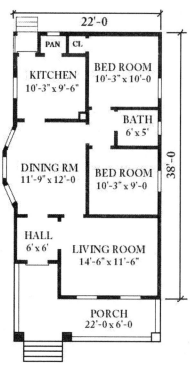

Aurora - (1917 Ready-Cut)
1917 ($774)

"How different and yet how pleasing is the design of this five-room home from the average home of like size. When built on a terraced lawn its wide steps and semi-open porch presents such a very striking appearance that it is sure to attract the eye of the passerby. The neat reception hall leads into either the dining room or large front living room. Off the dining room our designers have the popular arrangement of small hallway with two bedrooms and bathroom opening from the same.
- 1917 Wardway Homes

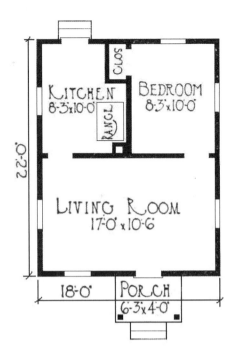

Bridgeport Cottage (1922-1927)

Gordon VanTine Design

1922 ($ 525), 1923 ($537), 1924 ($475), 1925 ($495), 1926 ($495)

"Three rooms of comfort and convenience at a price which makes this one of the biggest home bargains of the year, we believe. ... All materials are cut to fit - all you have to do is nail them together. Any handy man can erect this cottage without the help of skilled labor."

- 1923 Wardway Homes

Phoenix (1922-1923 Ready-Cut)

Gordon-VanTine Design

1922 ($1270), 1923 ($1289)

"It is unusual to find real architecture in a four-room home. Generally the design of such a place is left to chance and the carpenter, but this cottage has really good lines and proportions and a plan which affords comfort and convenience. Both front and rear door are glazed, furnishing additional light for living room and kitchen. In the living room the matter of wall space has been carefully taken into consideration. This room is lighted by two big windows. Each of the bedrooms is of really fine size and each has a window in opposite walls"

- 1923 Wardway Homes

#310 (1912-1916 Not Ready-Cut)

1912 ($453 NRC), 1913, 1914 ($428 NRC), 1915 ($450 Panelized), 1916 ($428 Panelized)

"A Ready Made Home that is far more attractive than the usual four-room cottage put up by ordinary methods. Note the divided lights in the windows, the stucco effect in the gables produced by slate-surfaced roofing and panel strips, and the substantial effect of the porch. A desirable home in every respect at low cost. There are no dealers' or jobbers' profits in the material that goes into the house, and by making the sections in large quantities, by machine work instead of by hand, the cost of construction is kept very low. Ready Made house Number 310 is a good example of this saving, of which you get the benefit.

Important! Ready Made Houses require no tools except a hammer and a wrench. They are made in sections, assembled at the factory to see that they fit perfectly. We furnish full directions for setting up, so that you can do the work yourself with the help of a handy man"

- 1915 Book of Homes

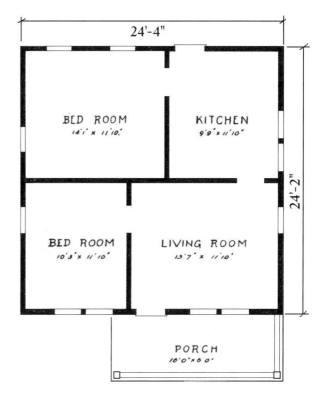

Barcelona (1929-1931 Ready-Cut)
1929 ($1575), 1930 ($1645), 1931 ($1597)

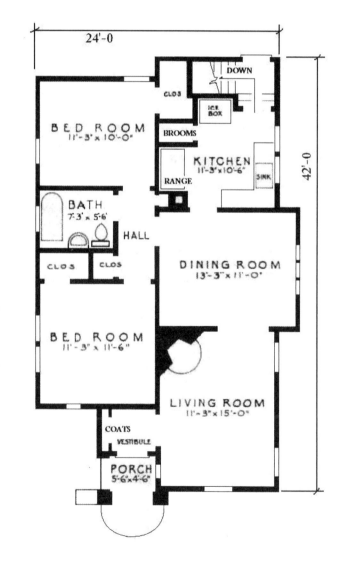

"The Barcelona has every latest Wardway feature. It is ultra modern from the brick step in front, through every room to the service entrance off the kitchen. The fashionable and architecturally excellent design comes from old Madrid in Sunny Spain. The Barcelona stands out, imposing, beautiful on any street. It marks the man of taste - discrimination - individuality! It brings you beauty that lasts.

Everyone says "It's the smartest home in town". Those who favor the bungalow say there is no home so beautiful, so fashionable and so comfortable as the new Barcelona. It's the home of homes to hundreds of people - to city man, suburbanite and country dweller alike.

The Spanish effect stucco is applied over metal lath on ship-lap - the best construction known. 5-2 Perfect Red Cedar - the best grade wood shingles made - are supplied for the roof. Stain them red and you will obtain a most striking and colorful effect, much admired by all."

- 1929 Wardway Homes

A *Barcelona* in Charleston, West Virginia (photograpgh by Rose Thornton).

The repairs to this *Barcelona* in Waterford, Michigan illustrate one of its design flaws, the roof valley between the entrance and the living room that had a tendency to leak (photograph by Dale Wolicki).

Sheridan (1927-1928 Ready-Cut)
Gordon VanTine Design
1927 ($2621), 1928 ($2697)

"The Sheridan is an excellent example of modern bungalow planning and designing. The low roof lines, the sturdy roof brackets and the rubble stone chimney all seem to blend in so perfectly and set this home off as one which has been designed by the hand of an expert. Note the size of the front porch – ten feet wide and twenty-one feet long. It will be the most popular part of the house during the warm summer months. The outside walls are sided with 8-inch bungalow siding, particularly adapted to this style of home. The interior is equally as modern and appealing as the exterior. There are six spacious rooms all cleverly arranged to use all available floor space to the best advantage.

You enter the long living room from the charming, inviting porch. This room has a massive fireplace which will give the entire family many hours of cheer and happiness on frigid days. Lighted by four big windows with Colonial top sash, this room will always be light, cheerful and well ventilated. A convenient coat closet is placed in the rear of this room. From the living room you enter the dining room through a wide cased opening. A fine bay window greets you at the right, and you realize that this room was most thoughtfully planned for a nice arrangement of dining room furniture."

- *1928 Wardway Home*

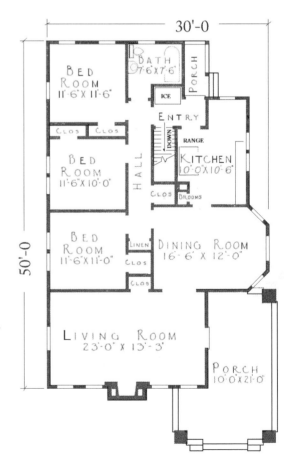

A Wardway *Sheridan* in Vinton, Virginia (photograph by Rose Thornton and Dale Wolicki).

Dresden - Renamed Webster in 1929 (1924-1931 Ready-Cut)

Gordon-VanTine Design

1924 ($2098), 1925 ($2058), 1926 ($2058), 1927 ($2144),
1928 ($2210), 1929 ($2385), 1930 ($2385), 1931 ($2340)

"Where "home" means more than shelter - where pride and hospitality, comfort and security, culture and a demand for real economy are the true motives, the Webster makes life-long friends. And the Webster is so good looking! In any climate - the middle west, south, east or the Pacific Coast states where the cozy bungalow type of home originated - it will conform well with the landscape. Its rugged rubble stone pillars and chimney add so much to its beauty, and even seem to emphasize the staunchness and solidity of this house. The uniquely spaced shingle sidewalls, exposed rafter ends, cornice brackets and fancy sawed verge boards are truly handsome architectural details. Picture yourself in this delightful, cozy home. Think of the cool autumn evenings when the family gathers around the cheer of a fire. For your wife, the Webster combines the conveniences of a well arranged city apartment with the advantages of a home of your own. Porch and terrace will be the center of activity all summer long. Everyone will praise the really beautiful Webster and you will own a home worth hundreds of dollars more than it will cost to build."

- 1929 Wardway Homes

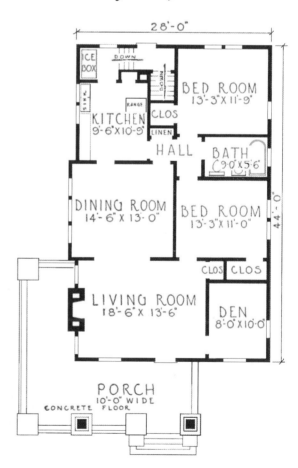

#137 - Renamed #172 in 1915; Iowa in 1917
(1911-1918 Not Ready-Cut; 1919-1921 Ready-Cut)

1911 ($865 NRC), 1912 ($910 NRC), 1913 (NRC), 1914 ($884 NRC), 1915 ($878 NRC), 1916 ($868 NRC), 1917 ($981 NRC), 1918 ($1393 NRC), 1919 ($1568), 1920 ($1523), 1921 ($1523)

"The attraction of Home Number 172 lies very largely in its straight, simple lines, which make for beauty as well as practicability of construction. In a home of such splendid proportions the effect of the unbroken roof line and wide eaves is very pleasing, while the construction of the porch under the main roof, with siding and short columns, gives an air of comfort and stability."

- 1915 Book of Homes

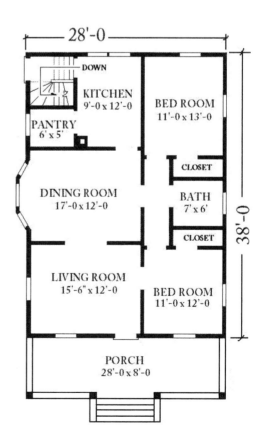

#172/Iowa as it appeared in the 1917 catalog

Florence (1918-1931 Ready-Cut)

Gordon-VanTine Design

1918 ($944), 1919 ($1125), 1920 ($1093), 1921 ($1093), 1922 ($1198),
1923 ($1282), 1924 ($1198), 1925 ($1198), 1926 ($1198), 1927 ($1556)
1928 ($1297), 1929 ($1390), 1930 ($1440), 1931 ($1425)

"The Florence is one of our favorites and we believe you, too, will be quick to appreciate the many fine qualities. The home is modern in every respect. How homelike and inviting is its appearance too with its low gabled roof, shingled side walls and cozy open porch? Its quaint Virginia windows and Craftsman door add their part, giving a particular touch of style to the home and thus making it just a little different from the ordinary house. An interior inspection reveals that this is just as convenient in arrangement as the exterior is in attractiveness. The living room with its four large windows is ideal. The dining room just beyond is another light, airy room with large double windows in one end. From the dining room we enter the kitchen through the double action door. Notice the convenient space here for placing the stove; the double window is arranged plenty high enough to give an ideal location for the sink just beneath, while there is yet plenty space for cabinet and table."

- 1918 Wardway Homes

A Wardway *Florence* in Elgin, Illinois (photograph by Rebecca Hunter).

Avondale (1926-1928 Ready-Cut)

Gordon-VanTine Design
1926 ($1352), 1927 ($1382), 1928 ($1425)

Identical to the *Florence* in appearance and size, the *Avondale* features a slightly different floor plan and arrangement of windows, most notably the entrance door without flanking sidelights.

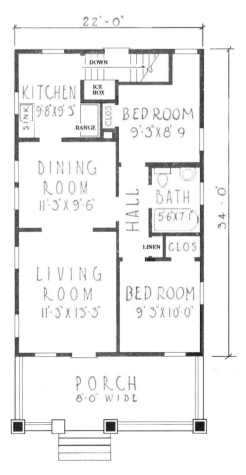

1 Story
Front Gable
Porch Under
Roof

#149 (1911-1914 Not Ready-Cut)
1911 ($905 NRC), 1912 ($950 NRC) , 1913 (NRC), 1914 ($1025 NRC)

"You have never seen a more desirable, large seven-room cottage, with veranda, and bath, at such a very small cost. If you buy the materials from us we give you, free of charge, a complete set of architectural plans that are worth sixty dollars. The rooms are all large and well-lighted. The bedrooms have good sized closets. For the price we quote, the house is finished with clear yellow pine trim, Western pine doors, and hard maple floor in the kitchen."

- 1912 Building Plans of Modern Homes

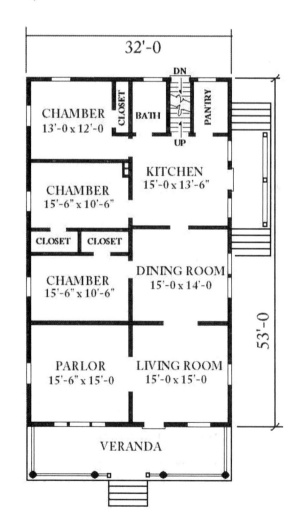

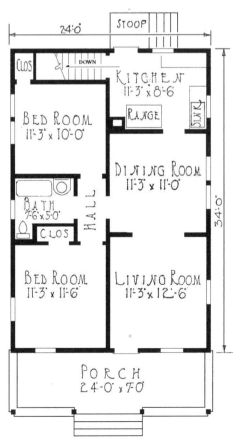

Glen Ellyn - Renamed Melrose in 1928; Montrose in 1929 (1925-1931 Ready-Cut)

Gordon-VanTine Design

1925 ($1398), 1926 ($1398), 1927 ($1435), 1928 ($1477),
1929 ($1547), 1930 ($1547), 1931 ($1524)

"This home is pleasant, comfortable and homelike. It gives the utmost livable space and convenience for the least outlay. The wide porch sheltered under the main roof gives a charming and inviting appearance and its box-rail permits easy screening. This practically adds another room to your home during the summer months. The interior arrangement is ideal for the small family.

The front door opens into a good sized living room, well lighted by windows on both sides, with a glazed front door. A wide cased opening between living and dining room throws these two rooms together and gives a spacious appearance. The dining room with twin windows make this room light and cheerful. Ample wall space for furniture is provided. A convenient swing door separates this room from kitchen. Windows on two sides permit good light and ventilation. Space is provided for kitchen sink near the dining room door."

- 1927 Wardway Homes

#131 (1909-1916 Not Ready-Cut)

1909 ($248 NRC), 1910 ($248 NRC), 1911 ($248 NRC), 1912 ($260 NRC),
1913, 1914 ($315 NRC), 1915 ($394 NRC), 1916 ($346 NRC)

*"This little house was designed as a summer cottage, or a
home for a small family in the rural or mining districts. While
it is a small house, still at the same time it is attractive for one
that can be built for such small expense. The quintet window
and window frame gives it a distinctive appearance. You will
note there is a convenient front porch with a neat front door
glazed with double strength glass; this door opens into the
kitchen, from which you enter either the living room or bed
room; this bed room also connects with the living room."*

- 1912 Building Plans of Modern Homes

1915 - 1916 Illustration

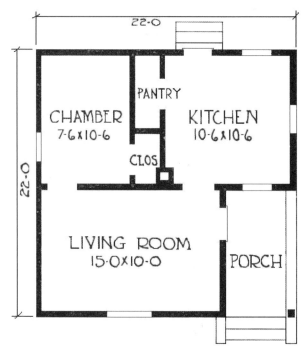

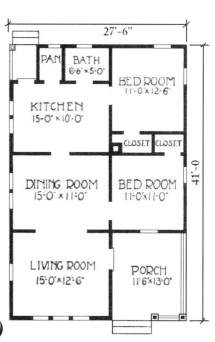

27'-6"

PAN. | BATH 6'-6" x 5'-0"
KITCHEN 15'-0" x 10'-0"
BED ROOM 11'-0" x 12'-6"
CLOSET | CLOSET
DINING ROOM 15'-0" x 11'-0"
BED ROOM 11'-0" x 11'-0"
LIVING ROOM 15'-0" x 12'-6"
PORCH 11'-6" x 13'-0"
41'-0"

#135 - Renamed Adams in 1917
(1915-1916 Not Ready-Cut; 1917-1918 Ready-Cut)
1915 ($652 NRC), 1916 ($687 NRC), 1917 ($863), 1918 ($1219)

"Many prospective builders prefer inset porches. For their approval we are offering the Adams with front and back porch both of this style. The front elevation of the Adams owes its attractiveness largely to the triple window with wide belt and panel work above. The interior is neatly arranged, compact, and convenient. One can make no mistake in selecting the Adams for a home of its type."

- 1917 Wardway Homes

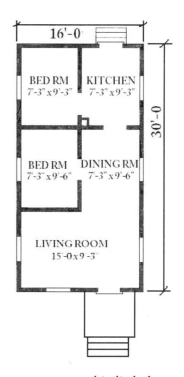

16'-0"

BED RM 7'-3" x 9'-3"
KITCHEN 7'-3" x 9'-3"
BED RM 7'-3" x 9'-6"
DINING RM 7'-3" x 9'-6"
LIVING ROOM 15'-0 x 9'-3"
30'-0"

Ford (1917 Ready-Cut)
1917 ($356)

"Well named is this little home for like the ever increasing popular car of the same name, this little house represents more for the money than any other we offer. Think of buying a five-room home complete for less than $350. Entering the home from the little porch with attractive hooded entrance we find a large living room fifteen feet wide and nearly ten feet deep, with three large windows and glazed front door, giving an abundance of light."

-1917 Wardway Homes

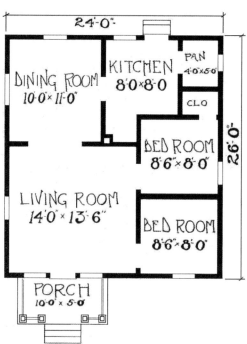

1 Story Front Gable Entrance Stoop

Sunshine (1918-1919 Ready-Cut)
1918 ($771), 1919 ($884), 1920 ($858), 1921 ($858)

"Isn't this home a little gem and all for less than $800 too? Most excellent taste has been shown in the planning and arrangement of this cozy design. The front porch is somewhat out of the ordinary. The siding below with sidewalls above, and attractive cornice brackets, give the house a very pleasing and modern touch. Five rooms and pantry compose the interior, the living and dining rooms being arranged in one large room. The two bedrooms of equal size are particularly well arranged for placing bedroom furniture."

- 1918 Wardway Homes

1 Story Front Gable Entrance Stoop

Colton (1922-1925 Ready-Cut)
Gordon-VanTine Design
1922 ($1039), 1923 ($1044), 1924 ($998), 1925 ($985)

"This unique little home with its most pleasing exterior, never fails to attract attention. The usual plain gable roof lines have been cleverly varied by the designer and the bracketed, hooded entrance not only serves to protect the front door from the weather, but also adds a most pleasing touch to the front of the home."

- 1924 Wardway Homes

Roseland - Renamed Glendale 1922 (1918-1926 Ready-Cut)

Gordon-VanTine Design

1918 ($919), 1919 ($668), 1920 ($649), 1921 ($649), 1922 ($925),
1923 ($933), 1924 ($878), 1925 ($860), 1926 ($860)

"If you are interested in a little bungalow of small cost and big value the Roseland should have your ready approval. While not large in size who would not agree that it is as attractive as any larger or more expensive home in the book? Hundreds of families of moderate means are building little homes like this every year and thus they stop using up their incomes in paying rent. If you have a few hundred dollars saved, write us and see how it can be arranged so you can build this attractive little home and pay the balance to some Building and Loan Association the same as you pay your rent now."

- 1918 Wardway Homes

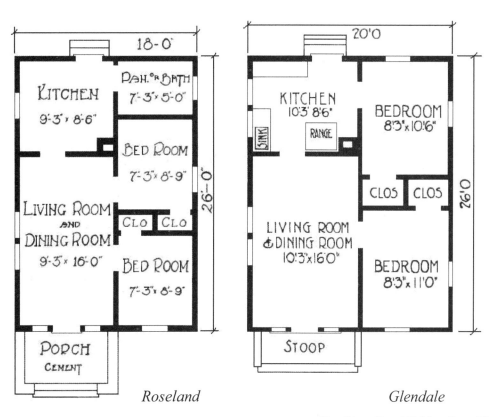

Roseland   Glendale

Garages, Cottages, Barns and other Building

Montgomery Ward offered mail-order auto garages, farm buildings and accessory structures, but sales were small in comparison to those of houses. Most garages and outbuildings were purchased from local companies. As an example, the *Toledo Portable House Company* was actually a local lumber yard that shipped and built hundreds of garages in northwest Ohio during the 1920s. They purchased materials in bulk, fabricated the garages at the mill and transported them to the site on trucks. This, together with their expertise in this field, allowed them to price their garages cheaper than the larger housing companies.

Early Montgomery Ward's plan book catalogs included barns for which blueprints and building materials could be ordered. These early barns are almost impossible to distinguish from traditionally built barns as the lumber is not stamped with assembly numbers. In 1917, Wardway began offering pre-cut kit barns (manufactured and shipped by Gordon Van Tine), which have assembly stamps marked on the framing lumber. Wards stopped offering barns in 1921 when Gordon Van Tine (which had its own catalog of barns and farm buildings) took over operations for Wardway Homes.

An unaltered Wardway *Lincoln* garage with its original folding three-part door, located in Bluffton, Ohio (1928 Wardway Homes catalog).

1914 *Building Plans for Modern Homes.*

The "Claremont"—*A Most Appealing Bungalow*

THE faithfulness with which each detail carries out the motive of the design, gives a most unusual but perfectly harmonious and pleasing appearance to this home. Battered gable ends are a striking departure from the usual, and most effective. The exterior beauty is further enhanced by the belt course extending around the house, which serves also as a head casing for all outside frames. Painted White, this is thrown into bold relief against the shingled side walls—creating an interesting effect.

The interior is as decidedly appealing to the discriminating buyer as the exterior, a practical floor plan making this a most desirable home.

Living Room: From the attractive porch you enter directly into a roomy living room, well lighted by twin windows on the side, and a single window in front. A note of cordial hospitality greets you in this room.

Dining Room: A wide cased opening separates the living room from the dining room, creating a spacious divided room effect that is impressive. Ample floor and wall space is provided for the placing of all dining room furniture. This is a most cheerful room, planned for convenience and comfort.

Kitchen: A convenient swing door in the rear wall of dining room leads into the nicely arranged, well lighted and airy kitchen. There is a twin window right over the work table of our large, built-in kitchen case "C," shown on Page 20, and a second window near the sink. Nothing interferes with passage to and from the dining room. The cellar steps are close by; descending just opposite rear door.

The entry between the kitchen and rear entrance serves admirably as a location for the ice box, and also permits entrance to cellar without passing through kitchen. This entry keeps the cold air out on wintry days, and provides a cool, convenient place for the ice box in summer and winter.

Bedrooms and Bath: A central hall sets off the bedrooms and bath from the rest of the house, which provides privacy and easy access to any room without passing through another. A room [...]

[...] the cellar [...] low grade, [...] but three [...]

This house [...] able point [...] costing [...]

FLOOR PLAN

KITCHEN 10'0"x9'6"

BEDROOM

DINING ROOM

BATH

HALL

CLOS

LIVING ROOM 13'0"x11'6"

BEDROOM

PORCH 20'0"x8'0"

Size of House, 26 feet wide by 24 feet long

One Story Side Gable

Danbury (1922-1929 Ready-Cut)

Gordon-VanTine Design

1922 (A. $2248, B. $2638), 1923 (A. $2178, B. $2552), 1924 (A. $2058, B. $2369), 1925 (A. $2038, B. $2340), 1926 (A. $2038, B. $2340), 1927 (A. $2129, B. $2417), 1928 (A.$2195, B. $2492), 1929 (A. $2440, B. $2655)

"The Danbury may be had in two arrangements, Plan A calls for the entire second floor being used as an attic, floored without partitions. Plan B has exactly the same downstairs as Plan A, but the upstairs as shown in the floor plan."

-1924 Wardway Homes

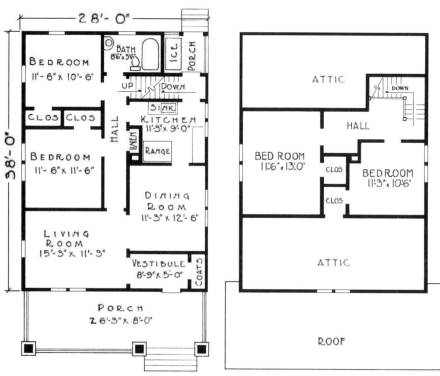

Plan A - 1st Floor   Plan B - 2nd Floor

1 Story
Side-Gable
Attached Porch
Full Width

Oakland (1926-1929 Ready-Cut)

Gordon-VanTine Design

1926 ($1835), 1927 ($1887), 1928 ($1945), 1929 ($2139)

"The Oakland gives you all the delightful features of convenience and comfort for which you have wished. Everything is in perfect proportion and it would be difficult to improve its exterior or its interior charm. Long sloping roof lines are broken by a well designed double window dormer. A large and pleasent front porch, projecting dining room wall and unique treatment of outside wall with a combination of siding and special spaced shingles"

- 1929 Wardway Homes

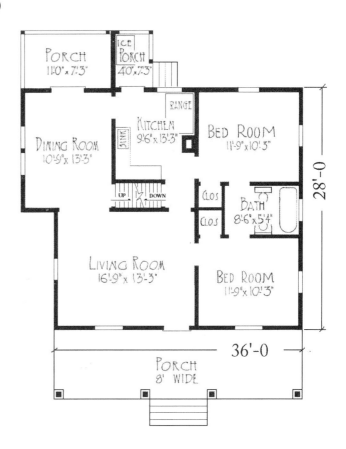

1 Story
Side-Gable
Attached Porch
Full Width

Maryland (1917-1931 Ready-Cut)

1917 ($911), 1918 ($1262), 1919 ($1437), 1920 ($1437), 1921 ($1437), 1922 ($1726), 1923 ($1830), 1924 ($1693), 1925 ($1693), 1926 ($1693), 1927 ($1677), 1928 ($1729), 1929 ($1807), 1930 ($1832), 1931 ($1797)

"For attractiveness of exterior and convenience of interior, few designs compare with the Maryland. Its individuality and charm are sure to attract the home buyer with discriminating taste."

- 1928 Wardway Homes

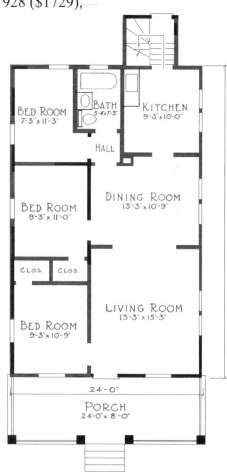

A Wardway *Maryland* In Sylvan Lake, Michigan (photograph by Dale Wolicki and Rebecca Hunter).

Corydon (1922-1931 Ready-Cut)

Gordon-VanTine Design

1922 ($1645), 1923 ($1576), 1924 ($1498), 1925 ($1470), 1926 ($1470),
1927 ($1588), 1928 ($1637), 1929 ($1794), 1930 ($1794), 1931 ($1748)

"The wide dormer, the changing slope of the roof at the porch, the hooded bay window and the large, square porch pillars make the exterior of this home exceedingly pleasing. The lines are simple, in perfect harmony and entirely practical, yet varied enough to command the attention of everyone. The exterior walls and square porch pillars are of stucco, for which we furnish Byrkitt patent sheathing. This home looks unusually well furnished this way, but should you prefer regular siding it will be furnished at slight additional cost. The exposed rafter ends of the dormer and main roof, the shingled dormer walls, the wide porch balusters and the outlined belt course, all contribute to the attractiveness of the Corydon. The correct handling of these details distinguishes the properly designed home from all others.

One is surprised to find a hall in a home of this size - yet it is here with a convenient coat closet opening off of it. This feature will be appreciated every day of the year. A large cased opening between the living and dining room makes these two practically one, yet preserves the identity of each. Fine twin windows in each insure a bright, cheery interior. The kitchen of this home will delight every housewife, as it is well arranged from every standpoint."

- 1924 Wardway Homes

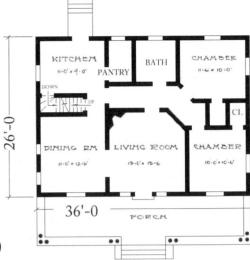

**1 Story
Side Gable
Attached Porch
Full Width**

#158 -Renamed Hinsdale in 1917
(Not Ready-Cut 1911-1916; Ready-Cut 1918)

1911 ($770 NRC), 1912 ($812 NRC), 1913 (NRC), 1914 ($808 NRC),
1915 ($871 NRC), 1916 ($932 NRC), 1917 ($1134 Ready-Cut)

"We have had so many calls for our house design Number 130 to be enlarged and made more elborate that we have designed this house on the same style but with more rooms in it, and of a higher class of architecture. It now is a home with a large living room and dining room, two bed rooms, a kitchen, pantry and bath. It also has a large Colonial porch with ten Colonial columns, set in groups of three on the corner and two each at the head of the steps leading to the porch; a large front door with side light on each side."

- 1914 Building Plans of Modern Homes

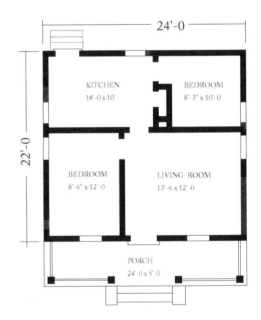

**1 Story
Side Gable
Attached Porch
Full Width**

#130 (1910-1916 Not Ready-Cut)

1910 ($267 NRC), 1911 ($287 NRC), 1912 ($306 NRC),
1913 (NRC), 1914 ($325), 1915 ($392 NRC), 1916 ($416 NRC)

"This little cottage has been sold more times than perhaps any other house shown in this book. For one of such small size and price it is exceptionally attractive. It has four rooms and closets, is finished throughout with yellow pine finish, and white pine doors. There is nothing special about the house of this size that one can say, except, perhaps, that it is house that can be built extremely cheap and give a better appearance for the amount of money spent than one would think possible. Many of the customers have built this for a home to live in permanently. Others have purchased it for a summer home, as it makes an ideal summer cottage."

- 1912 Building Plans of Modern Homes

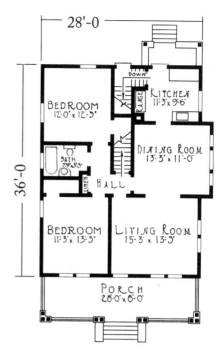

Arlington (1922-1924 Ready-Cut)

Gordon-VanTine Design
1922 ($2375), 1923 ($2280), 1924 ($2169)

"One of the most popular bungalow designs ever planned, our Arlington home, is giving great satisfaction to owners in every part of the United States. The broad roof coming low over the wide porch, and the shingled walls all the way to the ground line, give it a pleasing air of hospitality, and a very attractive exterior appearance. The wide dormer, the brackets supporting the cornice and the open rafter ends, are details which add greatly to the charm of this design."

- 1923 Wardway Homes

Michigan (1924-1927 Ready-Cut)

Gordon-VanTine Design
1924 ($1898), 1925 ($1888), 1926 ($1888), 1927 ($1938)

"In looking over the many designs of homes which are illustrated throughout this book, one is almost certain to hesitate when they reach the Michigan. We will venture to say that you have never seen a home quite like it. This is because very few homes have had the great amount of thought and care used in designing them that our architects have expended on this unusual bungalow."

- 1924 Wardway Homes

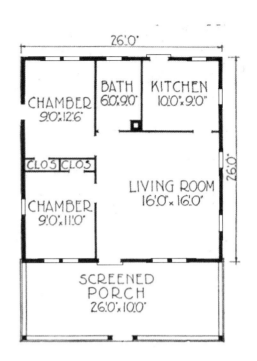

Bay View Cottage (1922-1928 Ready-Cut)

Gordon-VanTine Design

1922 ($715), 1923 ($707), 1924 ($707), 1925 ($707), 1926 ($707), 1927 ($698), 1928 ($698)

"One of the most practical and livable summer homes ever designed. Plenty of room - convenient arrangement - a good looking summer home in any community. Note the huge porch, 26 by 10 feet. The chimney is so placed that stoves can be used for heat in the spring and fall."

- 1923 Wardway Homes

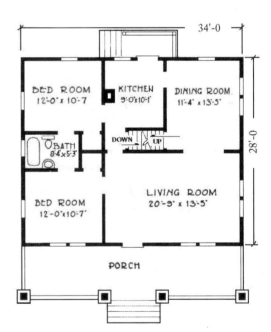

Carlton (1928-1930 Ready-Cut)

1928 ($2040), 1929 ($2127), 1930 ($2083)

"As you study the many different homes pictured in this book, you are sure to hesitate when you reach the Carlton. Seldom do you see a home like this, because very few homes have had the same amount of thought and care in planning them that our architects have expended on this unusual home. The well proportioned, correctly balanced dormers add greatly to this home, and prevent the low, squatty appearance which is noted in some homes of similar design and which greatly lessen their charm."

- 1928 Wardway Homes

#136
(1911-1914 Not Ready-Cut)
1911 ($1159 NRC), 1912 ($1230 NRC),
1913 (NRC), 1914 ($1230 NRC)

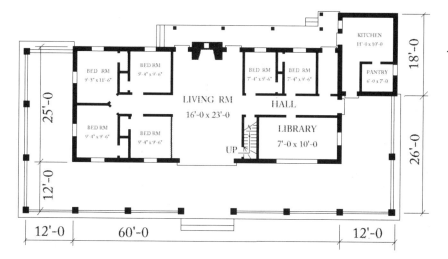

"Originally designed for one of our Florida customers, but it is so attractive that we offer it to you as an example of a very fine bungalow for those who live near the source of timber supply. The walls are constructed of peeled logs, squared on three sides, leaving the round face out. It is sheathed inside with sheathing boards and finished as any other building would be. We wish to call your special attention to the extremely large veranda, which is on three sides of the house."

- 1914 Building Plans of Modern Homes

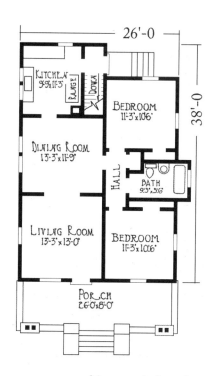

Santa Rosa (1922-1924 Ready-Cut)
Gordon-VanTine Design
1922 ($1990), 1923 ($1860)

"The unusual treatment of the porch gable and columns, and the broad eaves supported by sturdy brackets, give this delightful home a substantial appearance universally admired. The strength and dignity of the Santa Rosa is furthered by the porch wall of stone, capped with a cement rail. Material for this to be purchased locally. The roof over the bathroom projection is in perfect harmony with the main roof, while the projection itself furnishes a pleasing variation to the plain sidewall."

- 1923 Wardway Homes

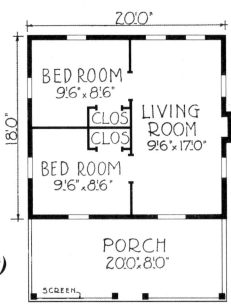

BED ROOM
9'6" x 8'6"

CLOS
CLOS

LIVING
ROOM
9'6" x 17'0"

BED ROOM
9'6" x 8'6"

20'0"

18'0"

PORCH
20'0" x 8'0"

SCREEN

1 Story
Side Gable
Attached Porch
Full Width

Avondale / Idlewood Cottage (1926 Ready-Cut)
Gordon VanTine Design
1926 ($475)

The catalog lists the model as the *Avondale* but the price list has it as the *Idlewood.*

"Of simple, easy, construction yet well arranged and roomy, this makes an ideal "shack" for those desiring comfort in the hot summer months. Big, cozy living room with cheery fireplace - wide porch that affords an unusual amount of outdoor living space - two large bedrooms, one of which may be used as a kitchen or dining room if necessary - all that one could ask for in a comfortable summer house."

- 1926 Wardway Homes

The PLAZA

AVERAGE MONTHLY
PAYMENTS
$30.00

Price $1597

1 Story
Side Gable
Attached Porch
Full Width

24'-0

KITCHEN
10'-0" x 6'-9"

RANGE

ICE BOX

BED ROOM
7'-9" x 10'-2"

LINEN

DINING ROOM
11'-3" x 8'-9"

CLOS

CLOS

BATH
7'-9" x 5'-6"

LIVING ROOM
13'-3" x 12'-3"

BED ROOM
11'-3" x 12'-3"

26'-0

30'-0

12'-3" x 7'-0"

Plaza (1930-1931 Ready-Cut)
1930 ($1597), 1931 ($1597)

"So pleasing and comfortable in design is the Plaza that every day you live in it will be one of increasing satisfaction. Snugly inviting, it offers a warm welcome to all your friends. That a home so charmingly simple could be so attractive is easily understood when you study its architectural features. A cozy trellis encased porchway with gabled roof and stately columns shelters the Colonial entrance. Shuttered windows, stained shingled sidewalls and gently sloping roof, all tend to increase its appearance of contentment."

- 1931 Wardway Homes

Claremont - Renamed Winslow 1929 (1922-1931 Ready-Cut)
Gordon-VanTine Design

1922 ($1720), 1923 ($1671), 1924 ($1568), 1925 ($1552), 1926 ($1552), 1927 ($1647), 1928 ($1698), 1929 ($1831), 1930 ($1831), 1931 ($1780)

"The faithfulness with which each detail carries out the motif of the design, gives an unusual but perfectly harmonious and pleasing appearance to this home. Battered gable ends are a striking departure from the usual, and most effective. The exterior beauty is further enhanced by the belt course extending around the house, which serves also as a head casing for all outside frames. Painted white, this is thrown into bold relief against the shingled sidewalls - creating an interesting effect."

- 1927 Wardway Homes

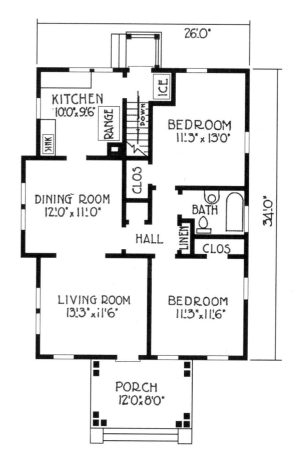

The *Winslow* offered 1929-1931

An unaltered Wardway *Claremont* in Ann Arbor, Michigan (photograph by Dale Wolicki).

A Rockford, Illinois *Winslow* (photograph by Rebecca Hunter).

A Wardway *Claremont* in Valspario, Illinois (photograph by Dale Wolicki).

A Wardway *Claremont* in Glen Ellen, Illinois (photograph by Rebecca Hunter).

Priscilla - Renamned Potomac in 1928 (1927-1931 Ready-Cut)
Gordon-VanTine Design
1927 ($1573), 1928 ($1656), 1929 ($1754), 1930 ($1754). 1931 ($1748)

When the Priscilla was introduced in 1927 the front elevation had larger single windows with 8/1 sash instead of the twin windows with 6/1 sash pictured above that were introduced in 1928.

The Priscilla can be distinguished from the Mount Vernon/Mayflower by the entrance door without side-lights, the short slope of clipped gables. There is no medallion above the entrance and the entrance gable features cornice returns.

"Everything about this home is Colonial in character. The distinctive hooded entrance affords the front door shelter and serves also to break up the otherwise plain roof lines. The Colonial door and shutters are especially harmonious. The thoughtfully designed, good lines, and nice proportions make this a beautiful and most desirable piece of Colonial architecture."

- *1927 Wardway Homes*

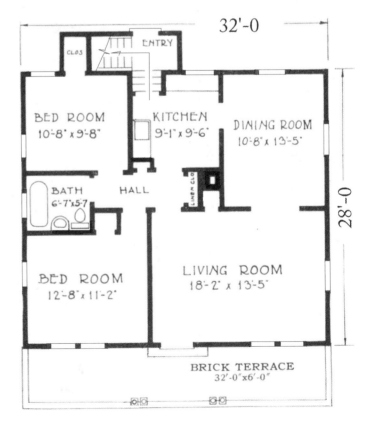

Mount Vernon - Renamed Mayflower in 1929 (1927-1931 Ready-Cut)

Gordon-VanTine Design

1927 (A.$1873, B.$2266), 1927 (A.$1931, B.$2336), 1928 (A.$1931, B.$2336),
1929 (A.$2101, B.$2520), 1930 (A.$2085, B.$2510), 1931 (A.$1984, B.$2386)

"Simple dignity - charm - and an air of refinement! Few houses create so aristocratic an impression as those of the Colonial style. And they are homelike, too - more truly home to the American than any other style house can possibly be, because they are closely associated with the traditions of the forefathers of this country. Perhaps that is why our Mount Vernon home has been one of the most popular houses pictured in this book. Its beautiful Colonial design has stood the test of time, and it is absolutely certain never to go out of style. The graceful architectural details are authentic, faithfully copied from fine old models. What a distinguished entrance with its nicely shaped and beautifully carved gable porch roof and slender columns! The battered gable ends, low overhanging eaves, big fireplace chimney, pretty trellises, and Colonial windows and window boxes, are delightful features. The long terrace adds architectural importance to the front - and will, of course, be ever so pleasant in summer. Our lovely Mount Vernon is unquestionably the greatest Colonial house bargain ever offered - and it will give you a lifetime of joy and service.

Two splendid floor plans - "A" and "B". Both of these floor plans for this house are skillfully designed, but they differ somewhat in size and arrangement. The Mount Vernon will minimize housework, since it is completely planned on the first floor - yet the bedrooms have desirable seclusion. The simple shape and spaciousness of the living rooms in plans "A" and "B" give you the freedom to create almost any interior effect."

- 1928 Wardway Homes

A *Mount Vernon* in Flint, Michigan has its original paired columns, paired windows with 6/1 window sash, clipped gables and ornamental medallion above the entrance door (photograph by Dale Wolicki).

The Mount Vernon/Mayflower can be distinguished from the Priscilla by the entrance door side-lights, the long sloping clipped gables and paired slender columns. The medallion above the entrance is unique to the Mount Vernon/Mayflower but may have been removed in subsequent renovations.

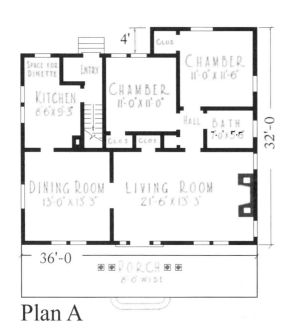

Plan A

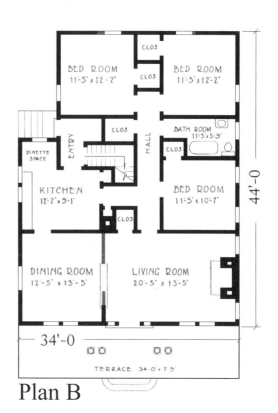

Plan B

A brick Mount *Vernon* in Roanoke, Virginia (photograph by Rose Thornton).

An Ann Arbor, Michigan *Mount Vernon* (photograph by Dale Wolicki).

A *Mount Vernon* in Georgetown, Kentucky with unclipped gables (photograph by Dale Wolicki).

A *Mount Vernon* in Greensboro, North Carolina (photograph by Dale Wolicki).

A Wardway *Mount Vernon* in Blacksburg, Virginia (photograph by Rose Thornton).

A Wardway *Mount Vernon* in Bluffton, Ohio (photograph by Dale Wolicki).

Edwards - Renamed Dellwood in 1928 (1924-1931 Ready-Cut)

Gordon-VanTine Design

1924 ($1332), 1925 ($1275), 1926 ($1275), 1927 ($1275),
1928 ($1384), 1929 ($1448), 1930 ($1429), 1931 ($1349)

"Many people prefer the small bungalow home to any of the larger houses, because a small house has quaintness and simplicity difficult to duplicate. It is therefore the cozy individuality of this little shingled bungalow which immediately attracts attention. The quaint exterior with its low sweeping roof lines, its battered gable ends and its unusually attractive Colonial porch, gives such an inviting appearance to the exterior that it bespeaks a cozy, convenient arrangement within. A wide triple window in the front, with divided upper sash, and flower boxes below, adds a final touch which makes the exterior nicely balanced and complete in every detail. The inviting interior supplies about everything one could wish in a four room home. The living room, which opens directly off the front porch, is a large, pleasant room, exceptionally well lighted by its three windows and door, the later which has six lights of bevel plate glass in the upper part."

- 1928 Wardway Homes

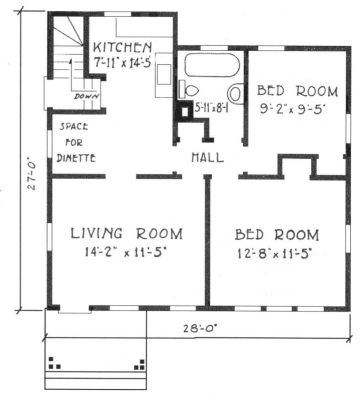

Marengo - Renamed Hillcrest in 1928 (1922-1931 Ready-Cut)

Gordon Van Tine Design

1922 ($1514), 1923 ($1480), 1924 ($1415), 1925 ($1385), 1926 ($1385),
1927 ($1429), 1928 ($1497), 1929 ($1573), 1930 ($1573), 1931 ($1548)

"The low, sweeping roof of this home and the shingled walls, give it the cozy, inviting appearance so much desired in a bungalow. This effect is increased by the wide steps flanked by the shingled buttresses. The careful design-ing to give this Wardway Home the most convenient room arrangement and to utilize every possible inch of floor space is evident in the floor plan. From the big porch one enters directly into the living room. Although there are four windows in this room, giving an abundance of light and air, still there is plenty of wall space for furniture. A broad cased opening directly opposite the front door gives an effect of distance which makes both rooms appear even larger. The kitchen, which adjoins the dining room, is com-pact and splendidly planned. The housewife can get a meal with very few steps, as sink, case and range are within reach when one stands in the center of the floor."

- 1923 Wardway Homes

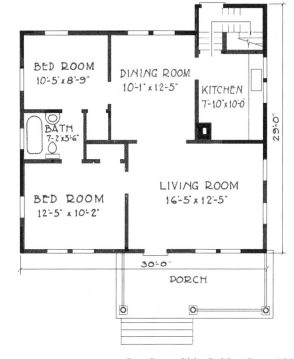

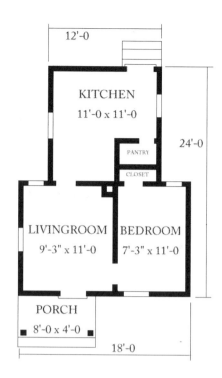

1 Story
Side Gable
Offset
Porch

KITCHEN
11'-0 x 11'-0

PANTRY

CLOSET

LIVINGROOM
9'-3" x 11'-0

BEDROOM
7'-3" x 11'-0

PORCH
8'-0 x 4'-0

12'-0

24'-0

18'-0

#134 (1910-1914 Not Ready-Cut)
1910 ($239 NRC), 1911 ($145), 1912 ($265 NRC),
1913 (NRC), 1914 ($313 NRC)

"This little cottage was designed especially for homesteaders who do not wish to go to the expense of building a full sized cottage or house. The principal merit of this building is the cheapness of construction. If you wish this this as a summer cottage and do not want plasterboard or double wall sheathing, write us and state your requirements. We will be glad to quote a price delivered at your depot."

- 1912 Building Plans of Modern Homes

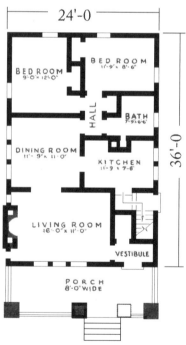

1 Story
Side Gable
Offset
Porch

BED ROOM
9'-0" x 12'-0"

BED ROOM
11'-9" x 8'-6"

HALL

BATH
7'-9" x 6'-6"

DINING ROOM
11'-9" x 11'-0"

KITCHEN
11'-9 x 7'-6

LIVING ROOM
16'-0" x 11'-0"

VESTIBULE

PORCH
8'-0" WIDE

24'-0

36'-0

Utica (1929-1931 Ready-Cut)
1929 ($1763), 1930 ($1887), 1931 ($1834)

"Throughout its five pleasant rooms the Utica is skillfully planned. In the vestibule you will find its first excellent feature, an unusually large coat closet. Through a plaster arch is the living room, and what a delightful one it is, with its three full sized windows and two casements besides the fireplace. Beyond through a second plastered arch, is the dining room with a most unique and pleasing arrangement of three casement windows. Two bedrooms are at the back of the house, away from the street noises, and shut off completely from the living rooms by a separating hall."

- 1931 Wardway Homes

#150 (1911-1915 Not Ready-Cut)

1911 ($1085 NRC), 1912 ($1139 NRC), 1913 (NRC), 1914 ($1090 NRC), 1915 ($1198 NRC)

"This is a very nicely arranged and attractive Bungalow. We wish to call attention to the fact that we supply the material to finish the dining room and living room in Craftsman Birch trim to be stained Mahogany finish. The dining room is to have beamed ceiling. Wall cornice, plate rail and panel strips, a nice mantel and a specially designed buffet, all in birch."

- 1914 Building Plans of Modern Homes

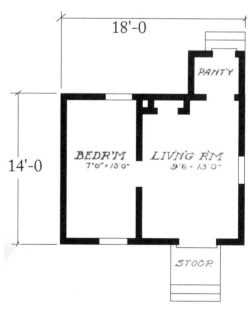

#135 - 1st (1910-1911 Not Ready-Cut)

1910 ($139 NRC), 1911 ($247 NRC)

"This is another homesteader's cottage that is inexpensive and that can later be utilized as a kitchen when you build your larger home. It also can be used very nicely as a summer cottage and is about the cheapest two room cottage that can be built."

- 1911 Building Plans of Modern Homes

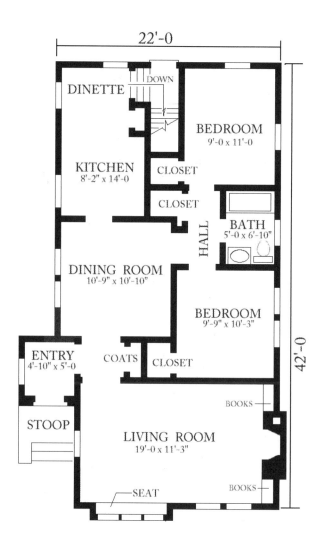

Yorkton (1931 Ready-Cut)

1931 ($1762)

"Those wide silvery gray sidewall shingles help to give the Yorkton its snug and cozy atmosphere. This pleasing effect is increased by the intriguing plank door whose hinges are decorative metal straps resembling wrought iron and whose window is small paned and circular. The architect has added still another charming touch - a wide flower box under the living room windows that you will want to fill with glowing geraniums. He also suggested an uncovered brick terrace as an appropriate threshold. So charming an exterior proclaims an equally delightful interior and you are not going to be disappointed. First of all the Yorkton has a studio living room. You enter it through a vestibule and a reception hall that has a convenient clothes closet. The arched ceiling of this spacious living room is a full story and a half high! There is a big open fireplace at the far end flanked with built-in, open bookshelves and of course there is a window seat placed in the arched bay of three casement windows."

- 1931 Wardway Homes

A brick *Yorkton* in Perrysburg, Ohio (photograph by Dale Wolicki).

A *Yorkton* in Mishawaka, Indiana that was used for the catalog illustration (photograph by Dale Wolicki).

Plymouth (1930-1931 Ready-Cut)
1930 (A. $1278, B. $1328), 1931 (A. $1278, B. $1328)

Plan B added a small breakfast nook that extended out from the kitchen.

"An inspired architect solved the home problem of many young married people when he planned the Plymouth. Strikingly graceful exterior lines combine with an unusually efficient interior arrangement to create a home for you, economical of space, low in price and rich in charm. Combining the living and dining rooms greatly reduces the cost of furnishing the Plymouth.

The beautiful entrance with its soaring upward sweep to a high peaked gable will impress even the most casual observer. Completing this French provincial suggestion is doorway arch of classic grace. The panel door has leaded diamond panes and opens into a formal roomy vestibule with closet for outer-garments at the right.

- 1930 Wardway Homes

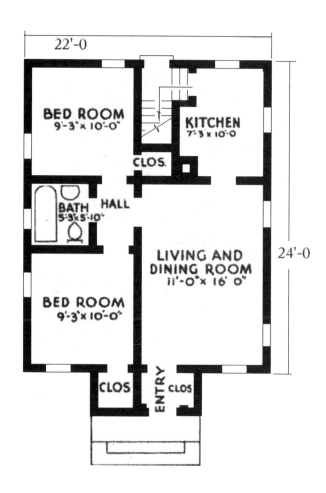

A brick *Plymouth* in Roseville, Michigan found with mortgage documents (photograph by Dale Wolicki).

A 1930 Wardway *Plymouth* in Lake Geneva, Wisconsin used for advertising (photograph by Rebecca Hunter).

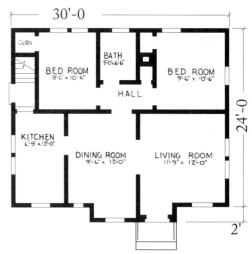

Drexel (1930-1931 Ready-Cut)

1930 ($1551), 1931 ($1523)

"How easily it can be yours - this pleasant low house with sidewalls of silver-gray shingles, brightened by boxes of geraniums at its quaint casement windows, or given an English touch by tiny evergreens at its prim door-stoop. With the sash and trim painted to contrast colorfully with the gray, and with the inside finished beautifully in the modern manner, the Drexel is more than a new house. It is your own charming home, expressing your good taste, and your sense of value."

- 1931 Wardway Homes

A *Drexel* in Mishawaka, Indiana (photograph by Dale Wolicki).

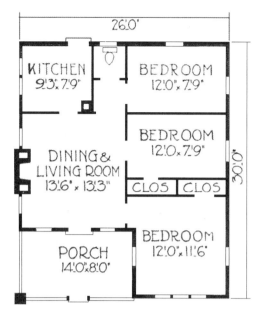

1 Story
Side Gable
Offset
Porch

KITCHEN
9'3" x 7'9"

BEDROOM
12'0" x 7'9"

BEDROOM
12'0" x 7'9"

DINING &
LIVING ROOM
13'6" x 13'3"

CLOS   CLOS

BEDROOM
12'0" x 11'6"

PORCH
14'0" x 8'0"

26'0"

30'0"

Charlevoix Cottage (1922-1928 Ready-Cut)

Gordon VanTine Design
1922 ($698), 1923 ($685), 1924 ($685), 1925 ($685),
1926 ($685), 1927 ($679), 1928 ($679)

"This beautiful little shingled cottage fits right in with any summer resort colony. It has an unusually good floor plan with plenty of room and plenty of conveniences which you do not expect in a summer cottage. Yet is not expensive and very easy to build. The porch screens are furnished. Everything with the exception of the masonry is shipped complete to build this cottage."

- 1926 Wardway Homes

1 Story
Side Gable
Offset
Porch

BEDROOM
10'0" x 10'6"

CLOS

CLOS

DINING ROOM
& KITCHEN
11'6" x 13'6"

BEDROOM
10'0" x 13'6"

LIVING ROOM
11'0" x 15'6"

PORCH
7'0" x 14'0"

26'-0

30'-0

Minnetonka Cottage (1922-1924 Ready-Cut)

Gordon VanTine Design
1922 ($717), 1923 ($897), 1924 ($690)

"A delightfully designed little summer cottage. Note the excellent floor plan with closet space provided. Wardway Ready-Cut System and complete specifications make this and our other summer homes so easy to erect and so low in cost that there is no reason for not having summer comfort."

- 1923 Wardway Homes

Wardway Home Locations

We are frequently asked, "Are there any Wardway Homes in my neighborhood?" Unfortunately, Montgomery Ward disposed of their records years ago, but our research indicates that Wardway Homes were built throughout the United States.

The majority of Wardway Homes can be found in eastern half of the United States, primarily the Midwest and Northeast. In no particular order, Ohio, Indiana, New York, New Jersey, Michigan, Maryland, Pennsylvania, Virginia, Illinois and Wisconsin have large numbers of Wardway Homes.

Although we do find kit-homes scattered throughout the countryside, by far the majority are located in villages and cities. The largest concentrations of kit-homes are typically in the villages and suburbs outside cities such as Chicago, Detroit, Cleveland, Washington D.C., Philadelphia, and New York City. Wardway Homes are found scattered among traditionally built homes, typically in neighborhoods that are within a few blocks of roads that once had street car lines.

Newspapers stories about home building may mention local Wardway Homes under construction (1931 Wardway Homes catalog).

This map illustrating the areas Montgomery Ward provided construction supervision helps to determine where concentrations of Wardway Homes can be found (1931 Wardway Homes catalog).

The "Leland" — A Charming Stucco Bungalow

A BIT of old English architecture combined with the latest features of modern home construction. The twenty-three attractive windows are arranged to give abundant light, yet mindful of space needed for furniture. The main roof extends over the porch, and the cornice projects sufficiently to insure plenty of shade. The boxed rail permits porch being screened at small expense. The attractive paneled gable eaves, supported by large brackets, help to make the exterior appealing. Beautiful flower boxes and supporting brackets are furnished.

Living Room: The interior arrangement cannot be excelled for convenience. The living room opens off the porch, and there are handsome French doors connecting the living room with the Sun Parlor. The latter has seven large windows and is indeed one of the most desirable features of this well arranged home. In the living room is a large fireplace which adds greatly to winter comfort and cheer.

Dining Room: A vestibule connects the living room. The two rooms span width of the home. The arranged and will seat a...

Hall: A central hall provides a degree of convenience otherwise unobtainable in furnishing easy access to and from the various rooms. Off the hall is a closet for mops, brooms, etc. At the rear end of the hall is a fine linen closet, while at the front is a closet for coats, wraps, etc.

Bedrooms and Bath: The three bedrooms are large and well grouped around the bathroom. There is an abundance of good light and ventilation. Note in these are also the quiet portions of the house. Each bedroom has a roomy closet for clothing, blankets, etc.

Kitchen: Placed in the center of the home, and uniquely arranged to save time and steps. The grouping of the range, sink, and two large built-in cases "B" and "D," shown on Page 30, and a smaller closet, is unusually well planned. The windows provide good light and...

One Story Cross Gable

Leland - Renamed Newcastle in 1929 (1924-1930 Ready-Cut)
Gordon-VanTine Design
1924 ($2129), 1925 ($2110), 1926 ($2110), 1927 ($2374), 1928 ($2447), 1929 ($2708), 1930 ($2695)

"A bit of old English architecture combined with the latest features of modern home construction. The twenty-three attractive windows are arranged to give abundant light, yet mindful of space needed for furniture. The main roof extends over the porch, and the cornice projects sufficiently to insure plenty of shade. The boxed rail permits porch being screened at small expense. The attractive gable eaves, supported by large brackets, help to make the exterior appealing. Beautiful flower boxes and supporting brackets are furnished. The exterior arrangement cannot be excelled for convenience. The living room opens off the porch, and there are handsome French doors connecting the living room with the sun parlor. The latter has seven large windows and is indeed one of the most desirable features of this well arranged home. In the living room is a large fireplace which adds greatly to winter comfort and cheer. A wide cased opening connects the living room with the dining room. The two rooms extending the full width of the home. The dining room is nicely arranged and will seat a large family."

- 1927 Wardway Homes

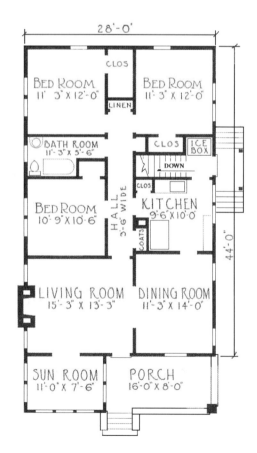

Assembly stamps helped Rebecca Hunter identify this Wardway *Leeland* in Lemont, Illinois.

1 Story
Cross Gable
Offset
Porch

Woodlawn (1927-1929 Ready-Cut)
Gordon-VanTine Design
1927 ($2379), 1928 ($2453), 1929 ($2734)

"If you are thinking of building a six-room bungalow home you will find much to interest you in our "Wood-lawn". The exterior with its broad roof expanse, its wide overhanging eaves supported by sturdy brackets and quaintly designed recess porch gives this home individuality and sets it part as quite different from the usual run of bungalows."

- 1927 Wardway Homes

#168 - Renamed Fairview in 1917 (1914-1921 Not Ready-Cut)

1914 ($1422 NRC), 1915 ($1392 NRC),
1916 ($1392 NRC), 1917 ($1497 NRC),
1918 ($2092 NRC), 1919 ($2261 NRC),
1920 ($2196 NRC), 1921 ($2196 NRC)

"Can any person help admiring this California Bungalow? Imagine yourself in a cozy rocker on one of those spacious porches watching a summer sunset. Your neighbor strolling leisurely by, stops to pass the time of day, and admiringly discusses with you the architectural merits of your new home. He, too is planning to build. The unusual treatment of the eaves with their projecting rafter-ends and numerous supporting brackets appeals to his fancy. The massive brick piers and grouped porch columns lend an air of solidity which conforms beautifully with the bungalow type of architecture."

- 1918 Wardway Homes

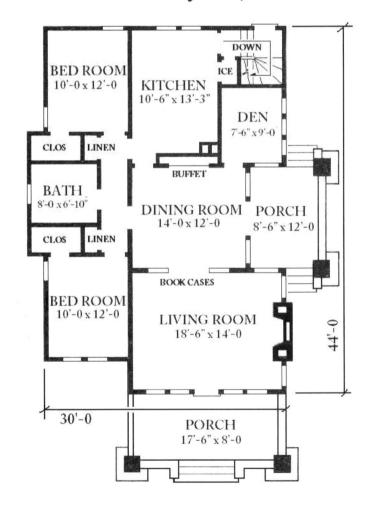

A *#168/Fairview* in Wood River, Illinois (photograph by Rose Thornton).

Crown Pointe, Illinois *#168/Fairview* (photograph by Rebecca Hunter and Dale Wolicki).

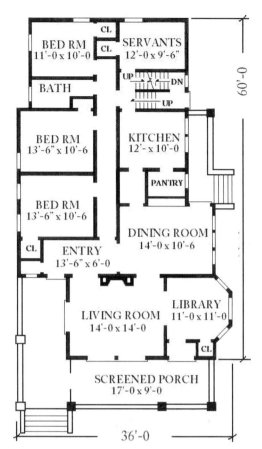

#170 (1914-1916 Not Ready-Cut)
1914 ($1324 NRC), 1915 ($1777 NRC), 1916 ($1777 NRC)

"The terrace and screened porch are perhaps the most striking features of this tasteful bungalow. Very pleasing, also, is the combination of shingle siding with a roof that is quite plain except for the brackets. The recesses in the gables are quite novel and attractive, providing a fitting background for a set of flower boxes. The Colonial windows and French doors and windows add just the right touch."

- 1915 Book of Homes

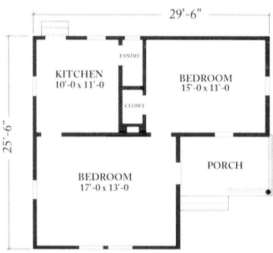

#126 (1909 -1914 Not Ready-Cut)
1909 ($381 NRC), 1910 ($381 NRC), 1911 ($370 NRC), 1912 ($394 NRC), 1913 (NRC), 1914 ($394 NRC)

"This little cottage, though quite small, and containing only three rooms, will, no doubt, catch the eye of those who desire a comfortable, cozy, inexpensive abode. It would make a very good ranch house for a couple of bachelors, or might be suited to the desires of a man and wife of modest means. It would certainly be just the thing for people who spend most of their time out of doors and want only a place to eat and sleep. It can easily be kept clean and tidy. Many houses of this type are seen in mountainous districts of the south and on the hot plains of the west."

- 1912 Building Plans of Modern Homes

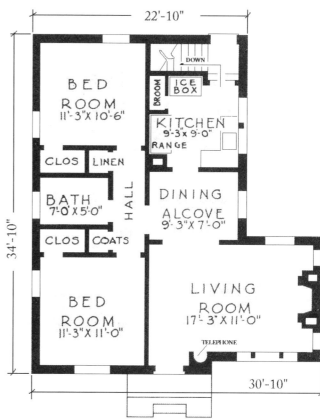

22'-10"

BED
ROOM
11'-3"X 10'-6"

DOWN

BROOM

ICE
BOX

KITCHEN
9'-3 x 9'-0"

RANGE

CLOS LINEN

BATH
7'-0" X 5'-0"

HALL

DINING
ALCOVE
9'-3" X 7'-0"

CLOS COATS

34'-10"

BED
ROOM
11'-3" X 11'-0"

LIVING
ROOM
17'-3" X 11'-0"

TELEPHONE

30'-10"

Berkley (1931 Ready-Cut)
Gordon-VanTine Design

1931 (A. $1651, B. $1503) A. was for an exterior of shingles, B. was framed for brick exterior

Although, the *Berkley* was popular, it was offered briefly, thus most examples of this house are actually Gordon-VanTine's *Rosemont (below)*. The two are identical in appearance, measurement and floorplan. Although the Berkley was illustrated with a round-top door flush with the wall, the Rosement featured a recessed standard square door under an ornamental fanlight that suggested a round-top door. The two entrances can be found with either model. To determine if the house is a Berkley you need to find written evidence or a shipping label.

Kelton (1929-1931 Ready-Cut)

Gordon-VanTine Design

1929 (A. $1397), 1930 (A. $1447), 1931 (A. $1441, B. $1553)

"Any prospective builders will find their ideals realized in this distinctive home. It affords an opportunity to give your decorative tastes free rein. The architect has suggested a bricked terrace, flower boxes and a box hedge as an appropriate setting for this harmonious home. The front entrance is through a formal vestibule, with closet for coats and outer garments. Vestibule and living room floored with oak. The cheery Living Room has two windows; the front window is provided with artistic shutters. Oak flooring furnished. Cozy Kitchen and Dining Nook - the big feature of this home. Two plaster arches span the rear of the kitchen. At the right is a dining space with two windows. Through the other arch is suggested space for the ice box, and stairs to the rear entry and cellar stairs."

- 1929 Wardway Homes

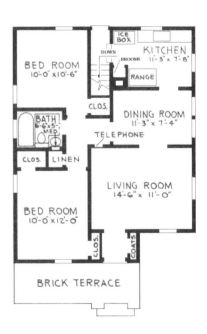

Plan A

Plan B

A Wardway *Kelton* in Mishawaka, Indiana (photograph by Barb Brownell).

A Wardway *Kelton* in Ann Arbor, Michigan (photograph by Dale Wolicki).

Dover (1929-1931 Ready-Cut)

1930 (A. $1564), 1931 (A. $1514, B. $1692)

"How comfortably you can settle down in the Dover! And how contentedly inviting will its snug appearance beckon to your friends! It's the kind of house you'd like to visit and the kind you'd like better to own. A modern home in every detail. It's one in which you can raise your children and know that, when they are ready to entertain in years to come, it's a house so correct in design that it will not be out of date. The simplicity of its beauty amplifies every tiny feature of design. Distinctive shutter windows, gently sweeping gables roof, concrete steps and stoop - add a box of flowers, a bit of shrub, a carpet of grass, and your setting is complete and enjoyable."

- *1930 Wardway Homes*

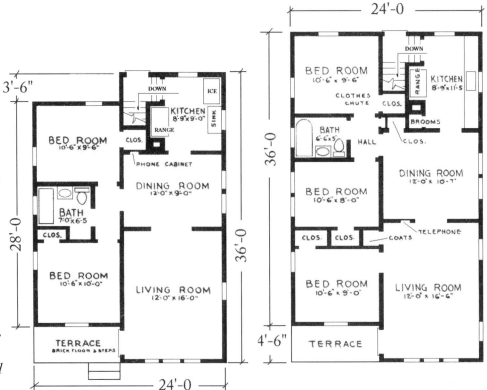

Plan A

Plan B

Mortgage records helped to locate this *Dover* in Grand Haven, Michigan (photograph by Dale Wolicki).

A *Dover* in East Lansing, Michigan (photograph by Dale Wolicki).

1 Story
Cross Gable
Entrance
Stoop

Avalon (1930-1931 Ready-Cut)
1930 ($1885), 1931 ($1795)

"The Avalon is a truly beautiful home and will prove an investment you may expect to pay big dividends as long as you have it, and pay a profit if you ever have occasion to sell. With the saving our price and ready-cut system offers you, with our special economical plan for easy payments, and with the real charm of the house itself, there is every reason in the world to congratulate yourself for choosing it. Outside, its sharp-peaked gables, its tiny-paned windows, its bright-painted shutters suggest the quaintness that is New England. Inside, there is everything you want for modern quickness and efficiency in housekeeping."

- 1930 Wardway Homes

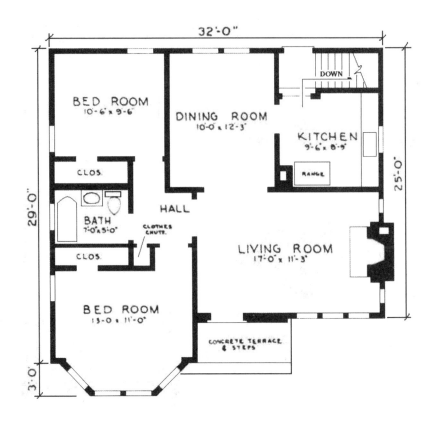

An *Avalon* in Port Huron, Michigan (photograph by Dale Wolicki).

An *Avalon* in Flint, Michigan (photograph by Dale Wolicki).

Pontiac (1930-1931 Ready-Cut)
1930 ($1527), 1931 ($1466)

"New grace - new style - new economy in a compact 5-room bungalow. Just visual the Pontiac as your home! Who can't help but admire its distinctive coziness - its quaint charm. The battered end front gable, attractive gray shingled sidewalls and Colonial windows with shutters, brings a suggestion of the old to an entirely new and modern design. It is a real home at an amazingly low price - one that you can buy with payments less than rent. In the Pontiac Wardway architects again demonstrate that even at a low price all modern conveniences and comforts with new beauty and style are retained in Wardway Homes."   -1930 Wardway Homes

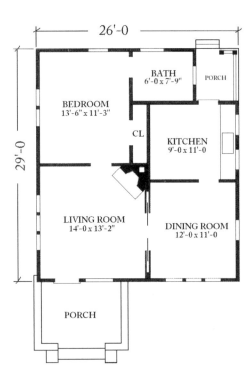

#164 - Renamed Woodlawn in 1917
(1912-1917 Not Ready-Cut)
1912 ($564 NRC), 1913 (NRC), 1914 ($574 NRC),
1915 ($649 NRC), 1916 ($585 NRC), 1917 ($693 NRC)

"A four-room bungalow, one that appeals alike to the follower of the practical and the lover of the artistic. Nothing freakish, nothing extravagant - but can you imagine a more charming exterior for a little home, or a more pleasing interior? Its charm lies in its very simplicity. Note the wide overhang of the eaves, the graceful lines of the roof, the inviting porch, the flower boxes around the windows."

- 1916 Book of Homes

Charming Modernized Swiss Cottage, $2500 or Under

Design No. 122—Size, exclusive of porches: width, 28 feet 6 inches; length, 32 feet 6 inches.

FIRST FLOOR PLAN

- PANTRY 5X4-6
- PORCH
- DINING ROOM. 12X15
- KITCHEN 10X10
- CLOS.
- DOWN
- HALL 9X11
- LIVING ROOM 13X14
- UP
- PORCH

Estimated Cost to Build $2200 to $2500, According to Location

Working Blue Prints consist of basement plans, first and second floor plans, front, rear and two side elevations; wall sections and all necessary interior details. Specifications are contained in a set of specially printed pages, bound in manila covers.

Price One Dollar

for complete set of Working Blue Prints, and set of printed and manila bound specifications, for design No. 122.

Without cost we will furnish an exact estimate of the cost of millwork with every set of plans.

SECOND FLOOR PLAN

- BED ROOM 10-6X11-6
- BED ROOM 11-6X11-6
- CLOS.
- CLOS.
- CLOS.
- BATH 8-6X6-6
- HALL
- DOWN

One & 1/2 Story Front Gable

#105 (1909-1916 Not Ready-Cut)

Radford Design

1909 ($575 NRC), 1910 ($575 NRC), 1911 ($632 NRC), 1912 ($717 NRC),
1913 (NRC), 1914 ($728 NRC), 1915 ($814 NRC), 1916 ($827 NRC)

"For $827.00 we furnish all the material to build this home of five rooms, bath and two porches, consisting of all the lumber, lath, shingles, finishing lumber, flooring, doors, windows, frames, trim, hardware, pipe and gutter, and painting material. We absolutely guarantee the material we furnish to be sufficient to build the house according to our plans and specifications. Home 105 represents quite a remarkable combination of handsome appearance, economy of construction, and convenient, comfortable arrangement. Throughout the entire house there is the pleasing sense of having plenty of "elbow room" while at the same time everything is so compactly arranged that the cost is kept low. Inside and out, every feature is pleasing, and it is equally suitable for a narrow city lot or a farm residence."
                    - 1915 Book of Homes

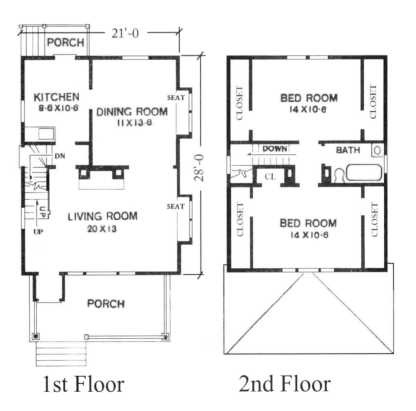

1st Floor   2nd Floor

Although this home in Elgin, Illinois has been updated, the three-part attic window and square bay windows on the side elevation are a distinctive detail of Montgomery Ward's *#105* (photographs by Rebecca Hunter).

#123 (1909-1914 Not Ready-Cut)

Radford Design

1909 ($654 NRC), 1910 ($654 NRC), 1911 ($794 NRC), 1912 ($899 NRC), 1913 (NRC), 1914 ($902 NRC)

"Design Number 123 is not the most elaborate and attractive house in this book, but it is one of the best sellers, due largely to the fact that the rooms are well arranged and that it has been and can be built at a very low price. The rooms are all of good size; an open stairway leads from the front hall to second floor; the living room has a mantel in one corner and is separated from hall and dining room by wide cased openings. On the second floor there are four bedrooms, bath and five closets. The interior finish is clear yellow pine with western pine doors. We have furnished this house in other wood to several of our customers and friends, and if you will write and tell how you wish this house arranged to meet your requirements, we shall be glad to give you our best attention."

- 1914 Building Plans of Modern Homes

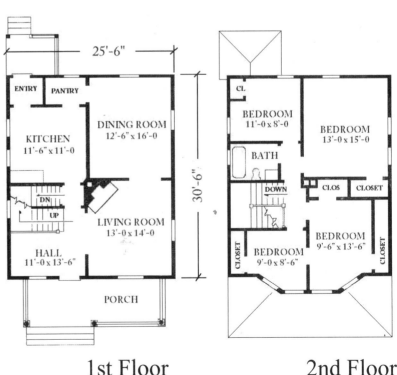

1st Floor   2nd Floor

Midland (1918-1921 Ready-Cut)

1918 ($1054), 1919 ($1242), 1920 ($1206), 1921 ($1206)

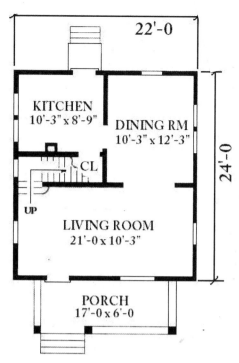

"The Midland is a substantial home of pleasing proportion, which cannot help but convey an impression of neatness and home comfort. An unusual treatment of the eaves lends an individuality and although there is no attempt at adornment, there is nevertheless a certain dignity associated with it. The interior arrangement leaves little to be desired. The living room is large, and ample wall space gives the housewife an opportunity to exercise her skill in placing her furniture attractively."
— 1918 Wardway Homes

#129 - Renamed Michigan in 1917 (1910-1916 Not Ready-Cut; 1917-1921 Ready-Cut)

1910 ($481 NRC), 1911 ($444 NRC), 1912 ($470 NRC), 1913 (NRC), 1914 ($482 NRC), 1915 ($599 NRC), 1916 ($570 NRC), 1917 ($695), 1918 ($1045), 1919 ($1260), 1920 ($1224), 1921 ($1224)

"For the small farm this home proves most desirable."
-1917 Book of Homes

The updated *#143/#183/Springfield* as it appeared in the 1917 catalog.

#143 - Renamed #183 in 1915, Springfield in 1917
(Not Ready-Cut 1911-1918; Ready-Cut 1919-1921)

1911 ($666 NRC), 1912 ($700 NRC), 1913 (NRC), 1914 ($776 NRC), 1915 ($826 NRC), 1916 ($795NRC), 1917 ($891 NRC), 1918 ($1310 NRC), 1919 ($1519), 1920 ($1475), 1921 ($1475)

"A remarkable little five-room house, because of its price, size and convenience. Simple lines have been fol-

lowed throughout, permitting only such few ornamentations as will harmonize with the general outside appearance. The large side dormer is a pleasing relief from the flat surface of the roof.

From the front porch you enter directly into the living room which is connected with the dining room by a cased arch, practically combining the two into one large room. Off the kitchen is a well lighted pantry, cellar stairs and a rear porch. A centrally located hall offers access to rear bedroom, bath and attic stairway. Another bedroom with large closet opens off the dining room. This home is a remarkably good investment."

- 1918 Wardway Homes

The original *#143* as it appeared in the 1914 catalog

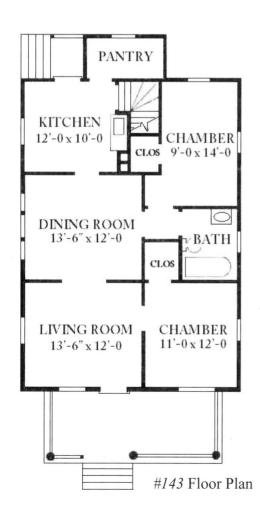

PANTRY

KITCHEN
12'-0 x 10'-0

CHAMBER
9'-0 x 14'-0

CLOS

DINING ROOM
13'-6" x 12'-0

BATH

CLOS

LIVING ROOM
13'-6" x 12'-0

CHAMBER
11'-0 x 12'-0

#143 Floor Plan

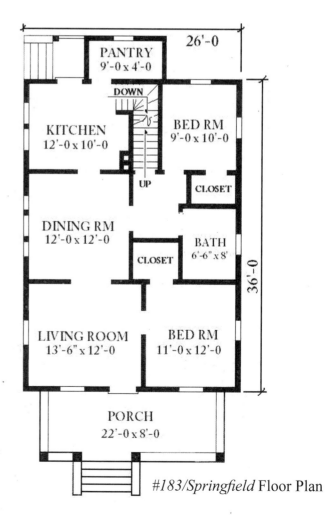

26'-0

PANTRY
9'-0 x 4'-0

DOWN

KITCHEN
12'-0 x 10'-0

BED RM
9'-0 x 10'-0

CLOSET

UP

DINING RM
12'-0 x 12'-0

CLOSET

BATH
6'-6" x 8'

36'-0

LIVING ROOM
13'-6" x 12'-0

BED RM
11'-0 x 12'-0

PORCH
22'-0 x 8'-0

#183/Springfield Floor Plan

Allerton - Renamed Newton in 1929 (1922-1928 Ready-Cut)

Gordon-Vantine Design

1922 ($2249), 1923 ($2150), 1924 ($1979), 1925 ($1995), 1926 ($1995),
1927 ($2106), 1928 (A.$2171, B.$2423), 1929 (A.$2215, B.$2614)

The Allerton was a one story model until 1928 when an optional finished attic was introduced.

"This home has that rare charm which gives it a universal appeal. The sensible, convenient floor plan makes it popular alike for town or country. Beautiful exterior treatment, comfort and conservatism are dominating notes. It is a type always in good style, and a home which, with its wide eaves, broad porch, and many windows, will always bespeak the comfort of those living in it."

- 1927 Wardway Homes

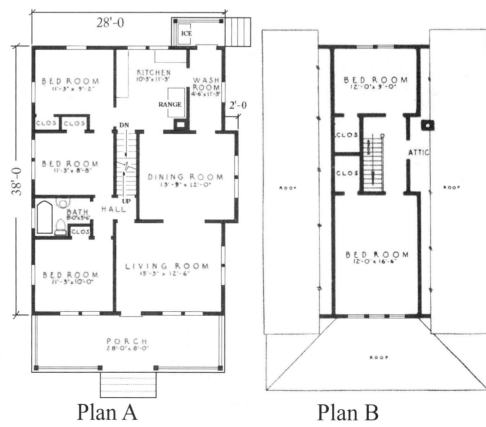

Plan A   Plan B

Mortgage records identified this *Allerton* in Howell, Michigan (photograph by Dale Wolicki).

#122 - Renamed Morse in 1917 (1909-1918 Not Ready-Cut)

Radford Design

1909 ($818 NRC), 1910 ($818 NRC), 1911 ($788 NRC),
1912 ($832 NRC), 1913 (NRC), 1914 ($851 NRC),
1915 ($907 NRC), 1916 ($907 NRC), 1917 ($997 NRC),
1918 ($1348 NRC)

Model #122 and the Morse have the same floorplan but the
#122 measures 23'-6" wide and 31'-0 in depth.

*"Your attention is called to the attractive and unusual ap-
pearance of the exterior. The windows are of the eastern type
- that is, one light of glass in the bottom sash and divided
lights in the upper sash. Note the large chimney, made of
rubble work. Note the peculiar and attractive style of finishing the balustrade."*

- 1914 Building Plans of Modern Homes

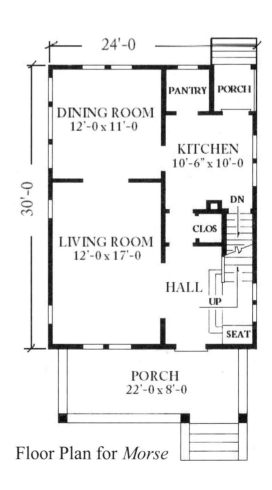

Floor Plan for *Morse*

1915 and 1916 llustration for the #122 without second floor bay window.

1917-1918 illustration for the *Morse*.

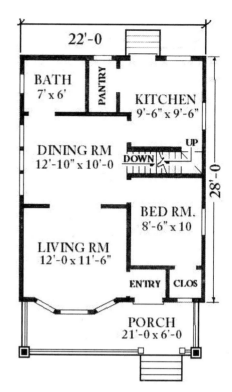

Gary "A" and "C" (1917 Ready-Cut)
1917 (A. $847, C. $851)

The Gary "A" is a front gable structure with a hip roof over the porch. The Gary "C" is a front gable structure with a front gable roof over the porch.

"Three of our very popular homes are shown in the Gary A, B and C. You will notice the same floor plan is used in each, but the roof and porch plans vary to avoid any tendency to monotony should a contractor desire to build several of these homes on adjacent lots."

- 1917 Book of Homes

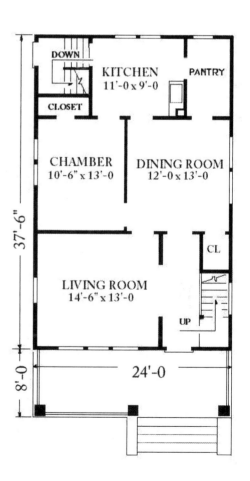

#138 - Renamed #178 in 1915
(1909-1914 Not Ready-Cut)
Similar to Sears *Niota*
1911 ($830 NRC), 1912 ($873 NRC), 1913 (NRC),
1914 ($871 NRC), 1915 ($935 NRC), 1916 ($913 NRC)

"There is a large and growing demand for stucco houses and in this two-story bungalow we have the perfection of architecture..."

- 1914 Building Plans of Modern Homes

Floor plan labels (Suburban):
PORCH | SUN·BREAKFAST·OR·SEWING ROOM 8'-0" X 7'-6"
KITCHEN 8'-6"X9'-6" | DINING ROOM 12'-0" X 15'-6"
ICE BOX | DOWN | BROOMS
LIVING ROOM 17'-6" X 13'-3"
COATS
PORCH 16'-0" X 8'-0"
22'-0" | 30'-0"

Suburban (1925-1928 Ready-Cut)

Gordon-VanTine Design
1925 ($2140), 1926 ($2140), 1927 ($2256), 1928 ($2326)

"Our Suburban design offers the discriminating builder an unusual opportunity to secure a typical English design home at a comparatively small cost. As the width is only 22 feet it may be built on narrow city lots as well as in suburban or rural districts"

— *1926 Wardway Homes*

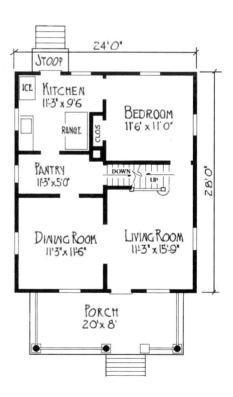

Floor plan labels (Jerome):
STOOP
ICE | KITCHEN 11'-3' x 9'6 | BEDROOM 11'6' x 11'0'
RANGE | CLOS
PANTRY 11'-3' x 5'0' | DOWN | UP
DINING ROOM 11'-3' x 11'6' | LIVING ROOM 11'-3' x 15'9'
PORCH 20'x 8'
24'0' | 28'0'

Jerome (1922-1924 Ready-Cut)

Gordon-VanTine Design
1922 ($1942), 1923 ($1840), 1924 ($1778)

"The story-and-a-half cottage is a type which is always popular and always in demand, for it gives you the most for your money in appearance and in living space. The home above illustrated is a splendid example of the type. Any effect of plainness is relieved by the fine enclosed cornice and the cornice returns at the end of the gables - also the dormer gables"

— *1923 Wardway Homes*

#179 - Renamed Princeton in 1917 (1914-1921 Not Ready-Cut)

1914 ($1100 NRC), 1915 ($1061 NRC), 1916 ($1114 NRC),
1917 ($1098 NRC), 1918 ($1746 NRC), 1919 ($1949 NRC),
1920 ($1893 NRC), 1921 ($1893 NRC)

"As neat a little Bungalow, considering the price, as was ever produced. Note the fine proportions throughout. A fine large porch, with
massive sided columns. This building has a concrete foundation to
grade, and is then built up of 2x4 studding, sheathed and sided on the
first floor with stucco or shingle finish for the gables and dormer. The
rafters of the roof are exposed and give a very finished appearance
to the building in its entirety. The ground plan is 28 feet x 41 feet 6
inches, and contains a large living room with a nook, spacious dining
room with a fireplace, both toward the front; while the kitchen, pantry, two bedrooms and bath can all be entered from a private hall. A
stairway leads to the attic, and an inside stairway to the basement can
also be arranged directly under the stairway. Provision for an ice box
is made in the rear entry. Particular attention is called to the fact that
all the plumbing is located so that same can be installed with the least
possible expense. This particular style of Bungalow meets with great
favor where the principal rooms are desired to front the street."

- 1914 Building Plans of Modern Homes

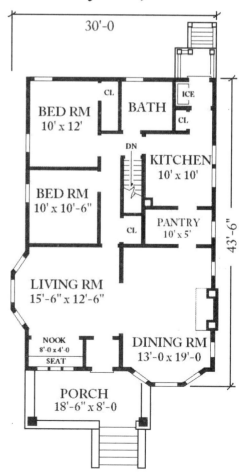

A *Princeton* in Elkins, West Virginia (photograph by Rose Thornton).

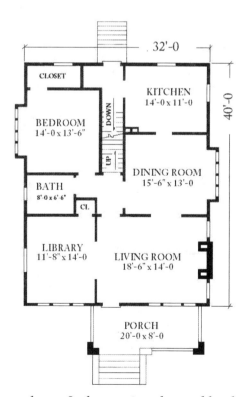

1 & 1/2
Front Gable
Attached Porch
Offset

#166 - Renamed Suburban in 1917
(1912-1921 Not Ready-Cut)

1912 ($1265 NRC), 1913 (NRC), 1914 ($1243), 1915 ($1256 NRC),
1916 ($1225 NRC), 1917 ($1398 NRC), 1918 ($2014 NRC),
1919 ($2442 NRC), 1920 ($2371 NRC), 1921 ($2371 NRC)

"Artistic indeed, but not overdone. This home appeals strongly to the home lover. Its beauty is enhanced by the clever treatment of details, such as the scrolled ends on the verge boards, supporting brackets, stuccoed front gable. The porch itself with solid brick rail and piers offers a solidity of aspect which is in harmonious contrast to the ornamentation."

- 1918 Wardway Homes

#118 (1909-1914 Not Ready-Cut)

Radford Design

1909 ($658 NRC), 1910 ($658 NRC), 1911 ($585 NRC),
1912 ($675 NRC), 1913 (NRC), 1914 ($652 NRC)

*"For $658.50 we furnish the materials to build this house, in-
cluding millwork, lumber, plumbing, hardware, lath and paint;
in short, all material except lime, stone, cement and brick, which
with the labor would make the total cost of construction about
$1211.75. Working blueprints consist of basement plan; first and
second floor plans, front, rear and two side elevations; wall sections and all necessary interior details."*

- 1910 Book of Building Plans

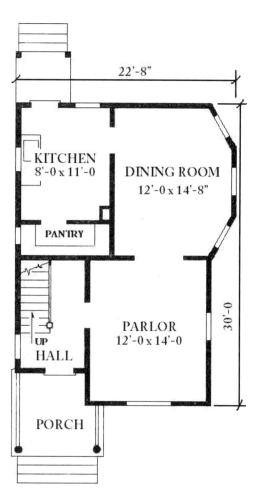

Iowa - Renamed Lakehurst in 1929 (1924-1927 Ready-Cut)

Gordon-VanTine Design

1924 ($1658), 1925 ($1628), 1926 ($1628), 1927 ($1715),
1928($1768), 1929 ($1997)

"Here's a small home that is quite out of the ordinary - an out-standing example of architectural unity as applied to structural values. The long, sloping roof surfaces and dormers on two sides make an instant appeal to people of good taste, but do not detract from its clean-cut neatness. A simple hooded entrance shades and protects the front stoop. A generous porch is provided at the side, with French doors opening into the living room. All but one room has light and ventilation on two sides. Beautiful clear oak floors included in the living room and dining room without extra charge. Entering the front door, we are in the spacious living room, showing a glimpse through a cased opening of the dining room behind, while at the right is the front stairs. Doors lead into the kitchen from both living room and dining room. It is roomy and conveniently laid out for all necessary equipment ... A large bedroom extends across the front of the house. Two in the rear are separated by roomy closets. All bedrooms open off a central hall and each has two windows for ample light and ventilation. A home like this will always be in style."

- *1929 Wardway Homes*

1st Floor

2nd Floor

Opposition to Pre-Cut Homes

Buying direct from us means the elimination of wholesalers, jobbers and retail dealers with their customary high profits. It means that you have no expensive plans to buy from an architect.
- 1919 Lewis Homes catalog

Skilled labor is really unnecessary in the erection and completion of an Aladdin house, because we supply skilled labor in our mills, preparing the entire house for you to fit and nail together in a few days
- 1913 Aladdin Homes catalog

Not everyone agreed mail-order homes were the best value for the dollar. Local building trades and unions, particularly carpenters - the very people whose livelihoods were threatened by the growing pre-cut home industry - lobbied for laws and ordinances that made it difficult to erect pre-cut homes. The most effective rule was the requirement that contractors could refuse to install any materials they had not supplied themselves, thus carpenters, plumbers and electricians, refused to install materials supplied by Montgomery Ward and others. "Builders are not particularly friendly to the ready-cut system", noted Business Week March 2, 1930, "for it leaves less for them to do. So the prospective home-owner who buys the ready-cut material may find difficulty in getting it put up."

Architects saw pre-cut homes as an intrusion into their practice. In response, the American Institute of Architects created the *Architects Small House Service Bureau*, a mail-order service that offered blueprints of architect designed residences in 1921.

"Far sighted economy dictates the wisdom of having an architect prepare plans and render service,", noted their 1921 home plan book *How to Plan, Finance and Build Your Homes*. "Too many builders, however, are disposed to eliminate the architect's service, and fail to avail themselves of a service which is the most useful tool in the entire home building operation. It therefore remained for some method of service to be evolved whereby the architect can render his talents, skill and counsel to small-home builders. The solution to this problem is presented to you in this publication."

Although their plan books offered a few smaller homes, the majority of ASHSB designs were fussy middle-class residences that reinforced the image that architects were unable to put economics ahead of style. The Architects Small House Service Bureau never offered any competition to the pre-cut housing industry, but their contempt for mail-order homes had an adverse impact on public opinion.

Another critic of the pre-cut housing industry was local lumber yards. In the early years they looked upon mail-order homes as a curiosity, spreading rumors of their poor quality materials and difficulty in assembly. Many wrote editorials to newspapers and magazines reminding reader's mail-order companies such as Montgomery Ward did not pay local taxes, had no local employees, and had no interest in community affairs.

During the building boom of the 1920's the opposition of local lumber yards subsided but the Depression brought frustrations back to the surface. "Dealers, particularly, have been harmed by the statements of mail order houses, couched in the alleged language of consumers, that you can save $500 to $2000 by building your home the mail order house way as compared with dealing with the local dealer", cried the Secretary-Manager of the National Retail Lumber Dealers in the June 1931 issue of American Builder and Building Age.

The
Curtis

$**1294**

Not
Ready-Cut

This particular style of house seems to be always growing more in favor. With its long sloping roof and large distinctive looking dormer it presents a very comfortable, substantial looking appearance.

The solid built-up rail on the porch with the privacy which it affords is a very desirable feature as well as making it a very simple matter to have the porch screened in during the summer months. The interior of the home is designed for the average family and is complete in every detail. The large well lighted living room and dining room leading from same are both most attractive. Note the ample closet room, each bedroom having a large closet under the projecting roof. The grade entrance is another very desirable feature. In fact how could this home be made more modern or convenient?

Curtis Specifications

Material list for this home follows the general specifications as given on pages 4-7. Size of porch, 20x8 feet. Ceilings, first floor, 9 feet, second floor, 8 feet, slightly hipped at side. Center sill, 6x8 inches. Floor joists, 2x8 inches. Studding, ceiling joists and rafters, 2x4 inches. Front door, 3x7 feet, style Van Dyke, glazed bevel plate. Rear and grade entrance doors, 2 feet 8 inches by 6 feet 8 inches, glazed. Inside doors, 5-cross panel. Windows, 2-light check rail with weights.

Possible Changes

Extra window at side bedroom. Omit kitchen door, using grade entrance for kitchen as well as basement. Using Pilgrim style of windows shown on page 20 in place of 2-light. Mission colonnade in archway between living and dining room. Estimates will be quickly furnished for any of the Possible Changes named for any house.

We do not quote
because temperature
costs with those
For Lighting
For Correct

Montgomery Ward & Co.

The above price is for the material uncut. Ready-cut price is

$**1366**

26 by 26 feet exclusive of porch

One & 1/2 Story Side Gable

Buena Vista (1922-1928 Ready-Cut)

Gordon-VanTine Design

1922 ($2915), 1923 ($2710), 1924 ($2572), 1925 ($2522), 1926 ($2522), 1927 ($2605), 1928 ($2686)

"Seldom do you see a more inviting and comfortable home than the Buena Vista. The keynote of the whole home, both inside and out, is given by the wide porch with its heavy beam supported by massive columns at both ends, and the broad steps flanked by the stone buttresses, giving an air of comfort and hospitality thoroughly carried out in the plan. The low dormer, with its overhanging roof supported by timber brackets, and the bay window extension in the dining room, are especially attractive features."

- 1924 Wardway Homes

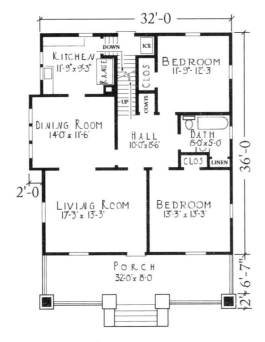

1st Floor

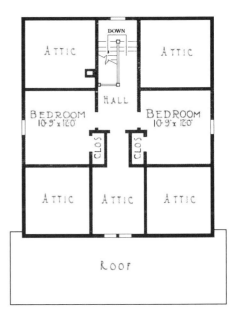

2nd Floor

Danbury (1922-1929 Ready-Cut)
Gordon-VanTine Design

1922 (A. $2248, B. $2638), 1923 (A. $2178, B. $2552), 1924 (A. $2058, B. $2369), 1925 (A. $2038, B. $2340), 1926 (A. $2038, B. $2340), 1927 (A. $2129, B. $2417), 1928 (A.$2195, B. $2492), 1929 (A. $2440, B. $2655)

"The Danbury may be had in two arrangements, Plan A calls for the entire second floor being used as an attic, floored without partitions. Plan B has exactly the same downstairs as Plan A, but the upstairs as shown in the floor plan. One of the chief reasons for the great popularity of this bungalow is the handsome, clean-cut appearance of the exterior. The main roof of the house is continued out over the porch and is always an attractive feature, and when it is supported by massive porch columns and wide cornices upheld by handsome timber brackets, it is particularly appealing. The lower half of the walls are sided with clear cypress siding, and above the belt course clear red cedar shingles are used."

-1924 Wardway Homes

1st Floor
Plan A

2nd Floor
Plan B

Hamilton (1919-1926 Not Ready-Cut)

1919 ($1955 NRC), 1920 ($1955 NRC), 1921 ($1955 NRC), 1922 ($2322 NRC),
1923 ($2344 NRC), 1924 ($2312 NRC), 1925 ($2312 NRC), 1926 ($2312 NRC)

"The Hamilton offers you all the charm and attractiveness of a bungalow design without the sacrifice of any of the features found in larger homes. The long sloping roof broken only by the splendid dormer, giving a most pleasing, artistic effect. The porch carried under the main roof line extends the full width of the house, and because of the boxed rail offers a splendid opportunity to screen at a small cost. The wide cornice together with the exposed rafter ends of the main roof and dormer, unite to give this home a most handsome exterior. "

- 1923 Wardway Homes

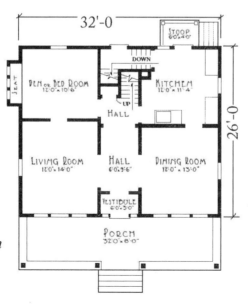

1st Floor

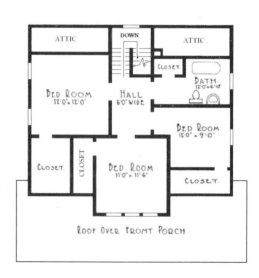

2nd Floor

One and One Half Story Side Gable - Page 146

Vincennes (1922-1926 Ready-Cut)

Gordon-VanTine Design

1922 ($2848), 1923 ($2612), 1924 ($2522), 1925 ($2470), 1926 ($2470), 1927 ($2517), 1928 ($2595)

"This splendid home follows the true bungalow style, but has as much room as a story-and-a-half house. The outside walls are sided up to the belt course, the gables and dormer being shingled. The most striking feature is the broad porch beam supported by cluster columns. This, together with the wide-open cornice supported by brackets and the siding walls extending clear to the grade line, is typical of genuine bungalow design. Our Vincennes home is one of the most popular, because it combines unusually generous living space with a handsome exterior at a very low cost."

- 1923 Wardway Homes

1st Floor   2nd Floor

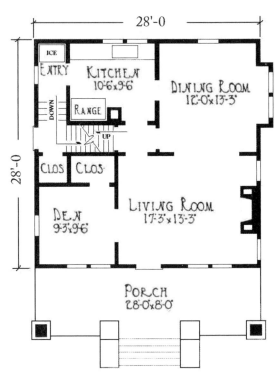

1 & 1/2
Side Gable
Attached Porch
Full-Width

28'-0

28'-0

ICE

ENTRY

KITCHEN
10'-6 x 9'-6

DINING ROOM
12'-0 x 13'-3

RANGE

DOWN

UP

CLOS

CLOS

DEN
9'-3 x 9'-6

LIVING ROOM
17'-3 x 13'-3

PORCH
28'-0 x 8'-0

Altamont (1922-1924 Ready-Cut)

Gordon-VanTine Design
1922 ($2415), 1923 ($2265), 1924 ($2133)

"This story-and-a-half bungalow, with its low, sweeping roof lines and broad porch, is a most popular type. In this particular Wardway Home these lines are enhanced by the splendidly designed dormer, the wide eaves supported by timber brackets, and the graceful treatment of the porch beam. The dining room bay window with its hooded roof breaking up the lines of the wall, is a feature which also deserves attention."

- 1923 Wardway Homes

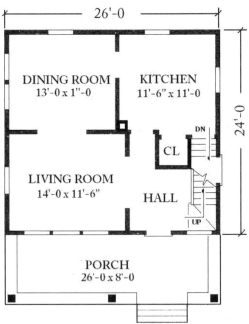

1 & 1/2
Side Gable
Attached Porch
Full-Width

26'-0

24'-0

DINING ROOM
13'-0 x 1"-0

KITCHEN
11'-6" x 11'-0

DN

CL

LIVING ROOM
14'-0 x 11'-6"

HALL

UP

PORCH
26'-0 x 8'-0

Madison (1917-1921 Not Ready-Cut)
1917 ($1096 NRC), 1918 ($1231 NRC), 1919 ($1469 NRC), 1920 ($1427 NRC), 1921 ($1427 NRC)

"There is a peculiar charm about this home which makes it immensely popular. It seldom fails of appeal to people of distinctive taste. It may be the clever treatment of the roof lines, the broad porch with its built up rail and square columns, or perhaps the well balanced arrangement of windows. We do not attempt to explain why but we do assert that it is popular and holds its place among our best sellers."

- 1917 Wardway Homes

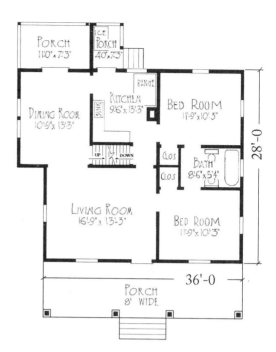

Oakland (1926-1929 Ready-Cut)
Gordon-VanTine Design
1926 ($1835), 1927 ($1887), 1928 ($1945), 1929 ($2139)

The *Oakland* is frequently mistaken for the *Cordova* because of the unique extended side-gable bay and an attic that is frequently converted into additional bedroom. The most distinctive difference is the roof of the Oakland has a distinctive break to a lower slope extending over the porch.

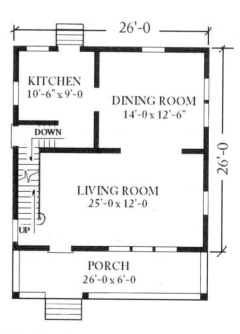

Curtis (1917-1920 Ready-Cut)
1917 ($1060 NRC), 1918 ($1366 NRC), 1919 ($1595 NRC), 1920 ($1521 NRC)

"This particular style of home seems to be always growing more in favor. With its long sloping roof and large distinctive looking dormer it presents a very comfortable, substantial looking appearance. The solid built up rail on the porch with the privacy which it affords is a very desirable feature as well as making it a very simple matter to have the porch screened in during the summer months. The interior of the house is designed for the average family and is complete in every detail."

- 1918 Wardway Homes

Waverly - Renamed Astoria in 1929 (1922- 1931 Ready-Cut)

Gordon-VanTine Design

1922 ($2040), 1923 ($2021), 1924 ($1890), 1925 ($1850), 1926 ($1850),
1927 ($1992), 1928 ($2054), 1929 ($2160), 1930 ($2149), 1931 ($2096)

"The wealth of room in this fine home is a constant source of surprise to all who see it. The front and rear dormers break up the plain roof line and add a distinctive touch to the exterior - also providing for full height ceilings on the second floor except for the small cut-offs in the front bedrooms at the side of the dormers, where the ceiling slopes down to a height of 5 feet 6 inches at the wall. The exterior is stucco on Byrkitt sheathing up to the belt line. From here up it is covered with shingles over shiplap and building paper. The unusually wide cornice is supported by handsome timber brackets."

- 1923 Wardway Homes

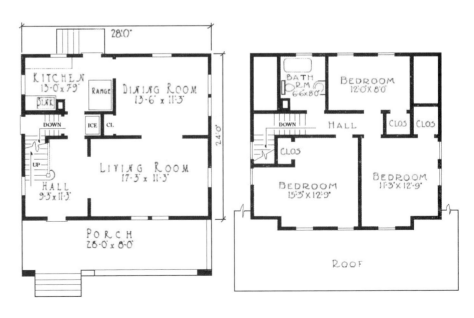

1st Floor   2nd Floor

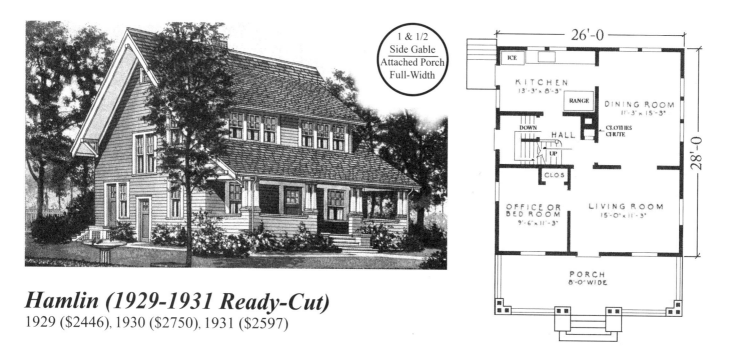

1 & 1/2 Side Gable Attached Porch Full-Width

Hamlin (1929-1931 Ready-Cut)
1929 ($2446), 1930 ($2750), 1931 ($2597)

"Your first impression of the Hamlin is that here is found new-fashioned modern comfort in an old-fashioned setting. Its general appearance is like that of many of our ancestral homes in the East and South, but its arrangement of details provides up-to-the-minute conveniences never thought of in those early days."

- 1930 Wardway Homes

A *Hamlin* in Ferndale, Michigan (photograph by Dale Wolicki).

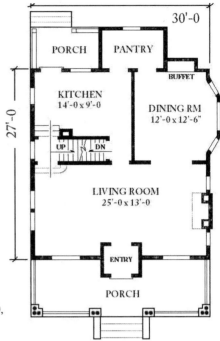

1 & 1/2
Side Gable
Attached Porch
Full-Width

PORCH   PANTRY   30'-0
BUFFET
KITCHEN
14'-0 x 9'-0
DINING RM
12'-0 x 12'-6"
27'-0
UP   DN
LIVING ROOM
25'-0 x 13'-0
ENTRY
PORCH

#157 (1911-1916 Not Ready-Cut)

1911 ($1031 NRC), 1912 ($1097 NRC), 1913 (NRC), 1914 ($1075 NRC),
1915 ($1152 (NRC), 1916 ($1188 NRC)

"We had so many calls for a house of this style that we were compelled to get out a design of home with its roof sloping to the front. We believe that we have designed a house that will meet with approval of our customers who desire this style of home. It is modern in every respect. Note the colonial columns in groups, set on brick piers, with colonial balusters and rail between the piers; concrete stairway; the roomy vestibule, and the extremely large living room."   *- 1914 Building Plans of Modern Homes*

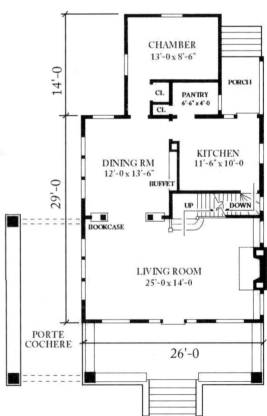

1 & 1/2
Side Gable
Attached Porch
Full-Width

CHAMBER
13'-0 x 8'-6"
PORCH
CL
PANTRY
CL   6'-6" x 4'-0
14'-0
DINING RM
12'-0 x 13'-6"
KITCHEN
11'-6" x 10'-0
BUFFET
29'-0
UP   DOWN
BOOKCASE
LIVING ROOM
25'-0 x 14'-0
PORTE
COCHERE
26'-0

#177 (1914-1915 Not Ready-Cut)

1914 ($1081 NRC), 1915 ($1398 NRC)

"Here is a very classy two-story stucco house, with Bungalow effect. This building is designed with a large porch across the front, a 1-3/4 inch white pine front door, glazed bevel plate and side lights of art glass. Most of the windows in this house are glazed with art glass or divided bars, which make a very pretty effect."

- 1914 Building Plans of Modern Homes

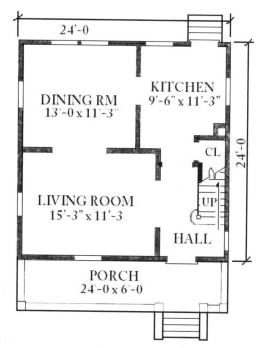

1 & 1/2
Side Gable
Attached Porch
Full-Width

24'-0

DINING RM
13'-0 x 11'-3"

KITCHEN
9'-6" x 11'-3"

CL

24'-0

LIVING ROOM
15'-3" x 11'-3

UP

HALL

PORCH
24'-0 x 6'-0

Webb (1917 Not Ready-Cut)
1917 ($973 NRC)

"This Wardway home is unique in that the porch has practically no wood in its construction, the rail being of brick and stone, the floor and front steps of concrete. Three massive square wood columns support the overhanging roof in a way that carries out the general lines of solidity and simplicity. The second floor dormer breaks any monotony coming from the long sloping front roof and at the same time it furnishes plenty of light for the two front rooms."

- 1917 Book of Homes

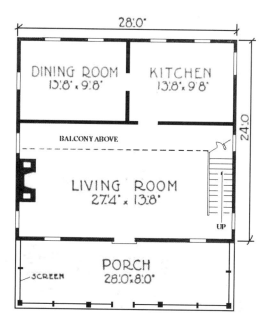

1 & 1/2
Side Gable
Attached Porch
Full-Width

28'0"

DINING ROOM
13'8" x 9'8"

KITCHEN
13'8" x 9'8"

24'0

BALCONY ABOVE

LIVING ROOM
27'4" x 13'8"

UP

SCREEN

PORCH
28'0" x 8'0"

Mackinac Cottage (1922-1927 Ready-Cut)

GordonVanTine Design
1922 ($880), 1923 ($850), 1924 ($850),
1925 ($715), 1926 ($885), 1927 ($890)

"Every detail that makes for summer comfort has been included in this wonderful design. Note the big screened porch and the high ceiling living room, fully two stories in extent. What you want in a summer cottage is plenty of light, air and room. The Mackinac provides all these in abundance. No matter how hot the days, it is bound to be cool, and if the weather is cool, the fine fireplace guarantees cozy comfort. Three bedrooms, a kitchen and dining room provide ample space for the practical needs of vacation life, and leave the living quarters free at all times. Although not a large cottage, there is a surprising amount of room in the Mackinac"

- 1927 Wardway Homes

Cordova (1922-1929 Ready-Cut)
Gordon-VanTine Design

1922 ($2725), 1923 ($2663), 1924 ($2492), 1925 ($2458),
1926 ($2458), 1927 ($2556), 1928 ($2635), 1929 ($2797)

"Compare the Cordova with the average farm home in your neighborhood - its striking beauty is immediately apparent. It combines the elements of appearance and comfort in a way that appeals strongly to those who long for the convenience of a city home in a story-and-a-half structure. Consider the charming exterior, the big porch and the shingled walls above the belt course. The interior of this wonderful home offers every advantage desired in a town or country home."

- 1923 Wardway Homes

A Wardway *Cordova* in Bedford, Virginia (photograph by Rose Thornton).

One and One Half Story Side Gable - Page 154

A Wardway *Cordova* in Chesapeake, Virginia (photography by Rose Thornton).

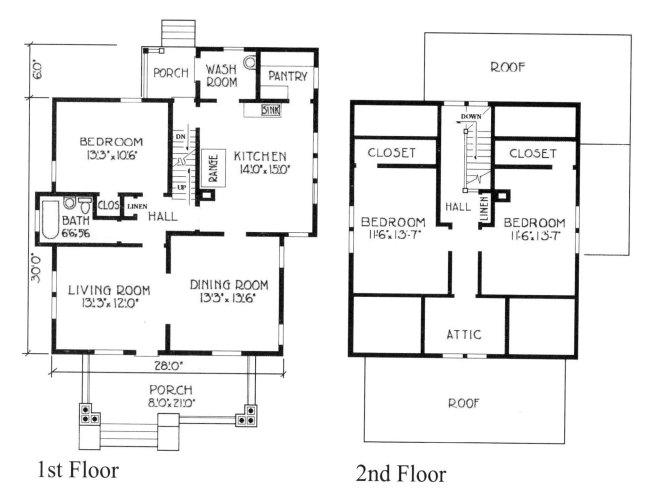

1st Floor

2nd Floor

1 & 1/2
Side Gable
Attached Porch
Centered

Washington (1918-1924 Not Ready-Cut)

1918 ($1348 NRC), 1919 ($1543 NRC), 1920 ($1523 NRC), 1921
($1523 NRC), 1922 ($1515 NRC), 1923 ($1963 NRC), 1924 ($1816 NRC)

*"For a home of distinction, style
and beauty the Washington is one
of our leaders. You wonder how we
can furnish so spacious and beautiful a home at so low a price. It is the
careful figuring of our architects so
that every inch of space is utilized,
keeping the house small and yet giving large comfortable rooms - that is
the reason. The floor plan we believe
you will agree is cleverly designed.
Note the placing of the windows at
the corners of the living room giving you a regular sun parlor right
in your living room. Then the big
bookcase archway leading to the
reception hall is another feature that
makes the living room an exceptionally pleasant room."*

  - 1918 Wardway Homes

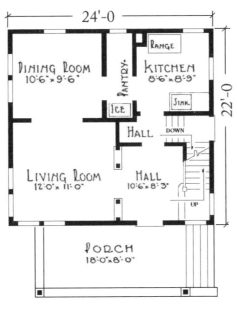

1st Floor

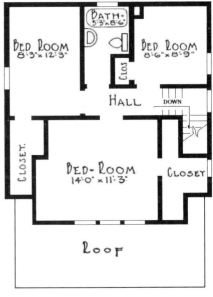

2nd Floor

Maywood (1917-1924 Ready-Cut)

1917 ($897), 1918 ($1213), 1919 ($1421), 1920 ($1380),
1921 ($1380), 1922 ($1705), 1923 ($1883), 1924 ($1742)

"Moderation is the keynote in this Wardway home of simple design. This particular type is sure to prove doubly so as to families of moderate size. Here you will note good example of care and forethought having been displayed in the easy blending of the gable and porch roof lines. By examining the floor plans of the Maywood you will note good judgment in the arrangement of the living and dining room, also what so many desire - a pleasant sleeping room on the first floor. This, of course, can be very easily used for a library or music room."

- 1918 Wardway Homes

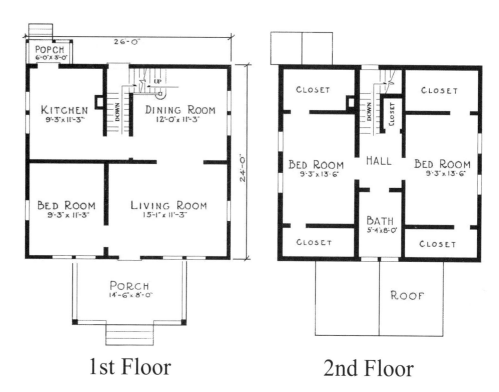

1st Floor   2nd Floor

Carlyle - Renamed Bedford in 1928 (1922-1929 Ready-Cut)

Gordon-VanTine Design

1922 ($2150), 1923 ($2100), 1924 ($1935), 1925 ($1896),
1926 ($1896), 1927 ($2039), 1928 ($2146), 1929 ($2216)

*"It is hard to believe that all the space
shown on the floor plan can be packed
into this charming little home, yet
when you enter the completed home
you will realize it has been done. The
exterior is all that good taste and
good architecture can desire. Especially attractive is the porch with its
heavy timbered construction and massive brackets. This "craftsman" note
is carefully carried out in the open
rafter ends of the cornice."*

-1923 Wardway Homes

1st Floor   2nd Floor

A Wardway *Carlyle* in Angola, Indiana (photograph by Dale Wolicki).

A Wardway *Carlyle* in Lynchberg, Virginia with unusual roof dormer (photograph by Rose Thornton).

Ferndale Duplex (1928-1931 Ready-Cut)

Similar to Sears *LaSalle*
1928 ($2265), 1929 ($2456), 1930 ($2526), 1931 ($2526)

The Ferndale was a offered as a Duplex but some examples have been converted into single-family residences.

"A doubly profitable investment! A wonderful opportunity to let your home actually pay for itself! Our new Ferndale with nine fine rooms and two baths is conveniently arranged for two families. The regular income from renting the upstairs apartment often takes care of your easy monthly payments for the home. The second floor is as splendidly arranged as many expensive city apartments. The hall, opening from the front porch, provides an entrance for the upstairs so private that your home downstairs need never be disturbed by anyone going above.

Houses like this have an exceptionally high re-sale value. The demand for them is constantly increasing. And whether you build it to live in or for re-sale, you will find the Ferndale an unusually practical choice. Its attractive Colonial architecture is always in excellent taste. The roof slopes gracefully – the porch always inviting – and details such as the shutters and small paned windows lend individuality. When you examine the floor plan you will immediately realize the convenience it assures."

- 1930 Wardway Homes

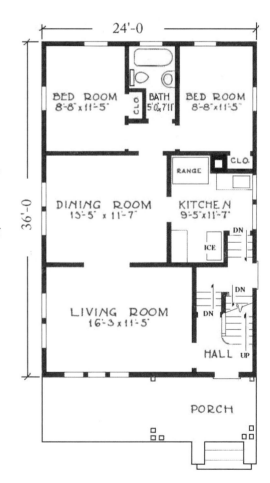

A *Ferndale* found in Rockford, Illinois through mortgage records (photograph by Rebecca Hunter).

A *Ferndale* duplex in Flint, Michigan (photograph by Dale Wolicki).

1 & 1/2
Side Gable
Recessed Porch
Offset

Trenton (1929-1931 Ready-Cut)

1929 ($2367), 1930 ($2598), 1931 ($2462)

Similar to Sterling Homes *Lawnsette* and othe popular Plan Books designs

"Here is an architectural masterpiece - a real gem of a home! And it's not necessary to have a large income or a big bank account to own the Trenton. It is remarkably low priced - easy and inexpensive to build. And Wards's will help you to finance its construction. As you stand out in front of the Trenton, you are impressed with the graceful sweep of the roof, the wonderful sun parlor, front porch with colonial columns - and the pleasing general effect. Step inside, and you are charmed by the inviting, cozy interior. Every room, you will note, has windows on at least two sides. the sun room with windows on four sides will especially appeal to you. Every detail - every feature is modern to the minute. Such a home is sure to please you and draw admiration of your friends.

A living room of real distinction. A charming background for your new or old furnishings. the fireplace lends an atmosphere of cheer and warmth and is one of those details which helps make this a really charming home. Oak floors are included - and like fine old furniture, time only serves to make them mellow. The completed room will reflect your own individuality. The "homey" inviting dining room. Real distinction in decoration is made easy in this inviting dining room. It has balance, charm and dignity which you will especially appreciate when entertaining. Your guests will long cherish recollections of the teas and luncheons you will serve them here and this room will create for you a reputation for bounteous hospitality."

- 1929 Wardway Homes

A 1929 Montgomery-Ward *Trenton* built for General Motors in Flint Michigan (photograph by Dale Wolicki).

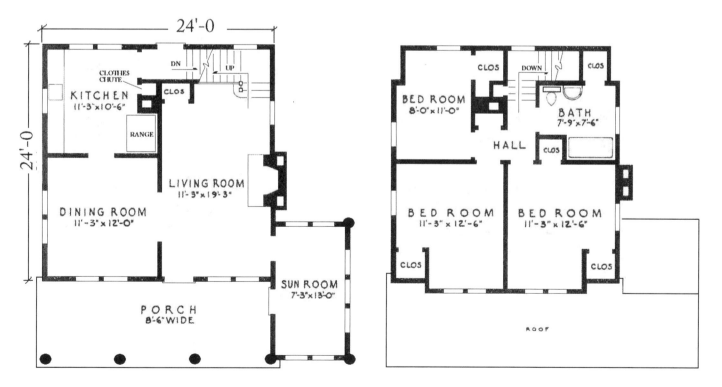

1st Floor

2nd Floor

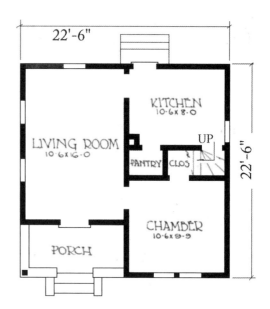

22'-6"

KITCHEN
10-6 x 8-0

LIVING ROOM
10-6 x 16-0

UP

PANTRY CLOS

22'-6"

CHAMBER
10-6 x 9-9

PORCH

#180 (1915-1916 Not Ready-Cut)
1915 ($406 NRC), 1916 ($406 NRC)

"From the inviting front porch a handsome door leads into the large, attractive living room. To the right, in front, is a chamber, lighted by double windows. Good sized closet. To the rear is the kitchen, which has pantry and attic stairs. Attic floored for one good size room. In a home of this size the living room, of course, is the main room, and is so arranged that it is possible to dine in this room, if desired. However, some other arrangement might suit your needs better, and we will be glad to make any changes you may desire."

- 1915 Book of Homes

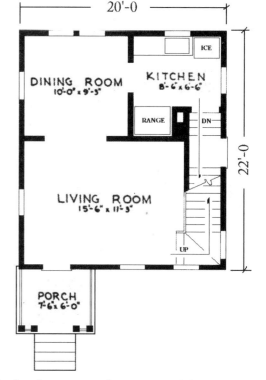

20'-0

ICE

DINING ROOM
10'-0" x 9'-3"

KITCHEN
8'-6" x 6'-6"

RANGE

DN

22'-0

LIVING ROOM
15'-6" x 11'-3"

UP

PORCH
7'-6" x 6'-0"

Ridgewood (1930-1931 Ready-Cut)
1930 ($1670), 1931 ($1647)

"A home of unmistakable beauty and distinction designed particularly for the narrow lot. Its carefully proportioned lines of roof and dormer produce an effect of greater width, so desirable on the lot of 25 or 30 feet wide. Refinements of design in the half timbered and stucco dormer and upper gable, the many-lighted windows and Colonial shutters, give the Ridgewood enduring charm and attractiveness."   *- 1930 Wardway Homes*

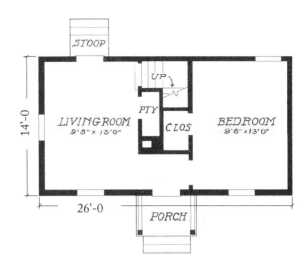

1 & 1/2
Side Gable
Entrance
Stoop

STOOP

UP

LIVING ROOM
9'8" x 13'0"

PTY

CLOS

BEDROOM
9'8" x 13'0"

14'-0

26'-0

PORCH

#132 (1910-1914 Not Ready-Cut)
1910 ($291 NRC), 1911 ($260 NRC), 1912 ($275 NRC), 1913 (NRC), 1914 ($294 NRC)

"The fact that this house is 26 feet wide gives it a much larger appearance than many homes that are actually larger. The first floor has two rooms, closet and pantry; the second floor is not finished, but at a small additional expense could be divided into two large bedrooms."

- 1912 Building Plans of Modern Homes

1 & 1/2
Side Gable
Entrance
Stoop

29'-0

ICE

DOWN

BATH

BED ROOM
9'-6"x10'-6"

RANGE

UP

HALL

26'-0

KITCHEN
8'-0" 13'-3"

LINEN

CLOS

CLOS

DINING ROOM
11'-3" x 11'-3"

LIVING ROOM
16'-3" x 11'-3"

STOOP

Rosehill (1929-1930 Ready-Cut)
1929 ($2223), 1930 ($2162)

"A breath of Old Quebec - an ultra modern home, copying the fine, stately French Colonial style of architecture that has lived through many centuries of ever-changing fads. The Rosehill, like the masterpieces of art, demonstrates the beauty of simplicity. The Rosehill is superbly suited to the American family, whether they live in the city, the suburb or the country."

- 1929 Wardway Homes

Girard (1922-1929 Ready-Cut)

Gordon-VanTine Design

1922 ($1875), 1923 ($1843), 1924 ($1748), 1925 ($1698), 1926 ($1698), 1927 ($1721), 1928 ($1774), 1929 ($1883)
Similar to Sears *Madella*

"Such details as the uneven roof design, wide cornice with returns, the raised roof over the two front windows, the perk little hood over the front entrance with its cornice continued across the front of the house and joining the porch - these things and the setting of the house low on the foundation - have made a distinctive and unusual home of the Girard. The front door leads into the reception hall, from which the stairs rise, and from which a cased opening leads into the fine, big living room. French doors open from this room onto the porch. A clothes closet is located in the hall. The living room is well arranged, comfortable and well lighted. Another cased opening between the living room and dining room contributes much to the spaciousness of the home. A swing door between dining room and kitchen is another feature. Our built-in kitchen case and work table is located in the kitchen."

-1927 Wardway Homes

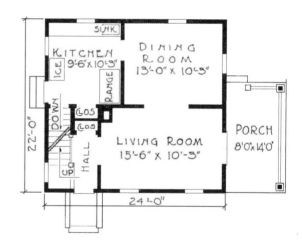

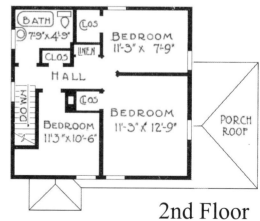

2nd Floor

A Wardway *Girard* in Sylvan Lake, Michigan (photograph by Dale Wolicki and Rebecca Hunter).

A Wardway *Girard* in Duquesne, Pennsylvania (photograph by Dale Wolicki).

Kenwood (1929-1931 Ready-Cut)
Gordon-VanTine Design
1929 ($2087), 1930 ($2087), 1931 ($1998)

The Kenwood is similar to the Sears *Dover* and Aladdin's *Lindbergh*, all being Neo-Tudor style homes with sloped entrance gables and accentuating chimneys. The Kenwood is easily identified by the one window aside the chimney, the paired windows on the opposite side and the recessed round-top entrance with thin attic vent above. The Kenwood has clipped gables but examples without clipped gables have been found, although they may actually be examples of Gordon-VanTine's *Burton*. The Kenwood was offered only a few years it was immensely popular.

"My wife and I had been thinking, planning - dreaming about a home all our own for years - ever since we were married, in fact, one of the first things I did was to buy a lot. But we never got right down to building the actual house until a few months ago when Ward's showed us how easy it is. And now we are so thrilled - so happy in our own home that we tell everybody about it."

- 1929 Wardway Homes

The Gordon-VanTine *Burton* from their 1932 catalog.

A perfect unaltered *Kenwood* in Aurora, Illinois (photograph by Rebecca Hunter).

1st Floor

2nd Floor

A Beckley, West Virginia *Kenwood* (photograph by Rose Thornton).

A LaPorte, Indiana *Kenwood* (photograph by Dale Wolicki).

A Clarkville, Indiana *Kenwood* (photograph by Dale Wolicki).

A *Kenwood* in Fairfield, Illinois (photograph by Rebecca Hunter).

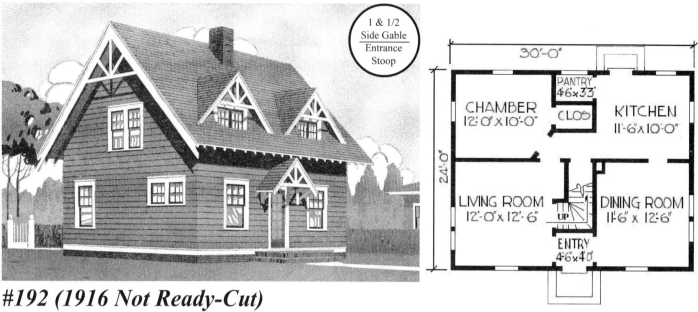

#192 (1916 Not Ready-Cut)
1916 ($744 NRC)

"A handsome French door leads through the entry into the living room and dining room. Living room is connected with kitchen and rear chamber by rear hall, with enclosed stairway leading to the second floor. This stairway can be made open at no extra cost. There is a closet under the stairs. Rear chamber has a large closet. Kitchen has a pantry which is fully equipped with shelves."

- 1916 Book of Homes

Rexton (1931 Ready-Cut)
1931 ($1945)

"If your lot is narrow, we recommend the Rexton. A clever modern architect has designed it especially for you. Its style is charming. The gracefully sloping roof is relieved by a quaint decorative eyebrow sash."

-1931 Wardway Homes

One and One Half Story Side Gable - Page 172

HOME No. 184

For $663.00 we will furnish the material to
built this home, consisting of all lumber, lath,
shingles, finishing lumber, flooring, doors, windows, frames, trim, sash weights, building
paper, hardware, pipe and gutter, and paint-
ing material. We absolutely guarantee the material we furnish to be
sufficient to build the home according to our plans and specifications.

A cottage home in which the high degree of practicability and
thoroughly satisfactory layout of Home No. 105 have been given a
little different form with most pleasing results. Note the effect
of the corbels and the siding and square columns of the porch. You
can build this home at a very reasonable cost and you will be more
than satisfied.

GENERAL SPECIFICATIONS

Built on a brick foundation, siding around porch. Double first floors, with one floor
of good inch lumber, over which is laid finish floor. Outside walls have matched
sheathing, building paper and clear Cypress siding. All framing material the best quality
Yellow Pine. Star A star Cedar shingles. No. 1 lath. Windows glazed "A" quality clear
glass. Excellent grade hardware. Painted two coats best Tower Brand paint outside, your
choice of colors, wood filler and varnish for interior. Read full description of each item in
our Building Material Catalogue.

By allowing a fair price for labor, brick, cement and plaster, which we do not furnish,
this home can be built for about $1,435.00.

FIRST FLOOR
Bevel plate front door opens into reception hall. To the right is the living room, connected with dining room by cased opening. The coffee side of dining room is a bay, with
three good sized windows, making an unusually light and cheerful room. Kitchen is conveniently located and arranged, with large, light pantry, sink, and rear porch. Finished
in Yellow Pine throughout. Ceilings, 9 feet high.

SECOND FLOOR
Choice Yellow Pine stair lands in corner, permitting a window and plenty of headroom.
In the opposite gable is the bathroom, and
with plenty of light and closet room.
Yellow Pine trim. Ceilings, 8 feet

Heating,

WRITE F

Warm Air Heating Plant, complete
Steam Heating Plant, complete
Hot Water Heating Plant, complete
Plumbing System, complete
Acetylene Lighting System

Size, exclusive of porches, 22 ft. 6 in.
wide by 30 ft. long

One and 1/2 Story Cross Gable

#184 - Renamed Boston in 1918 (1915-1921 Not Ready-Cut)

1915 ($699 NRC), 1916 ($663 NRC), 1917 (Not Offered), 1918 ($1082 NRC),
1919 ($1386 NRC), 1920 ($1346 NRC), 1921 ($1346 NRC)

"For $699.00 we will furnish the material to build this home, conisting of all lumber, lath, shingles, finishing lumber, flooring, doors, windows, frames, trim, sash weights, building paper, hardware, pipe and gutter, and painting material. We absolutely guarantee the material we furnish to be sufficient to build the homes according to our plans and specifications.

A cottage home in which the high degree of practicability and throughly satisfactory layout of Home Number 184 have been given a little different form with most pleasing results. Note the effect of the corbels and the siding and square columns of the porch. You can build this home at a very reasonable cost and you will be more than satisfied."

- 1916 Book of Modern Homes

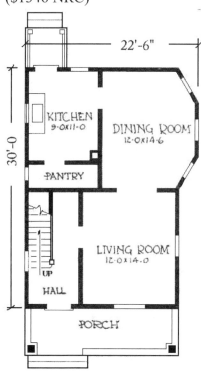

1st Floor

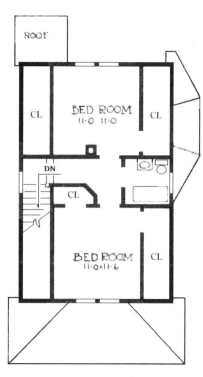

2nd Floor

#106 (1909-1916 Not Ready-Cut)
Radford Design

1909 ($975 NRC), 1910 ($975 NRC), 1911 ($894 NRC), 1912 ($960 NRC), 1913 (NRC), 1914 ($955 NRC), 1915 ($1044 NRC), 1916 ($1064 NRC)

"This house is, in our opinion, one of the prettiest of its type. Just look at it carefully; it rests on a brick foundation that extends under the house, and the width of the porch, which extends across the entire front. There is a grade door by which both kitchen and basement can be reached. We also call attention to the four gable roof with the peak cut off and sloping back, all shingled with first quality shingles. You will also note there is a large bay in the parlor and triple window in the front bedroom. As you enter the reception hall, to the left is an open stairway, to the right a parlor, back of which and seperated by a large sliding door is a dining room; in both parlor and dining is a neatly designed mantle and fire place; there is also a kitchen, pantry and butler's pantry."

-1914 Building Plans of Modern Homes

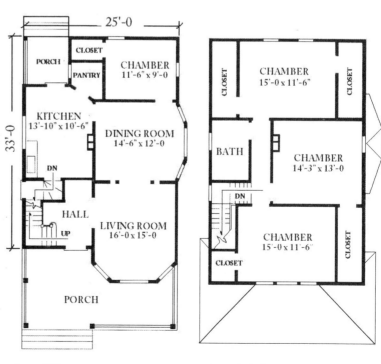

1st Floor   2nd Floor

#101 - Renamed Franklin in 1917 (1909-1921 Not Ready-Cut)
Radford Design
1909 ($1155 NRC), 1910 ($1155 NRC), 1911 ($982 NRC), 1912 ($1120 NRC),
1913 (NRC), 1914 ($1098 NRC), 1915 ($1406 NRC), 1916 ($1406 NRC), 1917 ($1341),
1918 ($2023), 1919 ($2356), 1920 ($2288), 1921 ($2288)

"A story and a half house of unusual convenience and beauty. The unique treatment of the roof, cornice and broken gable lines, place the Franklin in a class quite by itself. The treatment of the interior is even more interesting than the exterior. An arch opens the way into the living room, with its large bay window at one end and sliding doors at the other. The bay in the dining room affords an abundance of light and a view that cannot be had by windows in a straight wall. Behind the dining room is a bedroom and to one side the kitchen, leaving space in the right hand rear corner of the house for a closet off the bedroom, an entry, a toilet and a back porch. The second floor adds four good sized bedrooms, each with abundant closet room. A linen closet in the hall and bath complete the arrangement."

- 1918 Wardway Homes

1st Floor   2nd Floor

A perfect *#101* in Montvale, Virginia (photograph by Rose Thornton and Dale Wolicki).

#104 (1909-1916 Not Ready-Cut)

Radford Design

1909 ($1020 NRC), 1910 ($1020 NRC), 1911 ($910 NRC), 1912 ($1003 NRC), 1913 (NRC), 1914 ($958) NRC, 1915 ($1072 NRC), 1916 ($1085 NRC)

"A seven-room, story and three-quarter house, with two gables. All rooms on the second floor have vertical walls; there is no sloping of ceilings, so common in houses of this kind. We have designed this house so that the slope is in the closets. As you enter the hall from the large veranda, to the left is an open stairway, with a single sash, glazed with leaded crystal glass over the stair landing; to the right, through the wide cased opening, you see the living room, which has a large bay, in the center of which is placed a large cottage window, our Argyle pattern. From the living room you enter the dinning room, which also has a fine mantle; from the dining room you enter the kitchen, through the pantry. The kitchen has no direct connection with the front which enables one to keep all cooking orders from permeating the entire house."

- 1914 Building Plans of ModernHomes

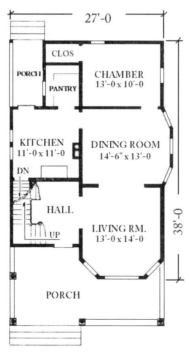

1st Floor

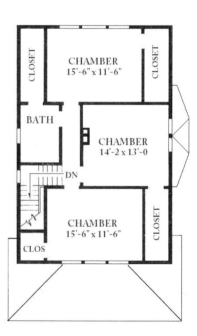

2nd Floor

#100 (1909-1916 Not Ready-Cut)

Radford Design

1909 ($850 NRC), 1910 ($844 NRC), 1911 ($774 NRC), 1912 ($844 NRC), 1913 (NRC), 1914 ($844 NRC), 1915 ($998 NRC), 1916 ($991 NRC)

"This design is one which has met with marked approval. Has a good size dining room from which an open stairway leads to the second floor. The dining room also has a china closet. The basement is reached by stairs from the pantry. The second floor has three bedrooms, bath and six closets. The general appearance of this cottage is very pleasing. The flooring on the first floor is hardwood. The balance of the interior trim is of yellow pine with western pine doors. All trim is strictly Number 1 in every respect. If you wish the house in another kind of wood, just write and state your wishes and we will gladly give you information that you desire. We furnish all millwork, lumber, hardware, lath and paint as listed in our latest Bill of Material, which material we guarantee to be sufficient to erect this building, as per our latest blue print. Our quotations are subject to market changes. We do not furnish stone, line, cement or brick."

- 1914 Building Plans of Modern Homes

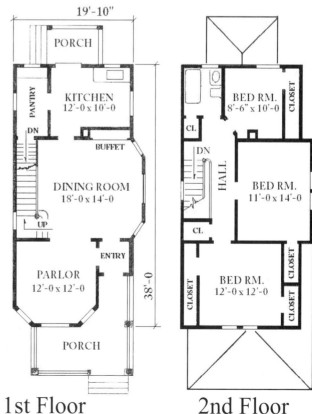

1st Floor   2nd Floor

PORCH
12'-0 x 5'-0

KITCHEN
7'-3" x 11'-3"

PANTRY

DN

DINING RM
11'-3" x 12'-3"

20'-0

30'-0

UP

LIVING ROOM
19'-0 x 11'-3"

PORCH
18'-0 x 7'-6"

Garfield (1917-1921 Not Ready-Cut)

1917 ($821 NRC), 1918 ($1060 NRC), 1919 ($1386 NRC),
1920 ($1346 NRC), 1921 ($1346 NRC)

"Here is a home of generous dimensions, built on original lines. Its exterior appearance presents a variation from the ordinary type of home, which is pleasing to the spectator. Siding for outside walls with shingles for the front gable has proven an effective combination."

- 1918 Wardway Homes

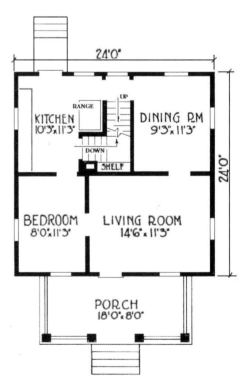

24'0"

RANGE

UP

KITCHEN
10'3"x11'3"

DINING RM
9'3"x11'3"

24'0"

DOWN

SHELF

BEDROOM
8'0"x11'3"

LIVING ROOM
14'6"x11'3"

PORCH
18'0"x8'0"

Meridan (1922-1923 Not Ready-Cut)

Gordon-VanTine Design

Similar to Sears *Cranmore*
1922 ($1585), 1923 ($1635)

"This home offers a wonderful degree of comfort and economy combined with a most pleasing exterior. The large porch and perfect balance of the two gables mark this as a home in which there has been no sacrifice of design to provide it with seven rooms. It is really a remarkable home for farm or city, where one must have four bedrooms and must of necessity have a home reasonable in cost."
-1923 Wardway Homes

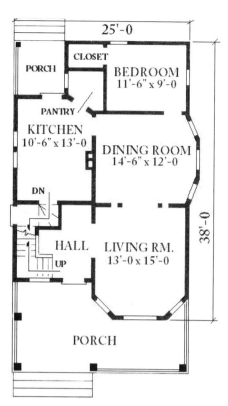

Floor plan labels (top, #190):
- 25'-0
- PORCH
- CLOSET
- BEDROOM 11'-6" x 9'-0
- PANTRY
- KITCHEN 10'-6" x 13'-0
- DINING ROOM 14'-6" x 12'-0
- DN
- HALL
- UP
- LIVING RM. 13'-0 x 15'-0
- 38'-0
- PORCH

Badge: 1 & 1/2 Cross Gable Classic Attached Porch

#190 - Renamed Plymouth in 1917
(1916-1921 Not Ready-Cut)

1916 ($1088 NRC), 1917 ($1256 NRC), 1918 ($1841 NRC),
1919 ($2264 NRC), 1920 ($2198), 1921 ($2198)

"For the lovers of the four-gable house, the Plymouth should be a pleasant surprise. Does it not appeal to you with its artistic designed exterior and large, well-arranged interior? The divided lights in front windows and wide, substantially constructed porch make the front elevation most inviting."   - 1918 Wardway Homes

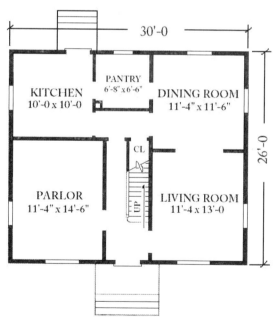

Floor plan labels (bottom, #152):
- 30'-0
- KITCHEN 10'-0 x 10'-0
- PANTRY 6'-8" x 6'-6"
- DINING ROOM 11'-4" x 11'-6"
- CL
- PARLOR 11'-4" x 14'-6"
- UP
- LIVING ROOM 11'-4 x 13'-0
- 26'-0

Badge: 1 & 1/2 Cross Gable Classic Attached Porch

#152 (1911- 1914 Not Ready-Cut)

1911 ($688), 1912 ($725 NRC), 1913 (NRC), 1914 ($772 NRC)

"We designed this house to give the greatest amount of floor space possible for the amount we charge for this material. Four rooms and pantry on the first floor and on the second floor three sleeping rooms, alcove, bath and six closets. The closet space is one thing about this home that we know the ladies of the household will appreciate. The reason why we can sell the material for so large a house at such a low price is because we have selected the sizes of lumber and material that are cheaper than others and then made a plan to fit the material."   - 1914 Wardway Homes

#191 - Renamed Ohio in 1917 (1916-1926 Not Ready-Cut)

1916 ($1142 NRC), 1917 ($1183 NRC), 1918 ($1593 NRC), 1919 ($1973 NRC),
1920 ($1916 NRC), 1921 ($1916 NRC),1922 ($1807 NRC), 1923 ($2423 NRC),
1924 ($2242 NRC), 1925 ($2175 NRC), 1926 ($2175 NRC)

"A home of the most interesting exterior appearance, perfect proportions and designed in the very best of taste. A porch the full width of the house with four handsome round columns, the broad roof with return cornice and the well-placed bay window, combine to give this home an air of dignity equaled only in the individually designed houses. Nothing is more depressing than a home whose interior is forever dark because of an insufficient number of windows. Twenty-two windows, a beautiful front door glazed with bevel plate and a glazed rear door, make this one of the cheeriest, best lighted homes that you will find anywhere."

- 1923 Wardway Homes

1st Floor

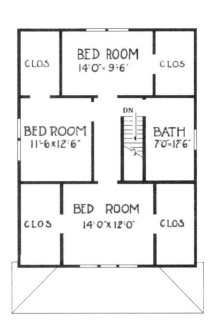

2nd Floor

A Wardway *Ohio* in Quinter, Kansas (photograph by Rose Thornton).

The Ringer Ranch – Quinter, Kansas

(photograph by Rose Thornton)

"We are well pleased with our Ohio which bought of you," wrote Mathias Ringer in the 1919 Wardway Homes catalog. "Everybody is welcome on the Ringer Ranch. Everything is modern and is from Montgomery Ward, furniture and all. We want to build two more of these later on" (page 44).

According to the catalog, this happy homeowner had built his Ohio in Quinter, Kansas. Intrigued by this testimonial, I sent several letters to the Ringers of Kansas, and was delighted to learn that the grandson of Mathias Ringer, 86-year-old Gail Ringer, had some wonderful memories to share about his grandfather's mail-order home.

In the early 1900s, my grandfather, Mathias Ringer was living in Somerset County, Pennsylvania when he developed black lung disease from working in the coal mines. He was 16 years old. The doctors told him he couldn't work in the mines anymore, so they gave him an office job. They also told him that if he went to western Kansas he'd live to be an old man. Well, he did as advised and Mathias lived to be 89 years old. His only hospitalization was just 10 days before he died. Mathias bought the land in Quinter, Kansas in 1905 and built a tiny two-room house on the property.

He and his brother worked the land and broke the sod enough so that they could farm it and run feed cattle. In 1916, he ordered The Ohio from Montgomery Ward. Mathias and his brother started building the house in 1916 and finished in 1917. It came in on the train, on a boxcar, and my grandfather and his twin sons hauled it out to the building site on a horse-drawn wagon. They brought in carpenters from Mitchell (about 120 miles east of the farm) to build the house. The carpenters were paid about 35 cents an hour. The only difference between our house and the original catalog picture is they didn't put in the window box when it was built. That's the only change they made.

Gail Ringer was born in his grandparents' home in 1921 and spent much of his childhood there on the Ringer Ranch. One of his fondest memories was staying with his grandma while his Grandfather drove a herd of cattle to the stockyards in Quinter. Gail recalls that their Ohio, ordered from the Montgomery Ward Building Plans of Modern Homes really was one of the most modern homes in the community.

It was the first house in the township that had a bathroom and kitchen with running water. Montgomery Ward sold a pressure pump outfit for use with a rural well. The pressure tank and plunger were in the basement and you pumped up the air pressure by hand. If you pumped up too much pressure, water would drain into the nearby laundry tub. The electricity was powered by a of a series of glass, acid-filled batteries. The 32-volt electrical system used a gasoline-powered, one-cycle engine to re-charge the batteries. Grandma always washed on Monday because that's when the batteries were freshly-charged and strong. Sunday night, the lights would start to go dim and that's how we knew it was time to recharge those batteries. Both the electrical system and the pressure pump outfit came from Ward's. My grandfather bought every thing from Ward's, including furniture, household items and even canned goods.

When the farm was sold in 1978, Gail Ringer couldn't bear to see the house destroyed, so he moved the house 10 miles to the town of Quinter. When the house was moved, he did some work to the structure.

It was a solid house with good lumber in it, I'll tell you that much. When we remodeled the house, we found that the trim moldings, window and door frames, all had "M. Ringer" stamped on the back of it. I saved one piece of that millwork and still have it.

The house remained in the Ringer family until 1987, when it was sold for about $40,000. The Ringers passed along the original 1916 Ward's Modern Homes catalog, from which Mathias Ringer ordered his "Ohio," along with the pressure pump outfit and 32-volt, battery-powered electrical system. .

And what happened to those other two kit homes that Mathias mentioned in his letter to Montgomery Ward? He'd intended to build the houses for his twin sons, Jonas (Gail's father) and Josiah. On a Sunday afternoon in 1923, a summer thunderstorm appeared while Jonas and Josiah were scurrying around to retrieve a few lost cattle on the Ringer ranch. Josiah was struck by lightning and killed instantly. Mathias Ringer, devastated by the loss of his son, never did build those other two Montgomery Ward homes.

The original water pressure tank in the Ringer house (photograph by Rose Thornton).

The original pine newel post and ballistrade of the Ringer House (photograph by Rose Thornton).

Stenciled customer information on back of piece of millwork trim (photograph by Rose Thornton).

#114 (1909-1916 Not Ready-Cut)

1909 ($997 NRC), 1910 ($997 NRC), 1911 ($918 NRC), 1912 ($970 NRC), 1913 (NRC), 1914 ($1024 NRC), 1915 ($1156 NRC), 1916 ($1169 NRC)

"Number 114 is a very convenient and well arranged house, at a low price; it consists of eight rooms, bath, three closets and a large attic. The dining room is exceptionally well lighted by a bay window. The right side has a grade door, by which the basement can be reached without having to go through the house. This house has a great many friends, due perhaps, as much to the good architectural appearance, as to the fact we are furnishing material for a large eight-room house at the price of a small one. The flooring on the first story is of hardwood; the balance of the interior trim is yellow pine; the doors of western pine, all good clear, first class material."

- 1914 Building Plans of Modern Homes

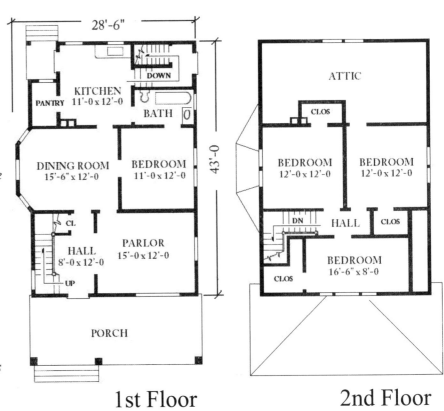

1st Floor   2nd Floor

#107 (1909-1914 Not Ready-Cut)

Radford Design

1909 ($1305), 1910 ($1305 NRC), 1911 ($1146 NRC),
1912 ($1203 NRC), 1913 (NRC), 1914 ($1304 NRC)

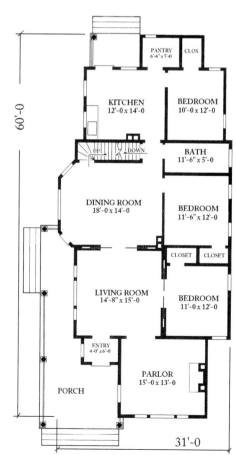

"To anyone desiring an attractive, homelike cottage which can be built at a moderate cost, we particularly recommend this one. The architecture is extremely good. With its large veranda supported by colonial columns, capped with composition cap of the Scamozzi Renaissance period and its triplet and Queen Anne windows, it makes a home of which anyone can well be proud. This cottage has three good sized bedrooms with plenty of closet room, and will be found large enough for a good sized family. The upstairs can be finished off into one or three rooms, as desired, at a very little additional expense. Should you prefer a house designed in different way, write and give us your ideas. Our Building Plan Department will be only too glad to assist."

- 1914 Building Plans of Moderate Homes

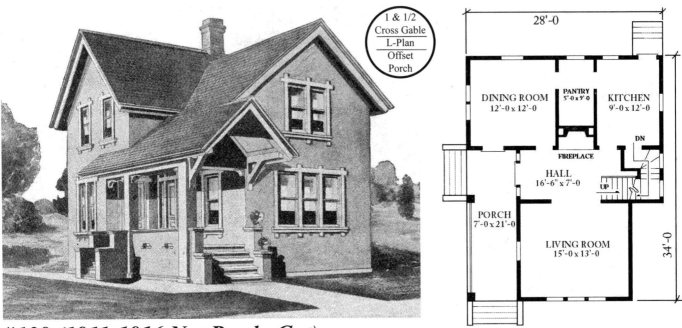

#139 (1911-1916 Not Ready-Cut)

1911 ($836 NRC), 1912 ($878 NRC), 1913 (NRC), 1914 ($726 NRC), 1915 ($866 NRC), 1916 ($837 NRC)

"This very modern home is one that demands attention by its imposing appearance. Has two sets of steps and two doors opening onto the porch, making it a suitable house for a corner lot. We call your attention to the outside casing of the frames, and to the way the porch is trimmed."

- 1912 Building Plans of Modern Homes

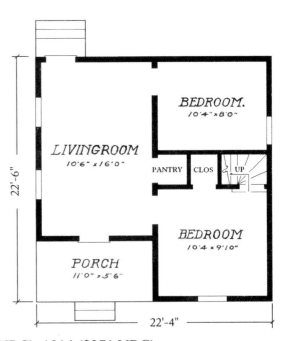

#133 (1910-1914 Not Ready-Cut)

1910 ($336 NRC), 1911 ($294 NRC), 1912 ($312 NRC), 1913 (NRC), 1914 ($371 NRC)

"It is impossible in one book of this size to show all the different styles of architecture. We have endeavored to design houses for those who wish either a large or small home. In a house of this size it is impossible to follow the lines of any particular style of architecture; still, at the same time, we feel sure that you will agree that for the price, we are offering plans and materials for a very attractive little cottage."

- 1914 Building Plans of Modern Homes

#182 (1915-1916 Not Ready-Cut)
1915 ($617 NRC), 1916 ($598 NRC)

Lanette (1922-1923 Not Ready-Cut)

Gordon-VanTine Design
Similar to Sears *Rossville* and Sears *Greenview*
1922 ($1698 NRC), 1923 ($1690 NRC)

It was not unusual for older models such as #182 to be redesigned and brought back with new names. The #182 is 22' wide while the Lanette is 24' wide.

The *Lanette* has a hip porch roof

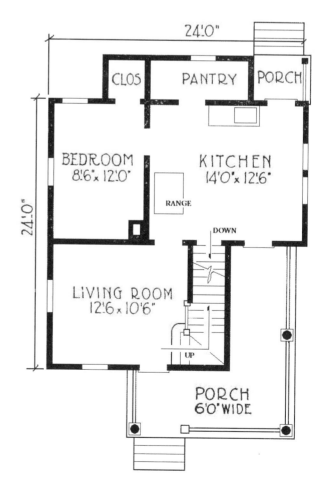

Custom Design

Finding Wardway Homes today can be especially challenging because homebuyers were encouraged to upgrade and customize their order. As early as 1910, the catalog said, "We do not confine your selection to the few plans this book contains, by any means. We are prepared to take your own ideas for any building – house, barn, store, block of buildings – anything you have in mind to build, and develop them for you at less than usual cost."

When Wardway introduced pre-cut homes in 1917 they all but eliminated the ability of customers to personalize their order.

The Ready-Cut home, like the ready-made suit of clothes does not lend itself easily to change. To do so, means not only an entire redrawing of the plans but the making over of an entirely new bill of materials. The original cost of this is about 5%, but in selling the same design fifty or a hundred times, the original cost for each purchase is trifling. This is not the case when dimensions are changed for just one sale. Some firms may say that they do not make any extra charge for special Ready-Cuts, but this extra expense must be borne by someone. We prefer to be frank. It may be this extra expense is charged up to general drafting costs, very evidently not fair to those not ask for changes. We prefer to state frankly, if a different size than that given for a Ready-Cut is desired it will cost the customer more for the same material than if he had bought a regular Ready-Cut design

- 1921 Wardway Homes catalog

SUBMIT YOUR OWN PLANS
and DESIGNS, IF YOU PREFER

Building Advice and Counsel FREE!

Just write Ward's Experts

IF you do not find the home you prefer to build in this book we are prepared to furnish materials for any home of special design that meets your need.

Even if it is only a rough pencil sketch, a bare idea of what you want—jot it down and send it to Ward's! Photographs, too, are sufficient to give our highly specialized architects and estimators a basis on which to prepare material estimates for your future home. So do not hesitate to send them. We are always glad to furnish you with estimates. You will be amazed at the low prices made possible by our large-scale operations in homes, building material and supplies.

Should you select one of the homes pictured in this book, and wish to change the floor space or plan in any way, we are prepared to furnish material for your home exactly as you desire it.

These are actual photographs of homes built by Ward's from the owners' own plans and designs. We extend the same service to you.

These homes are located in suburbs of Chicago

1931 Wardway Homes catalog.

One and One Half Story Cross Gable - Page 190

Even though Wardway Homes discouraged home builders from customizing their designs, they did permit them many choices, such as pine millwork or oak, window and door patterns, exterior sidings (shakes or clapboard or masonry), and reversed floor plans.

In 1929, Wardway went back to encouraging customized designs.

Changes can be made in the plans for any of our Wardway Homes, or we will supply you with materials for a special plan job. Our plans of Wardway Homes shown in this book are drawn to meet the requirements of the average family, and it our aim to make each home a model of convenience – perfect in floor arrangement. You may find that some alteration will make your home more comfortable, more convenient to meet some individual requirement. We will gladly arrange for any changes you wish.

In 1929, Sears went a step further and announced that they would offer full construction services for their own ready-cut houses. In 1930, Wardway introduced an identical program.

If you want a good local contractor to take over the entire job and be responsible to you we are prepared to recommend one to you", noted the 1931 catalog. "Ward's will act as your contractor and build your home complete from cellar to attic if you so desire – hire skilled local building tradesman to do the work – hand you the keys to your home. Completely finished and ready to live in. You need not be concerned or bothered with a single detail of work. Our construction department will direct the job from beginning to end.

The architectural staff at Gordon-VanTine kept busy throughout 1930 and 1931, drafting simple requests such as alterations and additions to pre-cut model homes, and providing full architectural services for Wardway customers wanting homes designed specifically for them. When Wardway Homes closed in January 1932 the architectural staff at Gordon-Van-Tine adapted popular Wardway Home designs as their own.

The Theon Literary Society Fraternity House at Michigan State University was built of Montgomery Ward materials by Wardway approved contractors (photograph by Dale Wolicki).

This North Muskegon, Michigan residence designed by Wardway architects was featured in a 1931 promotional brochure (photograph by Dale Wolicki).

Devonshire (1929-1931 Ready-Cut)
1929 ($2051), 1930 ($2453), 1931 ($2396)

"This charming home of many gables and half timbered effect in front, strikes a new note in home building. The Devonshire is bound to please. No matter how exacting you are, you will get full measure of satisfaction from such features as the sun porch, fireplace, side porch, and generous window space. Whether it be built on a large or small lot, it will proudly beautify whatever landscaping you decide upon, so well proportioned is it in every outward detail.

A house where a great many architectural perfections blend into a gracious, informal simplicity. Nor is the attractive exterior of the Devonshire its only merit, for inside it lives up to the myriad qualities so evident to the passerby. A first glance might give the idea that the Devonshire is hard to build, but in reality it is very simple. The plans are so through, the instructions so complete, that step by step can be followed without any trouble. If you are handy with tools you can do some of the work yourself and reduce building costs. Besides it is great fun, as many customers have told us.

Another decided advantage is the Easy Payment Plan which enables you to enjoy living in the Devonshire while paying for it as you formerly paid month rent, with only receipts to show for it afterward. These plans are explained in detail. Turn to these pages now and see for yourself how Wards' monthly payment plan will work in your case, how easy Ward's makes everything to enable you to own your own Home"

- 1930 Wardway Homes

A perfect *Devonshire* in Orchard Lake, Michigan (photograph by Dale Wolicki).

1st
Floor

PORCH
5'-6" x 11'-0"

DINING ROOM
11'-6" X 10'-6"

KITCHEN
8'-0"x10'-6"

RANGE

CLOTHES CHUTE

VESTIBULE

BROOMS

LIVING ROOM
16'-3" X 10'-0"

UP

DN

VESTIBULE

COATS

SUN ROOM
10'-0"x 7'-0"

PORCH
12'-0"x 7'-6"

5'-6"   21'-0

22'-0

7'-6"

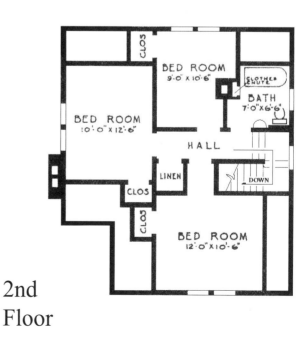

2nd
Floor

CLOS

BED ROOM
9'-0" X 10'-6"

CLOTHES CHUTE

BATH
7'-0"X 6'-6"

BED ROOM
10'-0" X 12'-6"

HALL

LINEN

CLOS

CLOS

CLOS

DOWN

BED ROOM
12'-0"X 10'-6"

1 & 1/2
Cross Gable
L-Plan
Offset
Porch

26'-0

DINING ROOM
12'-0" X 13'-3"

KITCHEN
12'-6" X 9'-3"

CLOS

ICE

CLOS

DOWN

LIVING ROOM
17'-0" X 13'-3"

HALL

UP

CLOS

28'-0

PORCH
9'-0" X 9'-0"

Parkway (1925-1928 Ready-Cut)

Gordon VanTine Design

1925 ($1950), 1926 ($1950), 1927 ($2059), 1928 ($2123)

"A beautiful example of English architecture. Dignity, quietude and restfulness are perfectly fused in a homey atmosphere. This type of home, with outside stucco walls nicely broken up with half-timbering, is increasingly rapidly in favor. The Parkway is one of those rare designs which blends perfectly with all surroundings"

- 1927 Wardway Homes

A *Parkway* in Champaign, Illinois (photograph by Dale Wolicki and Rebecca Hunter).

1 & 1/2
Cross Gable
L-Plan
Offset
Porch

Coventry (1931 Ready-Cut)
1931 ($2754)

"The smartest city suburb, where every lot contains an architectural masterpiece, will welcome the Coventry to its distinguished company of "Homes that are Unusual". We need not tell you how delightful it is from the out-side ... you can see for yourself the quaint charm of its tower entrance, and gables roof, of its casement windows that open above wide flower boxes. You can see, too, that the half timbered trim of windows and gables gives "atmosphere" that is decidedly interesting."
                                                                            - 1931 Wardway Homes

A rare *Coventry* in Elmhurst, Illinois (photograph by Rebecca Hunter).

Newport (1929-1931 Ready-Cut)

Gordon-VanTine Design

Similar to Sears *Mitchell*, Aladdin *University*, Bennett *Brentwood*,
Gordon-VanTine *Patrician* and Home Builders *Elyria*
1929 ($1930), 1930 ($1957), 1931 ($1926)

*"A modern version of the English cottage with its peaked roof,
numerous gables, arched doorway, and casement windows. Architecturally, it is one of the nicest small homes ever designed. Its floor
plan is perfect - embodying the modern architect's greatest achieve-
ments in scientific room arrangement. Particularly inviting is its
entrance. An uncovered brick terrace is the threshold for the old
style English style door, flanked on one side by the sturdy fireplace
chimney and on the other by the tiny look-out window."*
- 1931 Wardway Homes

Sears, Aladdin, Gordon-VanTine, and Montgomery Ward all had
versions of this particular house but the *Newport* is the easiest to
identify. Although the models are identical in measurements and
plan the Newport features a false round top door and a window
aside the fireplace. The front window arrangement varies. The
four-part casement window featured in the catalog illustration was
the most popular, with and without the accentuating transom, but
double-hung sash in groups of three or four can be found also.

A Wardway *Newport* in Woodstock, Illinois identified by shipping labels (photograph by Rebecca Hunter).

A brick *Newport* in Elkhorn, Wisconsin (photograph by Rebecca Hunter and Dale Wolicki).

A Wardway *Newport* in Barrington, Illinois used for advertising (photograph by Rebecca Hunter).

This attractive Wardway Home is to be found in Barrington, Ill.

The Wardway *Newport* is often mistaken for the Aladdin *University* (above) and Sears *Mitchell* (below).

Piermont (1929-1931 Ready-Cut)

Similar to Lewis Homes *St. Regis*
1929 ($2291), 1930 ($2395), 1931 ($2296)

"The rambling, free and easy air of an English country home. The distinctive handsome design, with the sharply sloping roofs - the unusual chimney - the wealth of artistic gables - the quaint shutters, divided light windows - all combine to create a general impression of inviting originality more than verified by the interior.

You step from the brick terrace into a friendly vestibule with clothes closet to the right. The living room is the sort that suggests well being and snug comfort. The fireplace - symbol of cheeriness - is truly impressive. Three windows afford excellent ventilation and a pleasant view. Home-like proportions offer wonderful possibilities for furnishing."

- *1929 Wardway Homes*

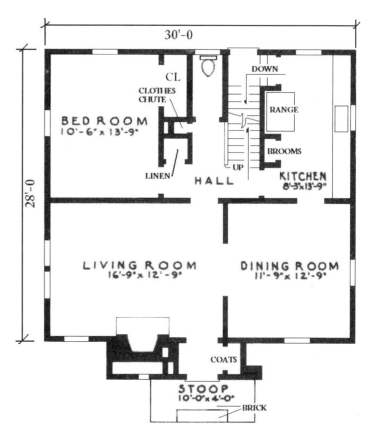

A *Piermont* in Union Grove, Wisconsin (photograph by Rebecca Hunter and Dale Wolicki).

A 1929 *Piermont* built in Flint, Michigan by General Motors (photograph by Dale Wolicki).

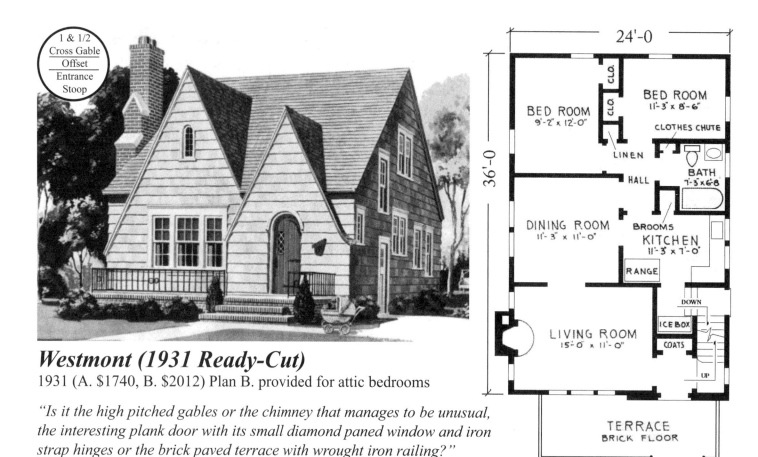

Westmont (1931 Ready-Cut)

1931 (A. $1740, B. $2012) Plan B. provided for attic bedrooms

"Is it the high pitched gables or the chimney that manages to be unusual, the interesting plank door with its small diamond paned window and iron strap hinges or the brick paved terrace with wrought iron railing?"

- 1931 Wardway Homes

Cortland Duplex (1930-1931 Ready-Cut)

1930 ($2687), 1931 ($2497)

"The Cortland offers convincing proof that two families can live in a home of unusual beauty and comfort for the amount of rent usually paid by one. If you are the owner of this fine duplex, you can collect rent, make it meet your payments and in a short time own the home outright."

- 1930 Wardway Homes

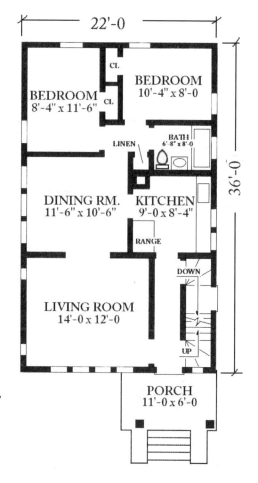

Winthrop (1931 Ready-Cut)
1931 ($2312)

"Nice to step in here for a later afternoon cup of tea and nicer still to be the gracious hostess dispensing hospitality in so charming a home. The Winthrop is quaintly picturesque and very English with its high pitched gables where simple half-timber work is used effectively, its plank door, its sturdy fireplace chimney and shuttered casement widows."

                                                   - 1931 Wardway Homes

Whitmore (1930-1931 Ready-Cut)
1930 ($2726), 1931 ($2680)

"Are you looking for a home in the very latest style? Do you want an individual and distinctive home that your neighbors will point to with pride - that will arrest the admiring attention of passers-by? Then you will go far to equal the undeniable attractiveness of the brick veneer Whitmore, our finest home. The peaked Gothic gables - broken patches of roof - picturesque half-timbered stucco will appeal to you. The unusual compactness and convenience of the interior layout, generous closet space and first floor lavatory are other features of this charming ultra modern Whitmore home."

                                                   - 1930 Wardway Homes

Parkside Duplex (1930-1931)

1930 ($3143), 1931 ($3143)

"You can build and live in this beautiful home, and let your tenant help pay for it. Brick veneer front with stucco and half-timbered front gables; sides and back stucco as pictured and priced. May also be built with all stucco gables, shingle or bevel siding if you prefer. Stairway leading upstairs direct from vestibule assures privacy to both apartments. Renting one floor often takes care of the easy monthly payments. The demand for houses like this is constantly increasing. Whether you build it to live in or for re-sale, you'll find the Parkside a thoroughly practical choice. Better grade of tenant and higher rent are to be expected for the Parkside because its appearance is like the fine modern type of one-family home."

- 1930 Wardway Homes

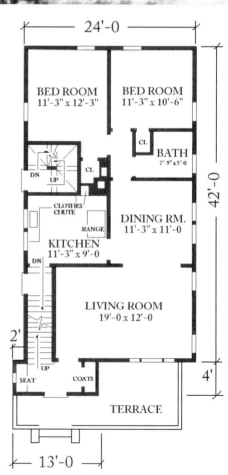

A Flint, Michigan *Parkside* found with a 1931 mortgage (photograph by Dale Wolicki).

A Jackson, Michigan *Parkside* (photograph by Dale Wolicki).

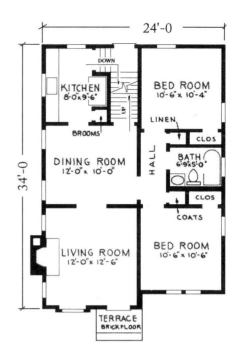

1 & 1/2
Cross Gable
Offset
Entrance
Stoop

24'-0

KITCHEN
8'-0"x9'-6"

DOWN

BED ROOM
10'-6" x 10'-4"

UP

BROOMS

LINEN

CLOS

34'-0

DINING ROOM
12'-0" x 10'-0"

HALL

BATH
6'-9"x5'-0"

CLOS

COATS

LIVING ROOM
12'-0" x 12'-6"

BED ROOM
10'-6" x 10'-6"

TERRACE
BRICK FLOOR

Fairfax (1931 Ready-Cut)
1931 ($1864)

"Charmingly and decidedly English is the Fairfax! And so unusually interesting ... with its smart half-timbered and stucco gable, with projecting casement in front - its square and diamond paned casement windows, and plank-type, strap-hinged doorway. Its novel 12-pane window in the dormer. Its use of ten-inch beveled siding. And the distinctive chimney treatment. Inside, the Fairfax is delightfully spacious. It is equipped with every modern feature of convenience and comfort."

- 1931 Wardway Homes

1 & 1/2
Cross Gable
Offset
Entrance
Stoop

25'-0

BED ROOM
10'-6" X 15'-0"

BREAKFAST
ROOM
6'-0" X 7'-0"

DOWN

BROOMS

CLOSET

CLOTHES
CHUTE

CLOSET

KITCHEN
9'-8" X 11'-4 1/2"

LINEN

RANGE

BATH
6'-8"x6'-10"

HALL

CLOS

DINING ROOM
12'-0" X 15'-0"

BED ROOM
10'-6" X 11'-6"

CLOS

LIVING ROOM
18'-9" X 12'-0"

UP

49'-0

VESTIBULE

COATS

STOOP
CONCRETE FLOOR

Bradford (1931 Ready-Cut)
1931 ($2086)

"Designed to meet the requirements of those desiring to build a residence of brick veneer, the Bradford represents a smart and striking advance in home beauty."

- 1931 Wardway Homes

The "Pinehurst" — A Handsome Half-Timbered Stucco

6 Rooms and Bath

$1726

Price Includes

Complete set of Plans. All Lumber, Lath, Shingles, Flooring, Inside and Outside Finish and Moldings, Doors, Windows, Frames, Built-in Kitchen Case and Towel Case, Nails, Hardware, Tinwork, Building Paper, Paint, Varnish. Everything to build your home with the exception of Heating, Lighting and Plumbing equipment and Masonry materials.

Unless otherwise requested, we furnish Dark Brown Paint for the Trim. Sidewalls are of Stucco.

Options

Oak Floors and Woodwork for Living Room, Dining Room and Stairs, $110.15 additional. Ruberoid Slate Surface Asphalt Shingles with tight roof sheathing, $33.70 additional. Galvanized Wire Screens for all windows and outside doors, $36.10 additional. Storm Sash and Doors, $49.30 additional. High grade Door and Window Shades, color optional, $14.41 additional.

See complete descriptions of all options on Page 19.

See complete specifications on Pages 10 and 11; also Heating, Plumbing and Wiring information on Pages 94 to 100.

YOU will rarely find as charming and well planned a small home as the "Pinehurst." Substantial, sturdy and individual—the half-timbered stucco house is still unusual enough to be distinctive. Every detail—the steep roof with its wide barge boards and supporting brackets, the broad windows, the hooded porch with its massive brick pedestals and its grouped pillars—all are architecturally perfect.

Living Room: Across the entire front of the house is one big, pleasant living room, with graceful stair at one end and light from three sides. It's the kind of a room every member of the family will thoroughly enjoy.

Dining Room: To the rear of the living room, and almost a part of it—through a wide cased opening, is the dining room, which is well lighted by a double window. An alcove in this room makes an effective setting for the buffet.

Kitchen: The wide window and closed door bring it light from two sides, so that stove, sink and built-in kitchen case "B," shown on Page 20, have direct sunlight all hours of the day. A door into the entry gives access to basement stairs, grade door and living room, bringing the kitchen within a few steps of the front door, yet shutting out its sounds and odor.

Bedrooms and Bath: Three large bedrooms are carefully arranged with the best of ventilation from windows on two sides, with extra large closets.

FIRST FLOOR PLAN

FOR FREE ESTIMATE

Two Story Front Gable

Pinehurst - Renamed Kelsey in 1928 (1926-1931 Ready-Cut)

Gordon-VanTine Design

1926 ($1536), 1927 ($1674), 1928 ($1726), 1929 ($1923), 1930 ($1947), 1931 ($1919)

"You will rarely find as charming and well planned a small home as the Pinehurst. Substantial, sturdy and individual - the half-timbered stucco home is still unusual enough to be distinctive. Every detail - the steep roof with its wide barge boards and supporting brackets, the broad windows, the hooded porch with its massive brick pedestals and its grouped pillars - all are architecturally perfect. Across the entire front of the house is one big, pleasant living room, with graceful stair at one end and light from three sides. It's the kind of room every member of the family will thoroughly enjoy. To the rear of the living room, and almost a part of it - through a wide cased opening, is the dining room."

- 1927 Wardway Homes

1st Floor   2nd Floor

#171 (1914 - 1916 Not Ready-Cut)
1914 ($1115 NRC), 1915 ($1316 NRC), 1916 ($1184 NRC)

"Anyone desiring a plain, spacious attractive home cannot make a mistake in selecting this well-studied plan. This frame building has a shingle roof with spacious front porch. The dimensions on the ground floor are 26 x 40, and the house contains 8 rooms, besides a neat reception hall with open staircase; also a stair leading from the kitchen to the grade level and thence to the basement, bathroom and pantry."

- 1914 Building Plans of Modern Homes

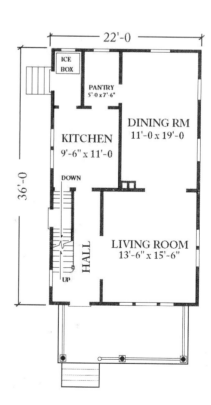

#173 (1914-1915 Not Ready-Cut)
1914 ($779 NRC), 1915 ($857 NRC)

"A well proportioned home, built entirely along straight lines. This form of construction permits the best use of space, so that while this house is suitable for a narrow lot; the rooms are of ample size, with ceilings full height. An attractive home for city or country, and a good value."

- 1915 Book of Homes

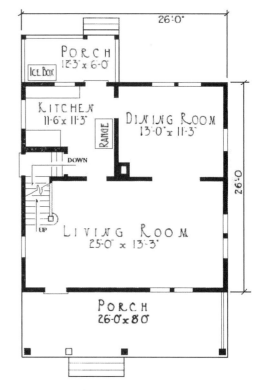

Hampden (1922-1925 Ready-Cut)
Gordon-VanTine Design
1922 ($2320), 1923 ($2300), 1924 ($2145), 1925 ($2112)

"The Hampton is a home which appeals to the conservative buyer who wants good appearance in his home without expensive trimmings, and the most room and convenience his money can buy. A simple, square home of splendid proportions."

- 1923 Wardway Homes

#147 (1911-1914 Not Ready-Cut)
1911 ($1063 NRC), 1912 ($1150 NRC), 1913 (NRC), 1914 ($1091 NRC)

"Brick houses create an impression of comfort, but they are of necessity plain in architecture. The manner of building the brick piers so that they extend a little above the porch rail, and then capping them with stone, makes an extremely fine looking veranda. There is also a balcony extending across the entire rear of the building. A balcony is always useful as well as ornamental."

- 1914 Building Plans of Modern Homes

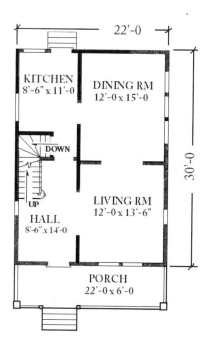

22'-0

KITCHEN
8'-6" x 11'-0

DINING RM
12'-0 x 15'-0

DOWN

30'-0

LIVING RM
12'-0 x 13'-6"

UP

HALL
8'-6" x 14'-0

PORCH
22'-0 x 6'-0

Hudson (1917-1918 Not Ready-Cut)

1917 ($956 NRC), 1918 ($1392 NRC)

"Here is a substantial looking home which at once gives the impression of stability and comfort. The heavy porch roof, supported by two large square columns, blends perfectly out to extend all the way around the house."

- 1918 Wardway Homes

STOOP

KITCHEN
9'-0" x 9'-3"

DINING ROOM
9'-6" x 12'-3"

RANGE

ICE

DOWN

26'-0'

LIVING ROOM
19'-0" x 12'-3"

UP

20'-0'

PORCH
10 x 8'

Hazelton (1922-1925 Ready-Cut)

Gordon-VanTine Design

1922 ($1782), 1923 ($1696), 1924 ($1595), 1925 ($1570)

"While only twenty feet wide and therefore especially suitable for a narrow lot, this home is fully two stories high and contains six big rooms, a bath and generous closet space. The complete harmony of the porch roof and the main roof, and the simplicity and dignity of design, suggest its true worth."

- 1923 Wardway Homes

2 Story
Front Gable
Entrance
Stoop

Mesa (1922-1924 Ready-Cut)
Gordon-VanTine Design
1922 ($2595), 1923 ($2547), 1924 ($2375)

The only way to distinguish between the Wardway *Mesa* and the Gordon-VanTine *#534* is to find the shipping label or mortgage documentation. They have identical measurements, floor plans, elevations and even share the same illustration in their catalogs. The Mesa was offered briefly, thus most examples are actually #534.

"The charm of the unusual appeals in this home at first glance, but when you analyze it you find that basically it is a simple square house, consequently an economical one to build; and its unusual charm is contributed to by the skillful handling of details. The outside walls have siding up to the belt course, and from there on shingles laid alternately two inches and seven inches to the weather, broken by half timbers. The distinctiveness gained by this arrangement is an example of what can be done by an expert designer without expense. The wide eaves with their open cornice and timber brackets, assist in contributing a craftsman effect to the whole. Perhaps the most unique idea is the continuing of the porch roof across the front of the house and joining it with the roof of the hooded entrance. The front door leads directly into a big living room, at the right end of which is a coat closet. Opposite this closet is a beautiful, artistic open stairway. French doors lead from the living room to the open porch, which may be screened for summer use. A plaster colonnade joins the dining room and living room. The dining room is well lighted with three windows. The kitchen is compact and convenient, containing our case design number 861 built into the rear wall, with room for all necessary kitchen equipment and supplies. A back porch is just off the kitchen."

- 1923 Wardway Homes

Among many Wardway Homes in Lapeer, Michigan, is this *Mesa* (photograph by Dale Wolicki).

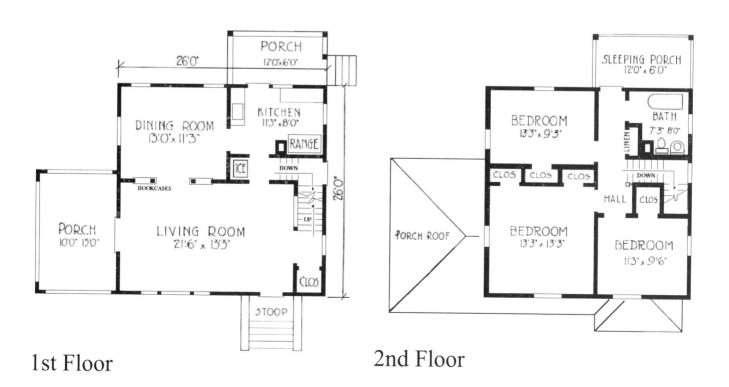

1st Floor

2nd Floor

2 Story
Front Gable
Entrance
Stoop

Cedars (1929-1931 Ready-Cut)

Gordon-VanTine Design

1929 ($2515), 1930 ($2694), 1931 ($2675)

"The Cedars - our home pictured on the front cover (of the catalog) - is a masterpiece of architectural beauty. And it is as distinctive and practical as it is beautiful and modern. The Cedars was designed by foremost architects to bring you the last word in a six-room home."

- 1929 Wardway Homes

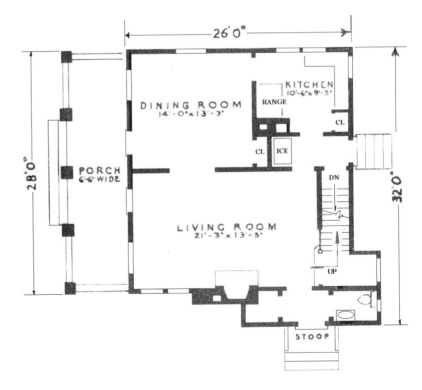

A 1931 *Cedars* in Kalamazoo, Michigan found by mortgage records (photograph by Dale Wolicki).

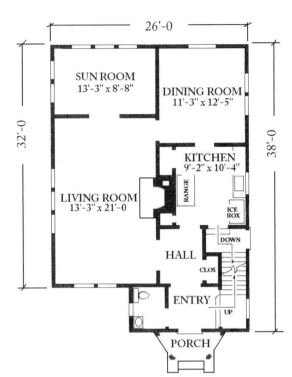

Sundale (1929-1930 Ready-Cut)
1929 ($2980), 1930 ($2835)

"The Sundale gets away from the commonplace by the use of gabled roofs, and interesting dormer windows with modernized shutters to add the enchanting touch so many desire. But withal, the freakish has been rigidly avoided - and the Sundale finds great favor with homeowners of conservative good taste."

-1929 Wardway Homes

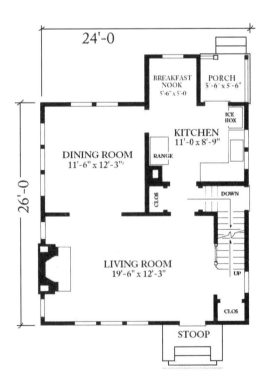

Northbrook (1929-1931 Ready-Cut)
1929 ($2248), 1930 ($2322), 1931 ($2272)

"The spirit of Old England and New England are united with the best American practice in this modern home - a model for those who desire the utmost in comfort and good taste.

- 1931 Wardway Homes

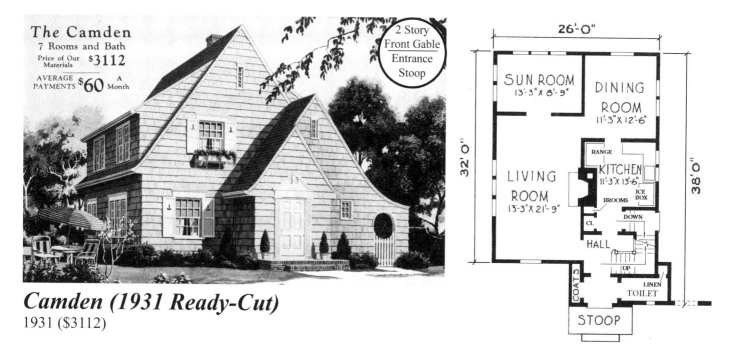

The Camden
7 Rooms and Bath
Price of Our Materials **$3112**
AVERAGE PAYMENTS **$60** A Month

2 Story Front Gable Entrance Stoop

SUN ROOM 13'-3" x 8'-9"

DINING ROOM 11'-3" x 12'-6"

LIVING ROOM 13'-3" x 21'-9"

RANGE

KITCHEN 11'-3" x 13'-6"

ICE BOX

BROOMS

CL.

DOWN

HALL

UP

COATS

LINEN

TOILET

STOOP

26'-0"

32'-0"

38'-0"

Camden (1931 Ready-Cut)
1931 ($3112)

"From the terraced brick porch you enter a pleasant vestibule, with lavatory at right, and a coat closet on the left. Just ahead from the spacious hall, a graceful staircase leads to three generous-sized second-floor bed rooms with plenty of cross-ventilation. The bathroom is easily accessible. Over the vestibule, on the second floor, a very convenient Sewing Room is also located. Downstairs, the 22-feet-long Living Room is delightfully spacious. Arched entries, a classic Colonial mantelpiece, and five windows giving illumination from two sides, make you more than welcome the moment you enter."
— *1931 Wardway Homes*

New Designs and the Spring Building Season

At the end of every building season (late October or early November), housing manufacturers estimated their sales for the approaching spring building season. Estimates were often optimistic. Building materials were purchased during the fall and winter. Extra building materials and fixtures could always be stored for future use but a shortage during the spring building season, particularly of lumber, would require it be purchased during the building season when prices were high.

At the same time, pre-cut housing companies would review their sales for the previous year and assess which models were selling and which models were unpopular. Each year, houses were added and others removed from their catalogs.

Overall, the pre-cut housing catalogs didn't undergo dramatic change from one year to the next. Revised editions typically featured a new home on the cover with updated prices inside. Catalogs were expensive to produce and required extensive preparation. Architects and builders were needed to design the houses, copywriters for the informative descriptions, artists and photographers for the illustrations, and special printers if there were color illustrations. Most catalogs were in development a full year before they were published and distributed.

Home Builders Catalog

Many houses of the 1920s and 1930s were built from blueprints purchased from *Home Builders*, a Chicago publisher that supplied architectural plan books to contractors and building material dealers. Much like William Radford, Home Builders offered designs from which customers could select the house that fit their life style and budget.

"Because of our experience and thorough knowledge of this line of work," noted the 1929 catalog, *"our large and capable staff of building experts, and the enormous volume of business we do, we are able to produce and furnish complete and accurate blue-print plans, specifications, material lists, etc. of higher quality and at a lower price than can be procured from any other reliable source."*

Home Builders offered several models that were strikingly similar to those offered by Wardway and other housing manufacturers, thus they are frequently identified incorrectly as pre-cut homes.

The CANDIA

Frank Lloyd Wright and Pre-Cut Homes

Disciples of the great American architect Frank Lloyd Wright often credit him erroneously with having perfected, even invented, the pre-cut house. Starting in 1911 Wright designed several bungalows, duplexes and apartment buildings for *American System Built Homes,* a Milwaukee pre-cut housing company that operated briefly before World War One. Although the Prairie style buildings were handsome only a few dozen American System Built Homes were erected before the company closed in 1917.

HOME No. 111

For $2,087.00 we will furnish the material to build this twelve-room double house, consisting of all lumber, lath, shingles, finishing lumber, flooring, doors, windows, frames, trim, mantels and grates, sash weights, hardware, pipe and gutter, and painting material. We absolutely guarantee the material furnished to be sufficient to build the house according to our plans and specifications.

A double house of a distinctive type. Where ground space is at a premium, a double house is often an exceedingly good investment, because it is more economical to build than two houses, and therefore produces more income in proportion to the amount invested. This is doubly true when you take into consideration the saving that the building of Home No. 111 will mean to you.

GENERAL SPECIFICATIONS

Brick foundation. Outside sheathing and building paper, double first floors. All framing material best quality Yellow Pine, Star A Star Cedar shingles, No. 1 lath. Excellent grade hardware. Windows glazed "A" quality glass. Painted two coats best Tower Brand Paint outside, your choice of colors, wood filler and varnish for interior. All materials specified are shown on Bill of Material furnished with our plans, and you can read full descriptions in our Building Material Catalogue.

By allowing a fair price for labor, stone, cement, brick, and plaster, which we do not furnish, this house can be built for about $4,375.00.

FIRST FLOOR

Each half of house on first floor contains vestibule, hall, parlor, dining-room, kitchen, pantry, rear porch and entry. Front porch is divided. Cased opening from hall to parlor, and from hall to dining-room. Dining-room has mantel and grate, and double windows with single sash between. Pantry located between dining-room and kitchen. Basement and back stairs from kitchen. Yellow Pine trim throughout. Ceilings, 9 feet high.

SECOND FLOOR

Three bedrooms, bath, and hall to each closet, and there is an extra room ... lighted from front and sides, and ... Ceilings, 8 feet 6 inches high.

BASEMENT

Excavated under entire house. ...

Heating

Two Warm Air Heating Plants	......
Two Steam Heating Plants	......
Two Hot Water Heating Plants	......

MONTGOMERY WARD & CO.

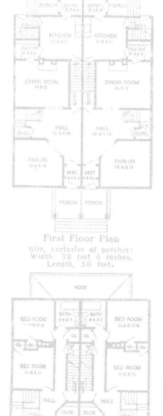

First Floor Plan
Size, exclusive of porches:
Width, 38 feet 6 inches.
Length, 50 feet.

Two Story Side Gable

#110 (1909-1915 Not Ready-Cut)

1909 ($1130 NRC), 1910 ($1130 NRC), 1911 ($1098 NRC), 1912 ($1155 NRC),
1913 (NRC, 1914 ($1197 NRC), 1915 ($1488 NRC)

"Our eastern friends admire this type of house very much. By looking at the floor plan you will note the large porch with nine large colonial columns set in groups of three. We enter and find a vestibule, reception hall with a closet, and an open stairway. The hall connects with the living room by a large opening, in which can be placed a colonnade. The living room in turn is connected with the dining room by a large opening, in which is placed a pair of sliding doors. There is a mantel and fireplace in both dining room and living room. The basement can be reached either from the kitchen or the grade door. All the interior trim is clear yellow pine, with Western pine doors of the cross panel type. All material is the best of its kind."

- 1914 Building Plans of Modern Homes

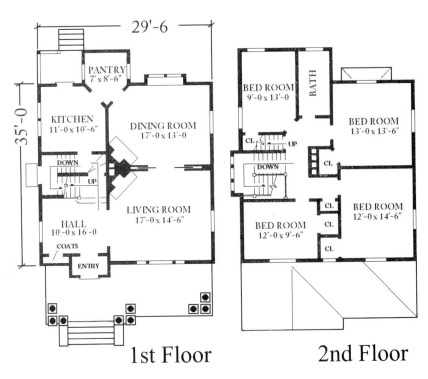

1st Floor   2nd Floor

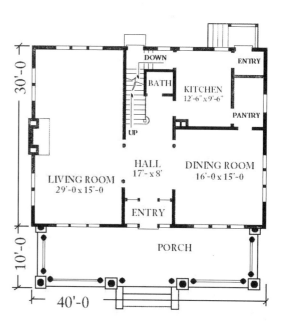

2 Story
Side Gable
Attached Porch
Full-Width

DOWN · ENTRY · BATH · KITCHEN 12'-6" x 9'-6" · PANTRY · UP · 30'-0 · HALL 17'- x 8' · DINING ROOM 16'-0 x 15'-0 · LIVING ROOM 29'-0 x 15'-0 · ENTRY · PORCH · 10'-0 · 40'-0

#146 (1911-1916 Not Ready-Cut)
1911 ($2042 NRC), 1912 ($2145 NRC), 1913 (NRC),
1914 ($2097 NRC), 1915 ($2133 NRC), 1916 ($2051 NRC)

*"For those who live South, or who desire the Southern or Colonial type of Architecture, this will make a conve-
nient and desirable home. Note the extremely large and attractive veranda, which from the front gives the appearance of a home costing at least four or five time the amount which we ask for this one. The house is finished
in oak, with hardwood floors, and oak veneered doors. Note the large living room, with open fireplace. Both the
large living room and dining room have oak beamed ceilings and connect with the hall by a large opening, with
oak interior columns in place of a colonnade."*

- 1912 Building Plans of Modern Homes

2 Story
Side Gable
Attached Porch
Full-Width

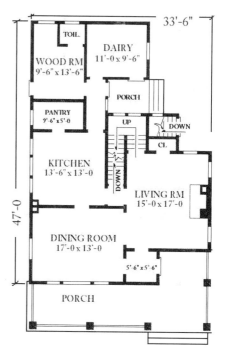

33'-6" · TOIL. · DAIRY 11'-0 x 9'-6" · WOOD RM 9'-6" x 13'-6" · PORCH · PANTRY 9'-6" x 5'-0 · UP · DOWN · CL · KITCHEN 13'-6" x 13'-0 · DOWN · LIVING RM 15'-0 x 17'-0 · 47'-0 · DINING ROOM 17'-0 x 13'-0 · 5'-6" x 5'-6" · PORCH

#112 (1909-1914 Not Ready-Cut)
1909 ($1230 NRC), 1910 ($1230 NRC), 1911 ($1262 NRC),
1912 ($1400 NRC), 1913 (NRC), 1914 ($1356 NRC)

*"House design Number 112 is a composite type having Colonial porch. The windows are of a style that is
mostly used in the east, and the roof is more often seen on a bungalow. It is designed to meet the needs of those
who wish a wood room and dairy connected with the house proper. If you intend to have a furnace or hot water
heat, you can change the wood room to the kitchen, the kitchen to the dining room, and the latter to the parlor,
thereby giving you four rooms and a dairy on the first story, which, with the four rooms and bath on the second,
will make a commodious and comfortable farm residence."* — *1912 Building Plans of Modern Homes*

Forsythe (1922-1926 Ready-Cut)

Gordon-VanTine Design
Similar to Aladdin Homes *Georgia*
1922 ($1770), 1923 ($1737), 1924 ($1649), 1925 ($1598), 1926 ($1598)

"The Forsythe is another one of our Wardway designs which has met with popular favor. It is an ideal home for the average family, combining so many essential features, such as a large living room, three spacious bedrooms and bath and an artistic cozy front porch. These are the details which always appeal to the purchasers of this home. It is a handsome two-story, three-bedroom home, combing all the things which make for convenience and comfort but with all the unnecessary features eliminated, making it one of the most economical homes in size and number of rooms ever designed."

- *1923 Wardway Homes*

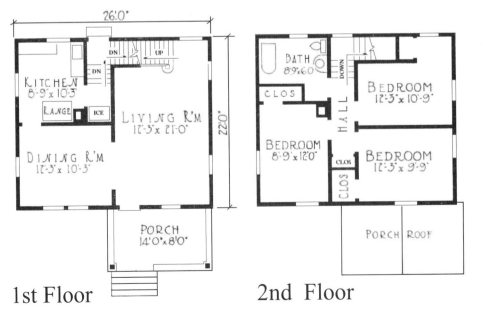

1st Floor   2nd Floor

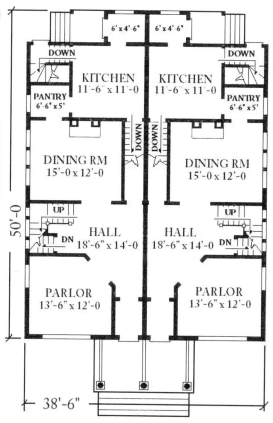

2 Story Side Gable Attached Porch Centered

6' x 4'-6"   6' x 4'-6"

DOWN   DOWN

KITCHEN 11'-6" x 11'-0   KITCHEN 11'-6" x 11'-0

PAN'TRY 6'-6" x 5'   PAN'TRY 6'-6" x 5'

DINING RM 15'-0 x 12'-0   DINING RM 15'-0 x 12'-0

DOWN

UP   UP

HALL 18'-6" x 14'-0   HALL 18'-6" x 14'-0

DN   DN

PARLOR 13'-6" x 12'-0   PARLOR 13'-6" x 12'-0

50'-0

38'-6"

#111 Duplex (1909-1915 Not Ready-Cut)

1909 ($1824 NRC), 1910 ($1824 NRC),
1911 ($1952 NRC), 1912 ($2050 NRC),
1913 (NRC), 1914 ($2007 (NRC), 1915 ($2087 NRC)

"Where one has sufficient ground room, it is a good idea to erect a double house, for you can build at much less expense than for two single houses."

- 1914 Building Plans of Modern Homes

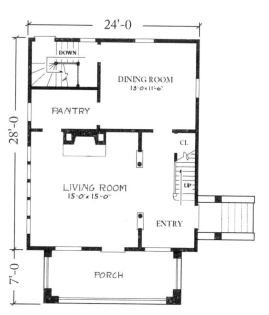

2 Story Side Gable Entrance Stoop

24'-0

DOWN

DINING ROOM 13'-0 x 11'-6"

PANTRY

CL.

LIVING ROOM 15'-0 x 15'-0

UP

ENTRY

28'-0

7'-0

PORCH

#141 (1911-1914 Not Ready-Cut)

1911 ($719 NRC), 1912 ($756 NRC), 1913 (NRC), 1914 ($752 NRC)

"Stucco houses are the quite the vogue nowadays, and are seen in all enterprising communities. There is an air of distinctiveness and smartness about them that cannot be found in an ordinary frame dwelling. This house has a pergola in front and the entrance is off to the side, making a house that should preferably be erected on a corner lot."

- 1914 Building Plans of Modern Homes

Beverly (1925-1927 Ready-Cut)
Gordon-VanTine Design
1925 ($2065), 1926 ($2065), 1927 ($2037)

The *Beverly* is similar to the *Rochelle* except the Beverly measures 26'-0 in depth, has a slightly different floor plan and the windows on the front elevation are equally spaced.

"This home with its picturesque appearance will make a strong appeal to those who favor Colonial style of architecture. Everything about this home seems to blend in harmoniously due to the care and thought used in its designing. The exterior stucco walls may be made particularly attractive by the use of clinging vines as shown. Notice the well-balanced manner in which the windows have been arranged and their specially designed crescent shutter, also the quaint entrance with its tall narrow columns, the brick floor and steps and the old fashioned wood paneled door, all of which are in harmony in this stately Colonial home. The large open porch, extending 20 feet along the right edge of the home sets close to the ground and provides a most inviting and delightful place to spend a hot summer afternoon or evening. On entering the home you will find the interior equally as attractive as the exterior. A vestibule and clothes closet for outside wraps are features not found in many homes, but these have not been overlooked in the Beverly. The spacious living room is well lighted by two large windows and the glazed French doors which lead out on to the open porch. The fireplace and attractive open staircase, also add greatly to the charm of this homey living room. The dining room is a pleasant, well lighted room and is connected with the living room by a wide cased opening. There is ample wall space for placing all dining room furniture without the slightest crowding."

- 1925 Wardway Homes

A brick *Beverly* in Detroit, Michigan used for advertising in 1931 (photograph by Dale Wolicki).

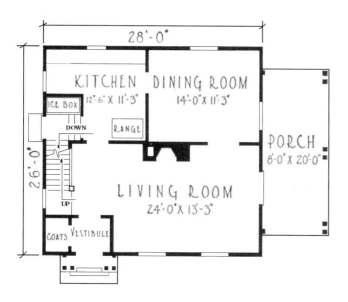

1st Floor

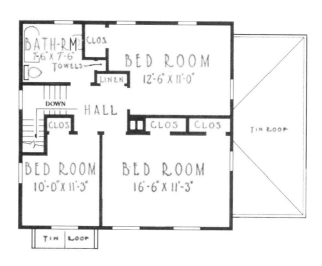

2nd Floor

Rochelle - Renamed Wallace in 1929 (1922-1931 Ready-Cut)

Gordon-VanTine Design

1922 ($2395), 1923 ($2100), 1924 ($2100), 1925 ($2072), 1926 ($2072), 1927 ($2168), 1928 ($2235), 1929 ($2559), 1930 ($2448), 1931 ($2424)

Similar to the *Beverly* except the *Rochelle* measures 24'-0 in depth, has a slightly different floorplan and an entrance door and window above offset slightly.

"An example of true Colonial architecture. The most discriminating will find this home desirable. It is built low to the ground into a most compact arrangements of six rooms. The hooded entrance, gable roof, shuttered windows and shingled walls combine in creating a most pleasing and harmonious appearance. The Rochelle is an aristocrat among the Colonial homes. It is charming and dignified appearance will make you justly proud no matter where it is built."

- 1927 Wardway Homes

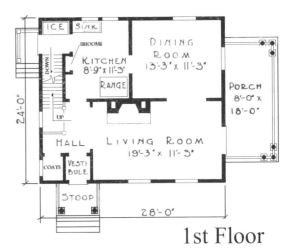

1st Floor

2nd Floor

Rosedale (1917-1919 Ready-Cut)

Gordon-VanTine Design
1917 ($1234) 1918 ($1648), 1919 ($1921)

The GVT model is identical in appearance but measures 28'-0 wide by 24'-0 deep.

"There is something striking about the Rosedale, somthing different, yet it is hard to select any single accountable feature. A gable roof sloping toward front and rear. Yes - this feature together with the large dormer on the front certainly has an influence. Besides, there is the front porch with its quaint and attractive roof - supported without the usual columns. The sun parlor lends distinction. An inspection of the interior is no less pleasing. from the recption hall one is greeted by the warm welcome of the fireplace at the end of the living room; whether in winter or summer, there is an abundance of light furnished by the large triple window in the front. The dining room, likewise, offers its attractions. A cheerful sun parlor is always acceptable. In this case it is epecially acceptable inasmuch as it may be used in connection of the dining room."

- 1918 Wardway Homes

First Floor

Second Floor

Maywood (1928-1931 Ready-Cut)

Gordon-VanTine Design

Similar to Sears *Barrington*

1928 ($2115), 1929 ($2295), 1930 ($2295), 1931 ($2278)

"The English cottage style has come into wide popularity because of its very evident charm, and also because it is particularly well adapted to our varying North American climate. The Maywood has many fascinating structural features. The perky front gable and quaint windowed dormer give the steep roof a delightful irregularity which is a truly English characteristic. The neat windows - small paned to preserve the scale of the house - are interestingly arranged; and the triple window frame in the front gives a charming effect to the living room both from without and within. A compact home with spacious rooms skillfully planned for comfortable family life. It has the beauty of the lovely little houses in the country sections of England, which have seldom been surpassed in charm. The Maywood - so far removed from the commonplace and so certain never to go out of favor - will prove a great asset if you should ever wish to sell it."

- 1930 Wardway Homes

An unaltered *Maywood* in Royal Oak, Michigan (photograph by Dale Wolicki).

The Maywood was Wardways version of the Sears *Barrington* and the two are frequently confused as they are identical in appearence and floorplan. Among the minor details that can distinguish the two, the Maywood has six/one window sash while the Barrington has six/six window sash. The Maywood many have a small round top window above the entrance gable instead of the square window featured in the illustration. Montgomery Ward allowed customers to substitute a gable roof for the small hip roof above the dormer. Although the Maywood was offered only a few years it was very popular.

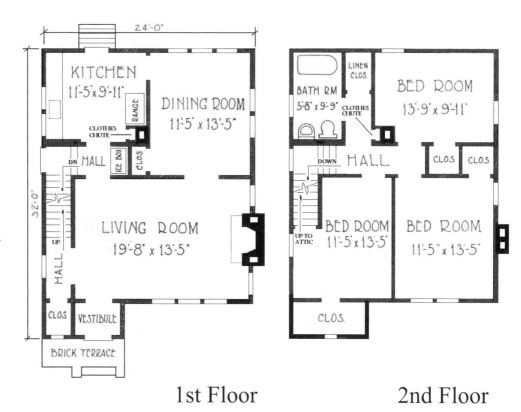

1st Floor   2nd Floor

This stately Wardway Home is one of the
many built in Battle Creek, Mich.

This *Maywood* in Battle
Creek, Michigan was used
in a 1931 promotional
brouchure for customized
Wardway Homes (photo-
graph by Dale Wolicki).

A Flint, Michigan *Maywood* with centered entrance door and shed roof dormer (photograph by Dale Wolicki).

The similarity of the Wardway Maywood and the Sears Barrington (above) is cause for frequent confusion.

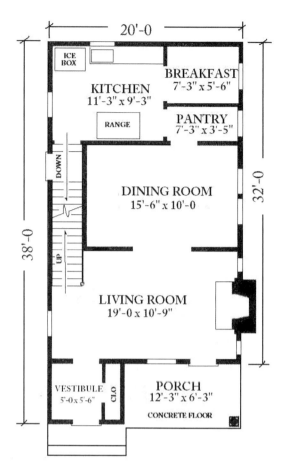

Newark (1931 Ready-Cut)
1930 ($2452)

"For all its well-groomed English air of smartness, the Newark is a very practical house for narrow city lots. You can build it on a twenty-five to thirty foot lot yet it has ample room for the average sized family."   *- 1930 Wardway Homes*

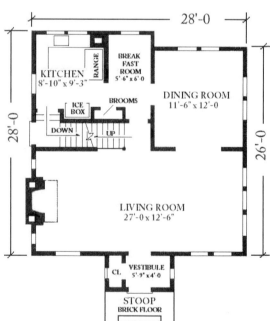

Dorchester (1930 Ready-Cut)
1930 ($2710)

"First impressions are most lasting - and the Dorchester will introduce itself very favorably to your friends. The charming gabled entrance and arched door is quaintly individual and appealing. Entering, you step into a home of graceful spaciousness, finished with a magic touch of modern beauty and convenience that makes every room more pleasant."   *- 1930 Wardway Homes*

HOME No. 174

$1,437.00

HOME No. 174

For $1,437.00 we will furnish the material to build this nine-room home, consisting of all lumber, lath, shingles, finishing lumber, flooring, doors, windows, frames, trim, china closet, medicine case, linen closet, hardware, sash weights, building paper, pipe and gutter, and painting material. We absolutely guarantee the material to be sufficient to build the home according to our plans and specifications.

A large, impressive appearing home, of a type that shows up to good advantage in any surroundings. The plan of the roof, with its wide, overhanging eaves, coupled with the generous dimensions of the house itself, gives an air of stability and strength, while just the right element of homelikeness is added by the extensive porch, the large amount of window space, and the ornamental sash. A home for a large family, and especially suitable for a corner lot, or other prominent location.

GENERAL SPECIFICATIONS

Built on a brick foundation. Lattice under porches. Double first floors. Side walls have sheating, building paper, and clear Cypress bevel siding. All interior material the best quality Yellow Pine. Star A Star Cedar shingles. No. 1 glass. Windows glazed "A" quality glass. Excellent grade hardware. Painted two coats best inner liquid paint outside, one coat of enamel, and one coat of varnish for interior. Full description of each article in our Building Material Catalogue.

By allowing a fair price for labor, brick, cement, and plaster, which we do not furnish, this home can be built for about $3,215.00.

FIRST FLOOR

Entrance into living room through vestibule having two inside doors. To right, through single sliding door, is parlor, with bay window in front. Directly beyond living room, through double doors, is the dining room, with another bay on side. It is a corner window, a large combination window and a side door. To the rear is a door in which are located the pantry and beyond is the kitchen. Pantry has abundance of bins and shelves, and two bottom cupboards, and is located so that the household one not have to pass through the pantry before any duty. To rear is stair with door to basement. To the right of living room is a bedroom. Yellow Pine throughout. Ceilings 9 feet 6 inches high.

SECOND FLOOR

Four large light bedrooms and bath on this floor, all opening from hall. Each room has closet. There is also a linen closet in hall and another one in bathroom. Yellow Pine trim throughout. Ceilings 8 feet 6 inches high.

BASEMENT

Excavated under entire house. Cement floor. Heater and storage, lighted by cellar sash. 8 one foot 6 inches.

Heating, Plumbing and Lighting
WRITE FOR DETAILED ESTIMATES

Warm Air Heating Plant, complete....................................
Steam Heating Plant, complete.......................................
Hot Water Heating Plant, complete...................................
Plumbing System, complete...
Acetylene Lighting System...

MONTGOMERY WARD & CO.

Size, exclusive of porches:
Width: 28 feet. Length, 35 feet.

Late Victorian

#109 - Renamed Farmland in 1917 (1909-1921 Not Ready-Cut)

Radford Design

1909 ($1225), 1910 ($1225 NRC), 1911 ($1112 NRC), 1912 ($1261 NRC), 1913 (NRC), 1914 ($1249 NRC), 1915 ($1463 NRC), 1916 ($1394 NRC), 1917 ($1725 NRC), 1918 ($2261 NRC), 1919 ($2709 NRC), 1920 ($2631 NRC), 1921 ($2631 NRC)

"For $1463.00 we will furnish the material to build this nine-room home, consisting of all lumber, lath, shingles, finishing lumber, flooring, doors, windows, frames, trim, hardware, sash weights, pipe and gutter, and painting materials. We absolutely guarantee the materials we furnish to be sufficient to build this house according to our plans and specifications. An imposing, nine-room home, with bath, plenty of closet room, front and back stairs, and two porches extending across the front and along practically one whole side. An especially pleasing design for a corner lot in town and equally desirable for a farm residence, because of the number of bedrooms, and the back stairs which eliminates the necessity of tracking through the front part of the house."

-1916 Book of Homes

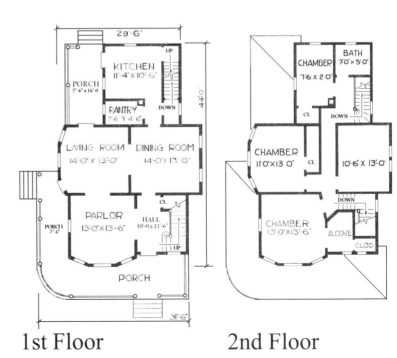

1st Floor   2nd Floor

#109/Farmland in Hardinsburg, Kentucky (photograph by Dale Wolicki).

A Henderson, Kentucky *#109/Farmland* (photograph by Dale Wolicki and Rebecca Hunter).

The Wallen-Cooper Residence
Ewen, Michigan

Although rough construction lumber was readily available in timber regions such as the Midwest and Northwest, millwork and architects were not, thus many remote northern towns have kit-homes. In 1889 August Wallen, a 23 year old Swiss immigrant, moved to Ewen, a small lumber town in the Upper Peninsula of Michigan. Working in the lumber mills he acquired extensive lands and interests in the area. Purchasing 70 acres on the western edge of Ewen he elected to build Montgomery Ward's *Farmland* in 1912.

The ornamental newel posts of the reception hall staircase (photograph by Ken Wheeler)

Grease pencil order number on the back of a piece of trim (photograph by Ken Wheeler)

The five panel double sliding doors between the living room and dining room are veneered with oak on one side and birch on the other (photograph by Dale Wolicki).

Always among the most prominent of local residences, the house was in need of renovations when Cindy and Roy Cooper purchased it in the summer of 2009. Having renovated their previous home, the Coopers were not discouraged by the outdated wiring and heating system, the missing porch spindles, the outdated kitchen or the clumsy garage addition. Instead they saw that the exterior of the house remained almost unaltered, its clapboards still straight and tight after ninety years of Michigan winters. A few window sashes had been replaced but not so as to distract from the historic character of the house. Inside, the main rooms remained unaltered with twelve foot ceiling original light fixtures and beautiful oak floors. The dining room and kitchen were finished in birch, while the upstairs bedrooms were finished in clear pine. The most striking feature was the golden oak millwork used generously for the main floor. Tall baseboards, corner guards, paneled doors, picture and plate rails, colonnade, door and window trim, and a magnificent reception hall staircase with artistic newel posts, handrail and spindles, all of golden oak that had never been painted or polyurethaned.

The Wallen residence was a Plan Book house, built from blueprints and materials supplied by Montgomery Ward. During the renovation the Coopers found the back of many trim boards had grease pencil writing identifying the length of the piece, a location reference, and the order number. As there was a sawmill only blocks away when the house was built, they suspect only the finished materials (millwork, flooring, light fixtures, windows and doors, hardware, and roofing) were ordered from Montgomery Ward.

#119 (1909-1916 Not Ready-Cut)

Radford Design

1909 ($1193 NRC), 1910 ($1193 NRC), 1911 (NRC), 1912 ($1189 NRC), 1913 (NRC), 1914 ($1166 NRC), 1915 ($1218 NRC), 1916 ($1329 NRC)

"This is without doubt one of our very neatest, prettiest and most attractive houses. It is true that this house, after all, is only a square house, which, as you know, gives the most room for a given amount of material; but the cottage roof, with four gables and one dormer, relieves it of the dry goods box appearance, so common with square houses."

- 1912 Building Plans of Modern Homes

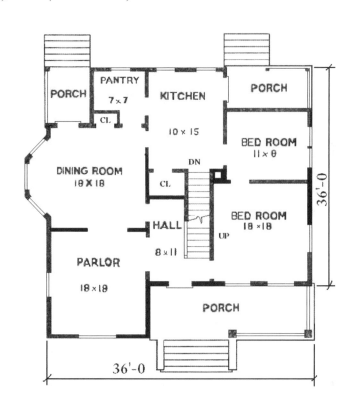

A *Model #119* in Coldwater, Ohio (photograph by Dale Wolicki).

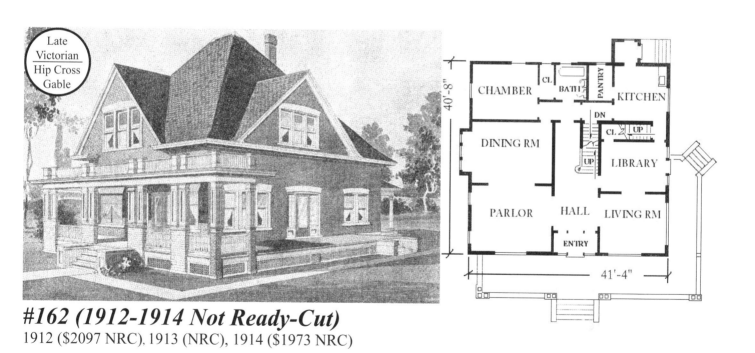

#162 (1912-1914 Not Ready-Cut)
1912 ($2097 NRC), 1913 (NRC), 1914 ($1973 NRC)

"Here we offer you a most attractive, well proportioned brick veneer home. The studs are 2x4's with 7/8 sheathing and then a brick veneer. The architecture is extremely fine. Note the very large veranda across the front, and the terrace leading half way down the right side. There are also 11 paneled square columns. Above the porch is a very nice balcony. From the porch leading into the vestibule is an extremely artistic door front, with art glass side lights; also, leading from the terrace into the library is another very attractive, artistic door."

- *1914 Building Plans of Modern Homes*

Late Victorian Hip Cross Gable

#174 (1914-1916 Not Ready-Cut)
1914 ($1289 NRC), 1915 ($1471 NRC), 1916 ($1437 NRC)

"The above design presents a very neat exterior. It is built entirely of frame, with shingle roof. The porch extends partly across the front and side, and is a very suitable design for a corner lot. The building on the ground floor is 26 x 39, and contains 9 rooms and bath."

- 1915 Book of Homes

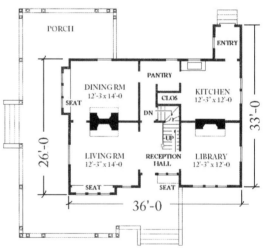

Late Victorian Hip Cross Gable

#165 (1912-1915 Not Ready-Cut)
1912 ($1759 NRC), 1913 (NRC), 1914 ($1643 NRC), 1915 ($1827 NRC)

"The first story is shingled and the second is stucco, with timber panel effect. Notice the large veranda on three sides of the house; look at the roof sloping four ways with the dormers to relieve the monotony of the long slopes. The windows are Queen Anne style. Just look at the first floor plan and you will see a recption hall, living room, library, dining room, butler's pantry, kitchen and closet. A fireplace is a feature of the dining room, living room and library."

- 1914 Building Plans of Modern Homes

#103 (1909-1916 Not Ready-Cut)
Radford Design

1909 ($730 NRC), 1910 ($730 NRC), 1911 ($666 NRC), 1912 ($719 NRC), 1913 (NRC), 1914 ($764 NRC), 1915 ($840 NRC), 1916 ($814 NRC)

"This house has five rooms, hall, bath, and two large alcoves, which are large enough for the bed, so that in reality, instead of two bedrooms, there are actually two suites, consisting of bed chamber, dressing room and clothes closet. Note the open stairway, with closet underneath, making it unnecessary to have a clothes rack in the hall. The alcove in the front has a pair of French Sash, glazed with leaded crystal glass, while the parlor has a leaded cottage window of our Argyle pattern. This house has a much larger and better appearance than you would think possible, considering the low price. This is brought about by the architecture of the roof, and the large porch with Colonial columns which always give a home a modern and substanual appearance. Hardwood floors first story. The flooring on the second floor and interior finish is of yellow pine, the doors being of Western Pine."

- 1914 Building Plans of Modern Homes

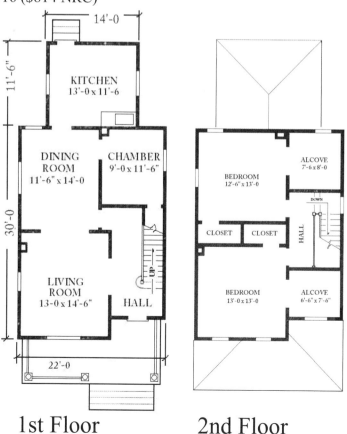

1st Floor   2nd Floor

Model #124 - Renamed Countryside in 1917 (1909-1921 Not Ready-Cut)

Radford Design

1909 ($1547 NRC), 1910 ($1547 NRC), 1911 ($1441 NRC), 1912 ($1520 NRC), 1913 (NRC), 1914 ($1477 NRC), 1915 ($1753 NRC), 1916 ($1685 NRC), 1917 ($1891 NRC), 1918 (Not Offered), 1919 ($1496 NRC), 1920 ($3298 NRC), 1921 ($3298 NRC)

"Exceedly attractive and at the same time one of the largest frame houses which we show. This is largely due to its roomy veranda, to the roof and to the bay window. As you enter the reception hall, to the right is the parlor, back of which is the living room, seperated from the parlor by a pair of sliding doors; in one corner of the room is a fireplace, set diagonially. To the left of this room, and directly back of the reception hall, is the dining room, back of which is the kitchen, pantry and cellar stairway. This house has also had a grade door, from which either kitchen or cellar is reached. We also call attention to the bay in both parlor and dining room, which is so arranged that a window seat could be placed in either."

- 1914 Building Plans of Modern Homes

1st Floor   2nd Floor

#108 (1909-1916 Not Ready-Cut)

Radford Design

1909 ($1473 NRC), 1910 ($1473 NRC), 1911 ($1406 NRC),
1912 ($1437 NRC), 1913 (NRC), 1914 ($1375 NRC),
1915 ($1638 NRC), 1916 ($1647 NRC)

*"Not a new style of house, but one that has
meet with the approval of a large percentage
of our customers. It is full two stories, with
attic above, and has a large porch across the
front and down one side. The kitchen is but
one story, with attic above. On the first floor
is the reception hall and parlor; to the right,
back of hall and parlor, you enter the living
room, leading from the right of which is a bedroom, with bathroom connected. Back of the
living room is the dining room, and to the right
is the kitchen. In one corner of the living room
is a mantel, and opening off the dining room is
a small closet"*

- 1914 Building Plans of Modern Homes

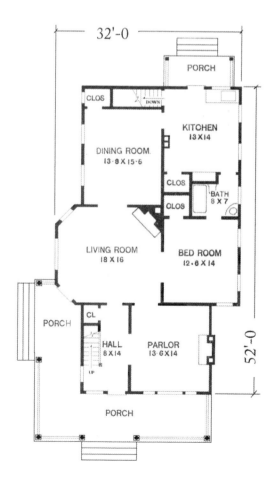

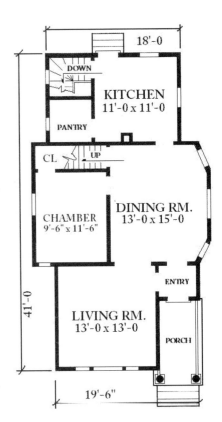

Late
Victorian
Cross
Gable

#102 (1909-1916 Not Ready-Cut)

Radford Design

1909 ($699 NRC), 1910 ($699 NRC), 1911 ($729 NRC), 1912 ($809 NRC), 1913 (NRC), 1914 ($815 (NRC), 1915 ($937 NRC), 1916 ($913 NRC)

"For $937.00 we will furnish the material to build this home, conisting of all lumber, lath, shingles, finishing lumber, flooring, doors, windoiws, frames, trim, hardware, sash weights, pipe and gutter, and painting materials."
           - 1915 Book of Homes

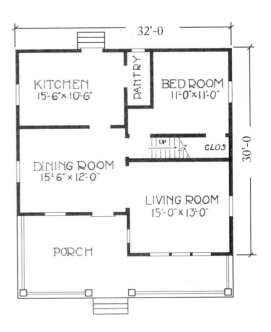

Late
Victorian
Cross
Gable

Wisconsin (1917 Not Ready-Cut)

1917 ($1091)

"A home of this type would be entirely out of keeping with any attempt at fancy decorations either in window, cornice or roof arrangement. These homes are substantial and typical of the style they represent. In interior arrangement, careful consideration has been given to light, convenience and size of rooms."
           - 1917 Book of Homes

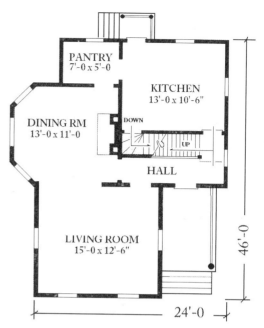

Late
Victorian
Cross
Gable

PANTRY
7'-0 x 5'-0

KITCHEN
13'-0 x 10'-6"

DINING RM
13'-0 x 11'-0

DOWN

UP

HALL

LIVING ROOM
15'-0 x 12'-6"

46'-0

24'-0

#142 (1911-1915 Not Ready-Cut)
1911 ($716 NRC), 1912 ($753 NRC), 1913 (NRC), 1914 ($756 NRC), 1915 ($851 NRC)

"Three rooms on the first floor and three chambers and bath on the second floor. Note the large closets connected with each bedroom, which always delight the housewife, being so necessary and convenient. The building is sided with bevel lapsiding two-thirds the way up, and the balance is shingled. A very desirable home for those who wish this style of architecture. "

- 1912 Book of Modern Homes

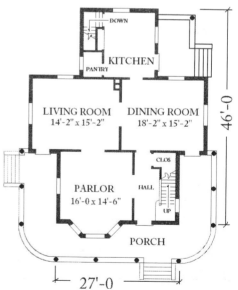

Late
Victorian
Cross
Gable

DOWN

KITCHEN

PANTRY

LIVING ROOM
14'-2" x 15'-2"

DINING ROOM
18'-2" x 15'-2"

CLOS

PARLOR
16'-0 x 14'-6"

HALL

UP

PORCH

46'-0

27'-0

#151 (1911-1914 Not Ready-Cut)
1911 ($1021 NRC), 1912 ($1075 NRC), 1913 (NRC), 1914 ($1069 NRC)

"Design 151 is another well arranged concrete block house. There are five rooms on the first floor, five rooms, bath and four closets on the second floor. This house has a very large porch extending across the entire front and half way down each side; also a back porch. Note the front porch has steps in both front and one side, making this a good house for a corner lot, giving a front and side entrance."

- 1914 Building Plans of Modern Home

#140 - Renamed #181 in 1915 (1911-1916 Not Ready-Cut)
1911 ($690 NRC), 1912 ($725 NRC), 1913 (NRC), 1914 ($801 NRC), 1915 ($956 NRC), 1916 ($886 NRC)

Montgomery Ward's *#140* was their version of Sears popular *Maytown*, and the two are commonly confused. While the Maytown measures 25' wide and features a simple roof above its turret, the *#140* measures 22' wide. In 1915 Montgomery Ward renamed the house the *#181*, widing it to 26', moving the bay window and extending the turret up and adding a witch's cap roof (below).

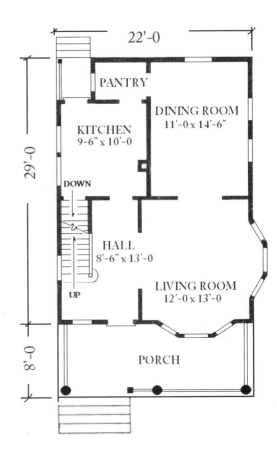

"The Aurora"—Material Supplied Either Ready-Cut or Not Ready-Cut

Everyone Admires This Splendid Bungalow

WHEREVER it is built, our "Aurora" home gains a host of admirers. The simplicity and dignity of the lines, combined with the air of hospitality given by the broad eaves and the recessed porch, make it a universal favorite.

The exterior is sided with clear cypress siding up to the belt course. From here to the wide, enclosed cornice, clear red cedar shingles are used. The heavy square columns and high piers give a solid, substantial effect which sets off the beauty of the whole house.

The floor plan must be considered carefully if none of its excellencies are to be missed. The front door opens directly into the living room, saving the space that usually goes into an entrance hall. The dining room is connected with this room by a wide cased opening. Notice how the dining room is made large and light by the square bay window. A coat closet opens from the dining room, as does the hall which leads to the bathroom and both bedrooms. The linen closet also opens off the hall. This hall arrangement gives perfect privacy to the sleeping quarters of the home and eliminates the objections so many have to the usual cramped bungalow plans with one bedroom leading from another.

Pay particular attention to the illustration of the linen closet on page 12. Here is a splendid feature and means much to the housewife. Note that each bedroom has its own ample closet. The kitchen is small enough to be extremely convenient and large enough to serve all practical needs. Space is provided for the big modern and washable near the window. This splendid pantry can be furnished with the house at an extra charge and is built into the wall. It is type No. 550, shown on Page 46. The cellar steps lead down from the kitchen, the door being near the rear entrance, at the most convenient place. There is room for the ice box in the rear porch where it is always cool, and where the ice man does not have to make a long trip to reach it. There is an abundance of windows in the kitchen.

As you will see by the specifications, this home is furnished and our customers may have.

Size of Home, 26 feet wide by 28 feet deep

See Prices on Pages 1 to 4
Specifications on Pages 10 and 11

Unless you request us to do otherwise, we ship paint for sidewalls, trim and White for trim.

See Page 4 for cost of home. For description of Rado Ashford and cost to you in water tight.

One Story Hip Roof

Detroit (1918-1929 Ready-Cut)

Similar to Gordon-VanTine #500

1918 ($886), 1919 ($951), 1920 ($951), 1921 ($971), 1922 ($971), 1923 ($1138), 1923 ($1218), 1924 ($1110), 1925 ($1110), 1926 ($1110), 1927 ($1150), 1928 ($1186), 1929 ($1218)

"The Detroit represents a style of architecture and arrangement of interior that is universally popular. Convenience of arrangment, abundance of light and low erection and upkeep cost are its distinguishing characteristics. It looks equally as well whether erected in the country or in the city, as it is a favorable with both our city and farm customers. The low, broad and comfortable lines of the bungalow give to this conveniently compact little home a most attractive appearance. The simple hip roof protects the front porch, while the dormer with shingled walls breaks the severe roofline and adds much to the attractiveness of the exterior"

- 1923 Wardway Homes

A near perfect *Detroit* In Perrysburg, Ohio (photograph by Dale Wolicki).

A Lancaster, Kentucky *Detroit* with taller roofline to provide an attic bedroom (photograph by Dale Wolicki).

Aurora-2nd - Renamed Tacoma 1928 (1922-1931 Ready-Cut)
Gordon-VanTine Design
1922 ($1782), 1923 ($1755), 1924 ($1625), 1925 ($1612), 1926 ($1612),
1927 ($1689), 1928 ($1778), 1929 ($1756), 1930 ($1779), 1931 ($1666)

"Wherever it is built, our Aurora home gains a host of admirers. The simplicity and dignity of the lines, combined with the air of hospitality given by the broad eaves and recessed porch, make it a universal favorite. The exterior is sided with cypress siding up to the belt course. From here to the wide, enclosed cornice, clear red cedar shingles are used. The heavy square columns and high piers give a solid, substantial effect which sets off the beauty of the whole house. The floor plan must be considered carefully if none of its excellencies are to be missed. The front door opens directly into the living room, saving the space that usually goes into an entrance hall. The dining room is connected with this room by a wide cased opening. Notice how the dining room is made large and light by the square bay window. A coat closet opens from the dining room, as does the hall which leads to the bathroom and both bedrooms."

- 1924 Wardway Homes

An updated Wardway *Aurora* in Wilmore, Kentucky (photograph by Dale Wolicki).

An *Aurora* in Kankakee, Illinois (photograph by Rebecca Hunter and Dale Wolicki).

Ardmore - Renamed Elsmore in 1928 (1925-1931 Ready-Cut)

Gordon-VanTine Design

1925 (A. $1175), 1926 (A. $1175), 1927 (A. $1242. B. $1394), 1928 (A. $1339, B. $1499),
1929 (A. $1411, B. $1618), 1930 (A. $1411, B. $1618), 1931 (A. $1411, B. $1566)

"The design of the Elsmore pleases the most critical. It is a very attractive in appearance. You have a choice of two floor plans, one 22 feet wide, the other 24 feet wide. Among the modern features included are telephone cabinet built into the wall and fine oak floors in living and dining room. A basement is specified under the entire house. All cellar windows and rear stairs are included. You can readily build this bungalow yourself. Very little skilled labor is required. In that way you will have a lovely home of your own, modern, handsome and comfortable at remarkably small cost. Or if you employ a carpenter to erect your Elsmore, our plan will save many hours of time."

- 1929 Wardway Homes

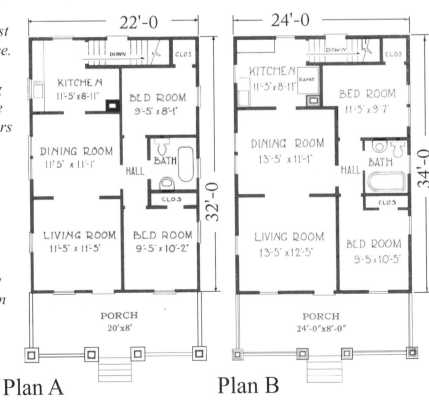

Plan A   Plan B

Clarendon - Renamed Broadview in 1928 (1922-1930 Ready-Cut)

Gordon-VanTine Design

1922 ($1742), 1923 ($1696), 1924 ($1566), 1925 ($1566), 1926 ($1566),
1927 ($1599), 1928 ($1683), 1929 ($1709), 1930 ($1709)

"Nowadays, when the bungalow is made an excuse for so many extreme and ofttimes outlandish effects, it is a relief to see a home of this type - simple and straightforward in design - owing its good looks to its lines and proportions rather than to freakish trimmings. The broad, low roof extending out over the porch with its open cornice, is a particularly effective feature, relieved as it is by the front dormer. The bay window extending from the dining room not only increases the size of the room, but by breaking up the line of the sidewall enhances the appearance of the home. The porch rail is sided clear to the ground.

The plan is a model of convenience and comfort. The front door opens directly into the fine general living room, which is in turn connected with the dining room by a cased opening. From the dining room a door opens into the little central hall which connects both bedrooms and bathroom. By this arrangement the bedrooms are each kept off from the rest of the house yet accessible. It is unnecessary to go through either to reach the bathroom. Each bedroom has two windows and its own closet."

- 1923 Wardway Homes

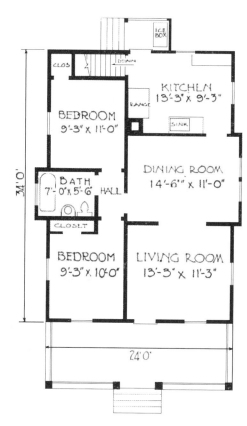

#156 - Renamed Edison in 1917
(1911-1916 Not Ready-Cut; 1917-1921 Ready-Cut)

1911 ($630 NRC), 1912 ($662 NRC), 1913 (NRC), 1914 ($806 NRC),
1915 ($998 NRC), 1916 ($894 NRC), 1917 ($1127), 1918 ($1421),
1919 ($1616), 1920 ($1598), 1921 ($1598)

*"Home Number 156 is probably the most popular type of home that
is being built today, for the reason that it combines to such good
advantage the elements of low cost in construction, utility in layout,
and attractiveness of appearance. In other words, it gives the most
value for the money expended. The exterior has that clean-cut appearance which is so much desired, while every foot of floor space
has been utilized in an unusually good arrangement, with three
bedrooms.*

*For $998.00 we will furnish the materials to build this home, con-
sisting of all lumber, lath, shingles, finishing lumber, flooring, doors,
windows, frames, trim, pantry case, sash weights, building paper,
hardware, pipe and gutter, and paint and varnish. We absolutely
guarantee the material we furnish to be sufficient to build the home
according to our plans and specifications."*

-1915 Books of Homes

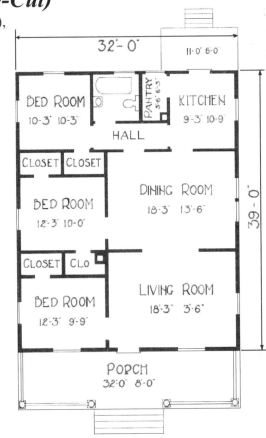

Roanoke - Renamed Wellington in 1929 (1922-1931 Ready-Cut)

Gordon-VanTine Design

1922 ($2045), 1923 ($1973), 1924 ($1879), 1925 ($1815), 1926 ($1815),
1927 ($1878), 1928 ($1936), 1929 ($2043), 1930 ($2089), 1931 ($1998)

"The charming Roanoke is always a popular bungalow among home lovers. Note how the main roof has been continued out over the porch. The shingled dormer with its replica of the hip-roof of the house breaks up the roof lines in a most attractive manner and adds to the broad, low appearance of the home. The unique handling of the outside walls indicates the extreme care given the designing of this home. They are sided up to the belt course, which incidentally takes the place of the top casing of the windows. Then to the open cornice, clear red cedar shingles are used. This gives a variety of effect particularly pleasing on a rather simple exterior.

You'll like the large living room with its two windows and wide cased opening leading into the dining room. The wall space is so well planned that you will be able to get almost any desired arrangement of furniture. It's one of those unusual rooms that will look well and be cheery and comfortable no matter how arranged. Directly back of the living room, through wide cased opening is the dining room, which has two windows and a door leading into both the kitchen and central hall - a most convenient and accessible layout."

-1927 Wardway Homes

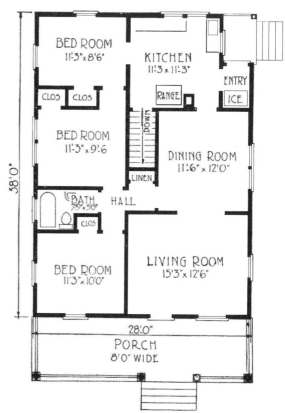

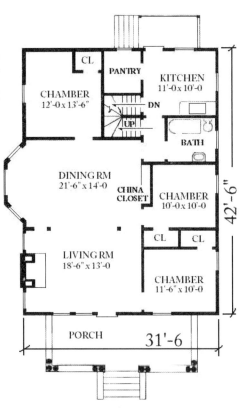

Floor plan labels:
CL — PANTRY — KITCHEN 11'-0 x 10'-0
CHAMBER 12'-0 x 13'-6" — DN — UP
BATH
DINING RM 21'-6" x 14'-0 — CHINA CLOSET — CHAMBER 10'-0 x 10'-0
CL — CL
LIVING RM 18'-6" x 13'-0 — CHAMBER 11'-6" x 10'-0
PORCH — 31'-6
42'-6"

1 Story Hip Roof Porch Under Roof

#144 (1911-1914 Not Ready-Cut)

1911 ($950 NRC), 1912 ($997 NRC), 1913 (NRC), 1914 ($1033 NRC)

"We offer what we believe to be one of the most attractive and convenient of Bungalows. Note the large veranda, with overhanging roof; the ten Colonial columns; the large living and dining room, seperated by two large oak columns, both rooms have beamed oak ceilings; a large open fireplace, with oak seat on each side, in the living room. Some of our customers wish these two rooms separated, which can be easily done at a very small extra expense, by leaving out the columns and putting in a partition between the two rooms."

- 1914 Building Plans of Modern Homes

Floor plan labels:
24'-0"
BED ROOM 8'-0" x 11'-3" — BATH 5'-0" x 7'-9 — KITCHEN 9'-0 x 11'-3
CLO — HALL
BED ROOM 8'-0" x 9'-3" — LIVING ROOM 14'-6" x 9'-3"
PORCH 24'-0" x 6'-0"
22'-0"

1 Story Hip Roof Porch Under Roof

Devon (1918-1921 Not Ready-Cut)

1918 ($792 NRC), 1919 ($934 NRC), 1920 ($924 NRC), 1921 ($924 NRC)

"If you are fond of bungalows with low sloping roofs and large airy porches you are sure to be pleased with the Devon. The interior has four good sized rooms and bath all well lighted with large wide windows. So many of the bungalows are built without basements that we have not shown any way of getting to the basement on the floor plan. Should basement be desired though it can be very easily effected by placing our addition Number 1 at the rear of the house."

- 1919 Wardway Homes

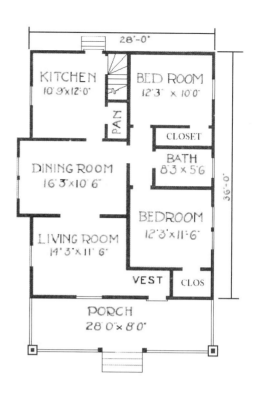

Whiting (1917-1921 Not Ready-Cut)
1917 ($989 NRC), 1918 ($1346 NRC), 1919 ($1543 NRC),
1920 ($1523 NRC), 1921 ($1523 NRC)

"The simple lines and fine proportion of this little home are among its chief attractions. The treatment of the dormer, narrow siding and heavy sided porch columns, all present a pleasing variation. The wide front porch, under the main roof, when screened in is practically an extra room."

- 1917 Wardway Homes

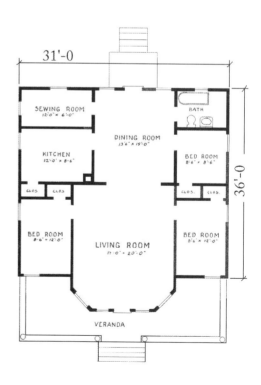

#167 (1912-1916 Not Ready-Cut)
1912 ($735 NRC), 1913 (NRC), 1914 ($745 NRC),
1915 ($788 (NRC), 1916 ($788 NRC)

"An unusual design that is worthy of careful study. The broad, simple lines of the exterior make a direct appeal, but the striking feature is the arrangement of the interior, in which the living room and dining room have been given the greatest space and prominence as the real center of the home. There is much to be said in favor of this idea, which is well worked out in Home Number 169."

- 1915 Wardway Homes

Fordyce (1922-1924 Ready-Cut)
Gordon-VanTine Design
1922 ($1412), 1923 ($1409), 1924 ($1348)

"The Fordyce is a practical, attractive little home with four rooms and a bath, at a very moderate price. It is the style of home which appeals to many prospective home buyers. Nor has appearance been sacrificed in the slightest degree. The simple hip roof, the wide closed cornice and the broad frieze which circles the home just below it, all combine to give one of the most favorable impressions."

-1924 Wardway Homes

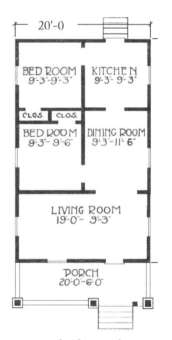

Ridgeway (1917 Ready-Cut)
1917 ($638)

"A cozy, convenient attractive home. That exactly describes the Ridgeway. It is as good a home for its size as money can buy and can all be built for from $950 to $1,100. For the man of moderate means who is located in such localities as to make a bathroom impractical, the Ridgeway offers exceptional value at the low price quoted. The large living room extending the full width of the house connected with the dining room by the wide open archway, the two bedrooms with closets off each, together with the porch of most attractive design, all features which are generally found in houses of a much higher price."

- 1917 Wardway Homes

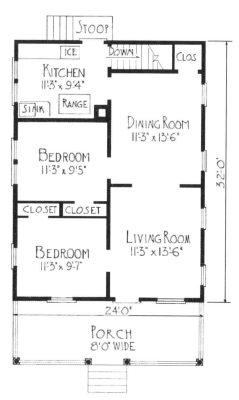

Elmwood (1922-1928 Ready-Cut)
Gordon-VanTine Design
1922 ($1425), 1923 ($1433), 1924 ($1318), 1925 ($1298),
1926 ($1298), 1927 ($1363), 1928 ($1405)

"The simplicity of this bungalow home is its chief charm. The low roof broken by the dormer, extends out over the porch, making it really a part of the home, and not just an afterthought tacked on, as are so many porches. The cornice is open, leaving the rafter ends exposed - a pleasing craftsman note." - 1923 Wardway Homes

Merrill (1931 Ready-Cut)
1931 ($1470)

"The Merrill room arrangement is our modernized plan for one of the most popular small family home we ever offered. Particularly noteworth is the arrangement of the bedrooms with connecting hall and bathroom opening from it. Such convenience is particularly desirable in the small home. Convenient plan, abundant light, low building and upkeep costs are distinguishinh characteristics of the Merrill. It is equally attractive for suburb or city. The simple hip roof has a dormer with siding walls to break up the roof line, adding attractiveness to the exterior."
　　　　　　　　　　　　　　　　　　　　　　　　　　- 1931 Wardway Homes

Euclid (1929-1931 Ready-Cut)
1929 ($1798), 1930 ($1973), 1931 ($1943)

"A picturesque bungalow - delightfully snug and cosy - yet so spacous for comfortable living. The reality of the dream house you have so often built! A real home - charming, delightful - where children get the most out of every moment in their precious childhood. A home every member of the family will enjoy and in which all will take sincere pride. Ideally contrived to combine genuine architectural beauty with practical conveniences. Everything is just where you would want it to be! In fact there are few homes that offer to such a high degree, the features of the Euclid. Its every detail proves it was specially designed for those who demand, besides livability - atmosphere - and true distinction in their surroundings."

- 1931 Wardway Homes

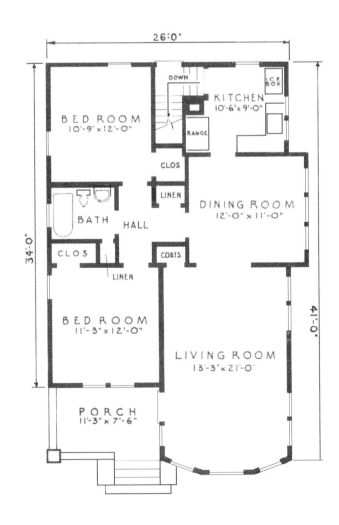

A perfect Wardway *Euclid* in Traverse City, Michigan (photograph by Dale Wolicki).

A Wardway *Euclid* in Woodstock, Illinois (photograph by Rebecca Hunter).

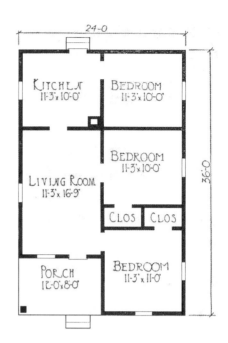

Akron Cottage (1922-1927 Ready-Cut)

Gordon-VanTine Design

1922 ($840), 1923 ($861), 1924 ($798),
1925 ($765), 1926 ($765), 1927 ($746)

"Note specifications for this home and the unusually low price quoted above. The timber and dimension lumber is Number 1 Yellow Pine, all timbers being of the most substanial to give solid construction. The roof boards are laid tight and the cornice and porch roofs are covered with Number 1 Yellow Pine ceiling. Realize too, that the construction cost of this house is very low on account of the amount of work done at the mills. An average workman, even though not skilled in carpentry can construct one of these houses, for practically all the difficult work is done at the mills, and the plans are very complete and easy to follow."

- 1927 Wardway Homes

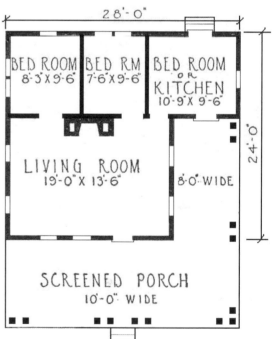

Linger Longer Cottage (1925 Ready-Cut)

Gordon-VanTine Design

1925 ($715)

"An ideal Summer Home. Just the spot at which you will want to linger longer. The spacous screened porch is very inviting and extends the entire width and part of the depth of the home. A living room with a fireplace, two bedrooms and a kitchen complete the arrangement of the Linger Longer."

- 1925 Wardway Homes

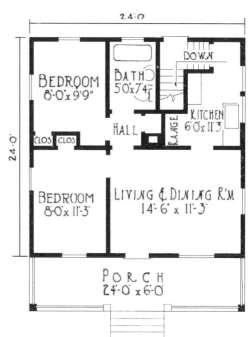

Vandalia (1922-1924 Ready-Cut)
Gordon-VanTine Design
1922 ($995), 1923 ($1282), 1924 ($1197)

"The dignified and attractive exterior of this little home with its four rooms and bath is sure to appeal to you. The dormer in the roof adds much to its appearance without greatly increasing the cost. The large front porch with steps planned to be of concrete, gives the impression of substanual worth often lacking in even more expensive homes."

- 1923 Wardway Homes

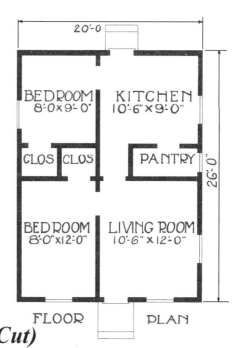

#189 - Renamed Eden in 1917
(1915-1916 Not Ready-Cut; 1917-1921 Ready Cut)
1915 ($294 NRC), 1916 ($325 NRC), 1917 ($358), 1918 ($565), 1919 ($684), 1920 ($646), 1920 ($646)

"A four-room home, designed with a view to giving room enough for the average size family, at the lowest cost possible. The same high grade of materials has been specified, the same high standards of construction adhered to, as in our higher priced homes"

- 1915 Book of Homes

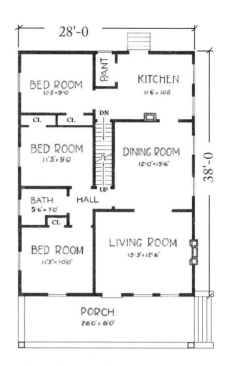

#193 - Renamed Yale in 1917
(1916-1917 Not Ready-Cut)
1916($946 NRC), 1917 ($1091 NRC)

"Many prefer the wide porch effect secured by front steps entering at the side. Where width of lot permits, this gives a very pleasing variation from the ordinary center front step entrance, and at the same time renders the porch more enclosed. It also enables a different style of lawn decorations. Our designers in planning the Yale feel certain there are many home builders that will be pleased not only with the side entrance, but also with the straight line architectural effects secured by cornice, hip roof, dormer and main roof."

- 1917 Wardway Homes

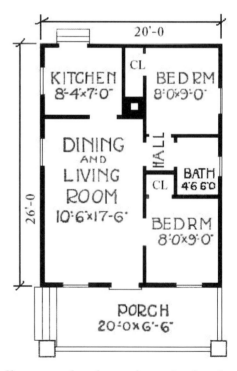

Florida (1917 Not Ready-Cut)
1917 ($653 NRC)

"Isn't this home a little gem and all for less than $700, too? Most excellent taste has been shown in the planning and arrangement of this cozy design. The front porch is somewhat out of the ordinary, the entrance being at the side, the high front rail thus gives a privacy to this part of the house. This plan allows the walk to be at the side of the lot and leaves the lawn complete for decorations. Four rooms and a bath compose the interior, the living and dining room being arranged in one long room."

- 1917 Wardway Homes

1 Story Hip Roof
Attached Porch Centered

Pullman A (1917-1921 Ready-Cut)
Pullman B - Renamed Rosedale in 1927 (1922-1931 Ready-Cut)

1917 (A. $435), 1918 (A. $594), 1919 (A. $706), 1920 (A. $686), 1921 (A. $686), 1922 (B. $820), 1923 (B. $877), 1920 (B. $686), 1924 (B. $812), 1925 (B. $812), 1926 (B. $812), 1927 (B. $838), 1928 (B.$864), 1929 (B. $998), 1930 (B. $998), 1931 (B. $998)

"If you are interested in a cozy home, with or without bath, at a small cost but representing big value, the Rosedale should make a very strong appeal to you. While not large in size, it is as attractive as many larger homes which cost considerably more. The ordinary objection of plain and unattractive appearance which is usually made against the small house does not apply to the Rosedale. It would be quite expensive to build a home of this character under ordinary conditions, but the cost of Wardway architectural service is distributed among so many homes it adds practically nothing to the cost of each."

- 1927 Wardway Homes

Plan A

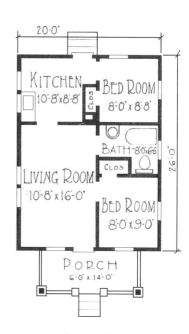

Plan B

#128 - Renamed Lincoln in 1917 (1909-1921 Not Ready-Cut)
Plan A offered 1917-1921
Plan B offered 1909-1921

1909 (B.$451), 1910 (B. $451 NRC), 1911 (B. $403 NRC), 1912 (B. $425 NRC), 1913 (NRC),
1914 (B. $448 NRC), 1915 (B. $461 NRC), 1916 (B. $403 NRC), 1917 (A. $528 NRC, B. $513 NRC),
1918 (A. $716 NRC, B. $702 NRC), 1919 (A. $822 NRC, B. $807 NRC),
1920 (A. $798 NRC, B. $784 NRC), 1921 (A. $798 NRC, B. $784 NRC)

"A square one-story house, with typical cottage roof sloping on four sides from a point in the center. This being simply a square cottage, nothing special can be said as to its architecture; but we wish to point out that there are four good sized rooms besides closet, bath and pantry; also two porches. There is a chimney in the center of the building, thereby enabling you to heat the house with stoves by the use of one chimney. The interior trim is of yellow pine, with western pine doors, all strictly Number 1 materials. If you wish any change that does not make it necessary to re-draw plans, we will make it free of charge, if you purchase the materials from us."

- 1914 Building Plans of Modern Homes

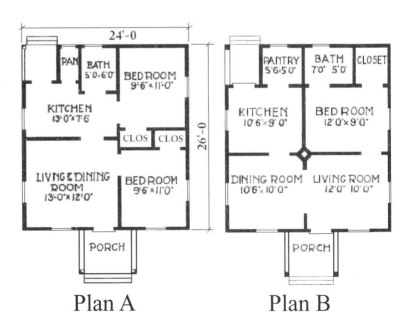

Plan A   Plan B

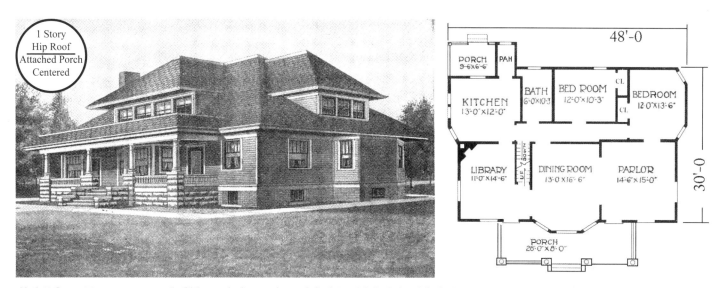

#159 - Renamed Sheridan in 1917 (1911-1921 Not Ready-Cut)

1911 ($1108 NRC), 1912 ($1165 NRC), 1913 (NRC), 1914 ($1138 NRC), 1915 ($1368 NRC), 1916 ($1379 NRC), 1917 ($1491 NRC), 1918 ($2134 NRC), 1919 ($2320 NRC), 1920 ($2253 NRC), 1921 ($2253 NRC)

"When you have determined to build a home, there are several big problems which confront you. To help you meet and overcome these difficulties is the aim and purpose of this book. We specify the cost of material needed to build and furnish building plans, which are simple and concise, and can be easily understood by anyone. The prices we quote are absolutely the lowest that you can secure anywhere for the same quality of material as we specify. House Number 159 is an attractive type of dwelling. It is a story-and-a-half house, with six rooms on the first floor and three on the upper, one of which is an unfinished room, that can be used as a storeroom or fitted up as nursery or sewing room."

- 1914 Building Plans of Modern Homes

A *Sheridan* in Monee, Illinois (photograph by Rebeeca Hunter and Dale Wolicki).

1 Story
Hip Roof
Attached Porch
Centered

PORCH

PANTRY

KITCHEN
10 X 18

BATH

29'-6"

BED ROOM
11X16

LIVING ROOM
18X16

DINING ROOM
11X16

37'-6"

#127 (1909-1914 Not Ready-Cut)

1909 ($545), 1910 ($545 NRC), 1911 ($474 NRC),
1912 ($521 NRC), 1913 (NRC), 1914 ($579 NRC)

"This cottage was designed for a small family, either in a village or on the farm. Many persons of small families will appreciate a home that does not cost much. The young farmer usually needs most of his resources to develop land and build farm buildings. The great advantage of this design is that while a small house, it still presents a very broad appearance from the front. When one becomes more prosperous or needs more room, all that is necessary is to raise the roof a few feet on the main building. This gives you a home of seven rooms at a cost of a few hundred dollars, which will have the appearance of having cost several thousand dollars."

- 1911 Building Plans of Modern Homes

1 Story
Hip Roof
Attached Porch
Centered

A. 24' / B. 26'

A. 24' / B. 26'

KITCHEN
11'-9"x 11'-3"

BEDROOM
10'-9"x 11'-3"

CL

CL

LIVING ROOM
11'-9"x 11'-3"

BEDROOM
10'-9"x 11'-3"

PORCH

Gary Cottage (1922-1927 Ready-Cut)

Gordon-VanTine Design

1922 (A. $662, B. $722), 1923 (A. $678, B. $740),
1924 (A. $625, B. $680), 1925 (A. $625, B. $680),
1926 (A. $625, B. $680), 1927 (A. $598, B. $640)

"A simple and logically arranged four-room cottage. This is our Gary design, which we can supply in two sizes - A and B - as shown below. This is a thoroughly comfortable, good looking home."

- 1927 Wardway Homes

Hymera (1922-1923 Not Ready-Cut)
Gordon-VanTine Design
1922 ($1475 NRC), 1923 ($1507 NRC)

"The Hymera is a practical, comfortable home at a remarkably low price, considering its six good sized rooms. Its simple straight lines are altogether pleasing and result in low construction cost and a saving in material. Its almost square shape permits the use of every inch of floor space."

- 1923 Wardway Homes

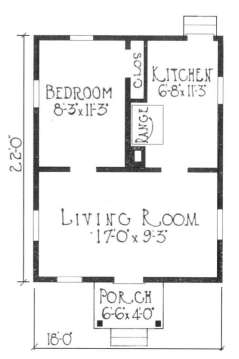

McKeesport Cottage (1922-1926 Ready-Cut)
Gordon-VanTine Design
1922 ($510), 1923($523), 1924 ($463), 1925 ($463), 1926 ($463)

"This snug little cottage provides ample living space, at a minimum cost, for the small family. All fancy details have been omitted in order to bring the cost of adequate shelter down to absolute rock bottom. The construction is so simple and our system of preparing materials ready-cut so complete, that two men can erect this house in astonishingly short space of time, even though they are not carpenters."

- 1924 Wardway Homes

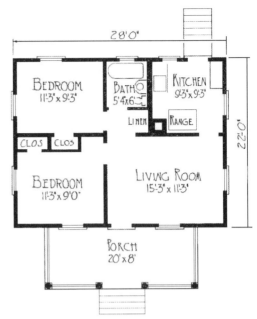

Royston (1922-1924 Ready-Cut)

Gordon-VanTine Design
1922 ($1155), 1923 ($1189), 1924 ($1118)

"The usual unattractive appearance of a low priced home is overcome in our Royton design. Economy without sacrifice of good appearance has been the aim of the architect and you will agree he has succeeeded. This neat little home with its broad porch and hip roof extending out to form the wide eaves, contains an exceptional amount of living space for the money it costs, and is completely equipped with the convenient features of the larger Wardway Homes."
                                                            - 1924 Wardway Homes

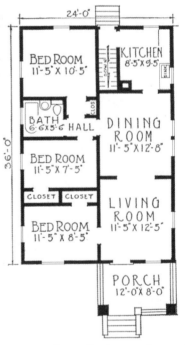

Rosewood (1924-1926 Ready-Cut)

Gordon-VanTine Design
1924 ($1398), 1925 ($1370), 1926 ($1370)

"When we speak of home, we think not of the materials which go into the construction of a house but rather the things which we associate with it and which makes it so dear to us. When you think of the Rosewood, you at once picture a cozy cottage with its vine covered front porch, its wide, pleasing front windows specially designed old fashioned shutters, and its dark stained shingled side walls with pure white trim, which gives it such a clean cut, pleasant appearance. Surely such a design as this is deserving of your most careful consideration"
                                                            - 1924 Wardway Homes

Berwyn - Renamed Garland in 1929 (1922-1931 Ready-Cut)
Gordon-VanTine Design
1922 ($1650), 1923 ($1604), 1924 ($1479), 1925 ($1450), 1926 ($1450),
1927 ($1498), 1928 ($1544), 1929 ($1695), 1930 ($1695), 1931 ($1668)

"A casual study of this cozy home is sure to win your interest. The interior is pleasing, convenient and attractive. There is genuine economy of space and money. The partly inset porch makes what might otherwise be a plain exterior very attractive indeed. The low, overhanging roof gives the much desired bungalow effect and shades the side walls from the hot summer sun.

You enter from the porch into a pleasing reception hall, off of which is a convenient coat closet. A cased opening leads directly into the splendid living room, which extends across the entire front of the house. This room is flooded with outside light from a twin front window and a large side window. There is nicely arranged wall space. There is also a wide cased opening between living room and dining room, which adds greatly to the spaciousness of this home. A swing door in the rear of the dining room leads into the kitchen. Twin windows flood this room with light."

- 1927 Wardway Homes

ICE

DOWN

BEDROOM
9'9" x 9'0"

BATH

RANGE

KITCHEN
8'9" x 8'0"

CLOSET   CL.

HALL

SINK

BEDROOM
12'3" x 11'6"

DINING ROOM
12'3" x 11'6"

36'-0"

CLOS   HALL
COATS 5'3" x 6'6"

LIVING ROOM
16'-6" x 11'-3"

PORCH
12' x 8'

26'-0"

Belmont - Renamed Howard in 1929 (1925-1931 Ready-Cut)

Gordon-VanTine Design

1925 ($995), 1926 ($995), 1927 ($1045), 1928 ($1077),
1929 ($1104), 1930 ($1104), 1931 ($1130)

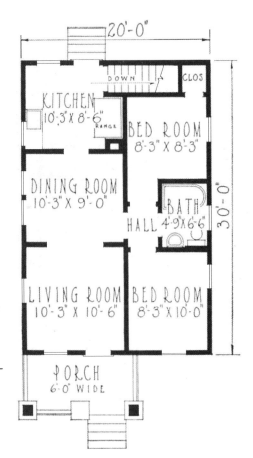

"This fine bungalow is a very popular type, and its low price makes it an exceptional bargain. It is well arranged and compact, with all the modern conveniences and comforts a small family could desire. Hip roof, wide overhanging eaves and exposed rafter ends create a pleasing effect and help to bring out the beauty of straight lines which are so popular in American architecture. It is nevertheless a true bungalow type - a home that looks well and gives an unusual satisfaction wherever it is built. The attractive and roomy front porch, with its overhanging roof and massive pillars, is a feature that adds much to this desirable home.

You appreciate this home the more as you cross the porch and enter the living room, which is nicely arranged as to wall space. From the living room you enter the dining room through a wide cased opening, which gives a most desirable and spacious appearance to these two rooms. The dining room is well lighted by wide twin windows. Another cased opening connects this room with hall. A swing door opens from the dining room into the kitchen. The large kitchen is just large enough to be a real step saving convenience to the housewife. The sink, located under the side window, is only a few steps from the range. Another window is located in the rear wall. Inside steps lead down to the cellar."

- 1927 Wardway Homes

Birchwood - Renamed Wilton in 1928 (1924-1931 Ready-Cut)
Gordon-VanTine Design
1924 ($1462), 1925 ($1433), 1926 ($1433), 1927 ($1487),
1928 ($1565), 1929 ($1586), 1930 ($1560), 1931 ($1492)

"For people who like spaciousness yet want a compact, easy-to-care-for home, the Wilton will have a special appeal. Designed for simplicity - with straight lines that cut down building costs. Yet it has those little attentions to details that set it apart from the usual bungalow sold at this price. Note the low hip roof, sheltering both the house and its porch; the wide belt course above the windows, and especially the extra width of all the windows. They give the maximum of light and cheeriness to the rooms.

The dining room bay breaks the long, straight sidewall, and gives you a little added space - without adding to the foundation costs. The porch buttresses are designed to be built of brick, the final detail in a home radiating comfort. Stepping directly into the living room you find it unusually bright and pleasant, due, in part to the fact thats its wide front window is not shaded by the porch. Living and dining room, joined by a wide arch, make one long pleasant room, and you will appreciate the added spaciousness which the dining room bay will give you."

- 1930 Wardway Homes

24'-0"

ICE BOX	DOWN	CLOS
PORCH 4'-0"x7'-0"	KITCHEN 11'-3"x8'-6"	BED ROOM 11'-3"x11'-3"
	RANGE	

HALL   BATH 7'x5'-9"

DINING RM 12'-3"x11'-3"

BED ROOM 11'-3"x17'-0"

36'-0"

LIVING ROOM 11'-3"x11'-3"

CLOS   CLOS

PORCH 18'-0"x8'-0"

Spanish Beauty

Sonora (1929-1931 Ready-Cut)
Gordon-VanTine Design
1929 ($1440), 1930 ($1490), 1931 ($1478)

"Modern adaptation of the Spanish. Beauty of line and architectural design carried out in smooth, water-proof stucco for lasting charm. This house lends itself particularly well to artistic landscaping. The interior arrangement veers sharply from the simplicity of the Spanish exterior, providing the most modern refinements and conveniences.

A plaster arch leads from the vestibule into a spacious living room with three windows. Dining room shows through another plaster arch at its back. The dining space is increased by a bay window. A door separates these rooms from a hall and sleeping room at the right. The kitchen is just the right size so that everything's conveniently within arm reach. Kitchen case, as well as an extra upper section to be placed over the ice box, is included. There is room for a large range and a nook for a broom closet, which is included. A door leads to the back entry and cellar stairs. The hall connecting the two large bedrooms provides space for a linen closet; each bedroom has ample closet space with shelves, and a towel case is placed above the clothes chute in the bathroom."

-1930 Wardway Homes

An altered *Sonora* in Waterford, Michigan (photograph by Rose Thornton and Dale Wolicki).

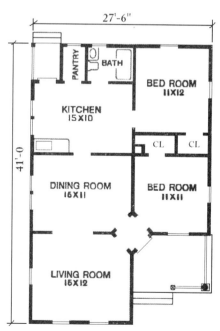

1 Story
Hip Roof
Other

#125 (1909-1914 Not Ready-Cut)
1909 ($574 NRC), 1910 ($574 NRC), 1911 ($ 539 NRC),
1912 ($568 NRC), 1913 (NRC), 1914 ($575 NRC)

"If you are a person of moderate means and desire to build a house that will not put too much strain on your pocketbook, you can put up this 5-room cottage at a small cost and be perfectly satisfied. The architecture is of no special period, and there are no fancy gables or other ornamental work that add to cost; but you can be assured that every stick of timber that we sell to put into this home is of a very good quality. You will notice the unique arrangement of the entrance eliminates all waste of room. Every square inch of space is available. At the same time this cottage has a very pleasing outside appearance."

- *1914 Building Plans of Modern Homes*

Winstead (1922-1928 Ready-Cut)

Gordon-VanTine Design

1922 ($2325), 1923 ($2253), 1924 ($2084), 1925 ($2038), 1926 ($2038), 1927 ($2116), 1928 ($2181)

"When you see the Winstead you feel instinctively that the interior is attractive and convenient. There is charm about the shingled walls, the timbered brackets and the clever handling of the roof lines which makes sure the architect has been as successful within the house as outside. You are not disappointed when you enter".

- 1928 Wardway Homes

A Wardway *Winstead* in Colonial Heights, Virginia
(photograph by Rose Thornton).

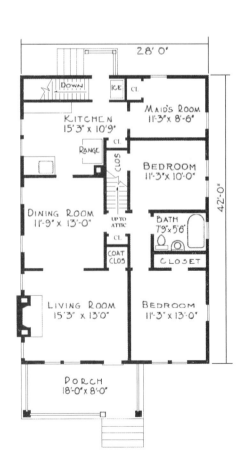

"The Panora"—Material Supplied Either Ready-Cut or Not Ready-Cut

A Universally Popular Four-Bedroom Home

Four-Square

#185 - Renamed Superior in 1917
(1915-1916 Not Ready-Cut, 1917-1929 Ready-Cut)

1915 ($732 NRC), 1916 ($755 NRC), 1917 ($1081), 1918 ($1293), 1919 ($1593),
1920 ($1547), 1921 ($1547), 1922 ($1872), 1923 ($1972), 1924 ($1824), 1925 ($1824),
1926 ($1824), 1927 ($1797), 1928 ($1945), 1929 ($1995)

"The ever popular square type of home is worthily presented in the Superior; such features as the broad cornice, hip roof and attractive dormer being essential to its style of architecture. A belt breaks the monotony of the exterior walls above which a variety of shingles are often used in preference to siding. The style of the porch is in keeping with the house properly."   - 1917 Book of Homes

When Model #185 was introduced it measured 22'-0 x 22'-6" but was enlarged to 24'-0 x 26'-0 in 1917. The polygonial bay window tucked under the front porch is the one feature that helps to identify this model. Model #121 is very similar but it has polygon bay window on one side elevation and a box bay entry on the other.

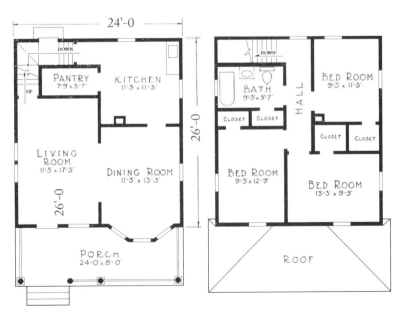

1st Floor   2nd Floor

Illinois (1917-1928 Ready-Cut)

1917 ($1437), 1918 ($2016), 1919 ($2421), 1920 ($2351), 1921 ($2351),
1922 ($2755), 1923 ($2987), 1924 ($2760), 1925 ($2698), 1926 ($2698), 1927 ($2888), 1928 ($2977)

"If you could talk with an owner of an Illinois he would quickly convince you of its merits and advantages. This stately home defies competition and boasts of an ideal interior arrangement. The attractiveness of the exterior is plainly shown in the picture, so we will direct attention to the interior. First of all, note the pleasant arrangement of living room and dining room, both at the front, equipped with sliding doors. An exceptionally large kitchen and a bedroom on the first floor are desirable features under any condition. The entrance to the stairway is cleverly arranged near the center of the house and connects directly with three of the first floor rooms. Four large bedrooms on the second floor offer plentiful sleeping quarters."

- *1918 Wardway Homes*

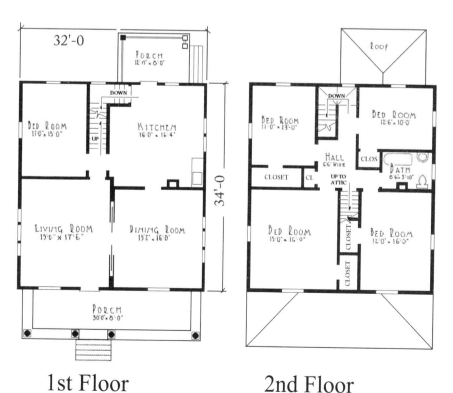

1st Floor   2nd Floor

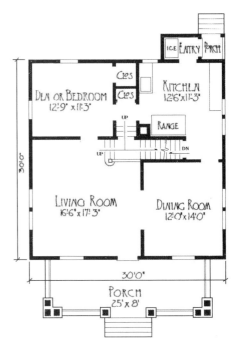

Orlando (1922-1928 Ready-Cut)
Gordon VanTine Design
1922 ($2898), 1923 ($2765), 1924 ($2618), 1925 ($2580), 1926 ($2580), 1927 ($2630), 1928 ($2711)

"This solid, substantial home appeals to all practical persons. The massive effect is produced by the heavy overhang of the main roof by the dormer, and particularly by the great supporting beam on the porch supported by the sturdy columns resting on boxed up piers"

- 1927 Wardway Homes

A perfect Wardway *Orlando* in Beckley, West Virginia (photograph by Rose Thornton).

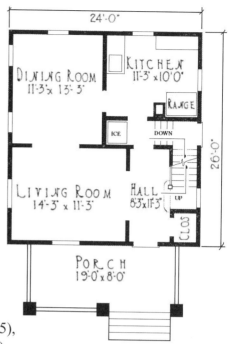

Bellevue - Renamed Milford in 1928
(1922-1931 Ready-Cut)

Gordon-VanTine Design

1922 ($2022), 1923 ($1942), 1924 ($1822), 1925 ($1785), 1926 ($1785), 1927 ($1843), 1928 ($1940), 1929 ($2107), 1930 ($2092), 1931 ($2052)

"For those who are seeking the most value for every dollar put into a house, there is no better choice than a square house. It gives more living space than any other design. Likewise, in the hands of a good architect, it is an impressive home, well lighted and convenient"

-1923 Wardway Homes

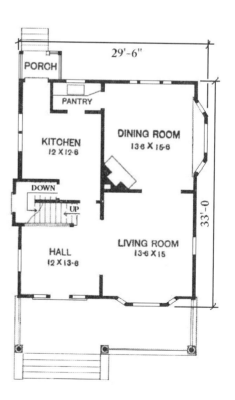

#121 (1909-1916 Not Ready-Cut)

Radford Design

1909 ($1155 NRC), 1910 ($1155 NRC), 1911 ($1001 NRC), 1912 ($1151 NRC), 1913 (NRC), 1914 ($1079 NRC), 1915 ($1232 NRC), 1916 ($1155 NRC)

"Sturdiness and stability stand out in every line of this house. Note how this effect is brought out by the way in which the stone or block foundation is continued to form the balustrade for the front steps. Even the charming bay at the side, instead of being on brackets, is extended to the ground to include the grade entrance, giving a substantial effect that is quite pleasing."

- 1915 Book of Homes

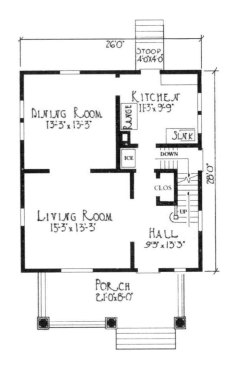

Shirley (1922-1927 Ready-Cut)

Gordon-VanTine Design

1922 ($1975), 1923 ($1958), 1924 ($1798), 1925 ($1765), 1926 ($1765), 1927 ($1928)

"This dignified, conservative home with square lines, hip roof and wide eaves, is very popular because it embodies economy of space, good appearance and maximum comfort. Side walls are of stucco. The porch columns rest on foundations of cement blocks which harmonize perfectly with the stucco walls. The interior could not be better plan for convenience, usable living space and economy."   -1927 Wardway Homes

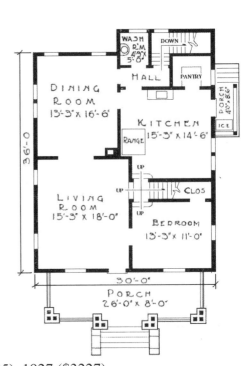

Warrenton (1922-1927 Ready-Cut)

Gordon-VanTine Design

1922 ($2490), 1923 ($3367), 1924 ($3150), 1925 ($3095), 1926 ($3095), 1927 ($3227)

"This handsome residence is planned for a large family. Especially suited to the farm and equally desirable for a city or suburban home. Big porch, massive dormers, broad eaves and twin divided light windows give it a truly distinctive tone. The living room is planned for a big family and the dining room will seat a large number without crowding. The stairways are arranged so they lead directly from living room, kitchen or front bedroom, which may be used as a library or den."   -1927 Wardway Homes

Montville (1922-1928 Ready-Cut)

Gordon-VanTine Design

1922 ($2438), 1923 ($2765), 1924 ($2225), 1925 ($2180), 1926 ($$2180), 1927 ($1947), 1928 ($2310)

"There is a substanial dignity in the handsomely designed and well built square house which makes it an ever popular type and a type always in style. To this advantage is added the maximum of room and the greatest possibilities for convenient arrangement. Before studing the floor plan of our Montville home, note the little arhitectural touches which make it distinctive."

-1923 Wardway Homes

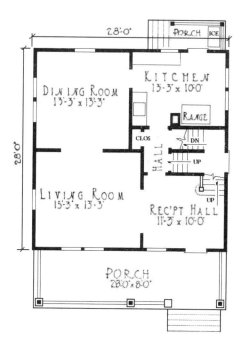

Panora (1922-1928 Ready-Cut)

Gordon-VanTine Design

1922 ($2642), 1923 ($2601), 1924 ($2422), 1925 ($2375), 1926 ($2375), 1927 ($2423), 1928 ($2498)

"The square hip-roof home, when expertly designed, always has an air of spacious dignity and comfort. In the Panora this impression is doubly enhanced by the wide eaves, the dormer, the broad front porch, and the clever placing of the two belt courses. The numerous Colonial windows likewise add to the handsome appearance of the exterior and to the light and cheer within."

-1927 Wardway Homes

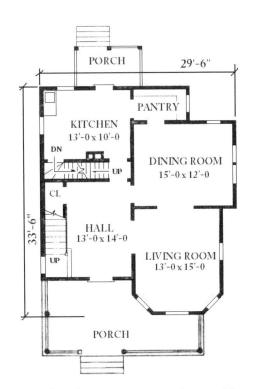

PORCH

29'-6"

PANTRY

KITCHEN
13'-0 x 10'-0

DN

UP

CL

DINING ROOM
15'-0 x 12'-0

33'-6"

HALL
13'-0 x 14'-0

UP

LIVING ROOM
13'-0 x 15'-0

PORCH

#113 (1909-1915 Not Ready-Cut)
1909 ($998 NRC), 1910 ($998 NRC),
1911 ($930 NRC), 1912 ($1076 NRC),
1913, 1914 ($1053), 1915 ($1133)

"Home #113 is a square design in which the squareness has been broken and a pleasing variety obtained by two front bays and by extending the upper floor a short distance over the porch. A belt course sets off the upper part of the house, which can be painted a different shade if desired, and the use of leaded sash and Colonial windows adds a pleasing note. An attractive home and a very good value at our price."

- 1915 Book of Homes

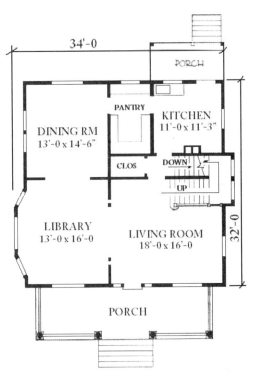

34'-0

PORCH

DINING RM
13'-0 x 14'-6"

PANTRY

KITCHEN
11'-0 x 11'-3"

CLOS

DOWN

UP

32'-0

LIBRARY
13'-0 x 16'-0

LIVING ROOM
18'-0 x 16'-0

PORCH

#120 (1909-1916 Not Ready-Cut)
1909 ($1310 NRC), 1910 ($1310 NRC), 1911 ($1273 NRC),
1912 ($1337 NRC), 1913 (NRC), 1914 ($1375 NRC),
1915 ($1368 NRC), 1916 ($1345 NRC)

"A large, comfortable home, old fashioned in the best sense - that of having plenty of room, especially for the part of the home that is lived in the most. While this home makes an impressive appearance in any location, there is no elborate attempt at ornamentation, and by following the square type a great deal of room is obtained. A good example of the savings our methods mean to home-builder"

-1916 Building Plans of Modern Homes

Norwood (1918-1928 Ready-Cut)

1918 ($1335), 1919 ($16390, 1920 ($1615), 1921 ($1615), 1922 ($1835),
1923 ($1996), 1924 ($1845), 1925 ($1846), 1926 ($1846), 1927 ($1973)

The *Norwood* was Montgomery Ward's version of the Aladdin *Standard* (1913-1922). The Norwood has a small window in the entry coat closet, a belt course above the second floor windows, and fewer windows along the living and dining room facade.

Aladdin Homes *Standard* from their 1918 catalog.

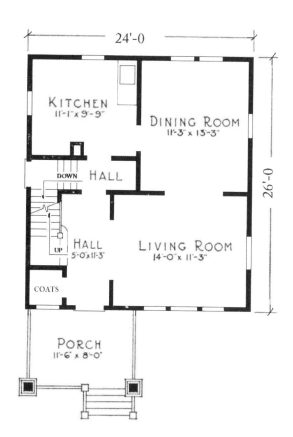

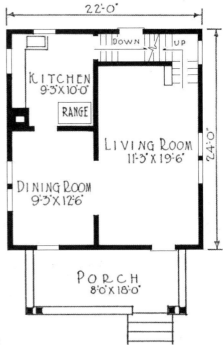

Huron (1924-1928 Ready-Cut)

Gordon-VanTine Design

1924 ($1616), 1925 ($1588), 1926 ($1588), 1927 ($1666), 1928 ($1718)

"This dignified, conservative home with square lines, hip roof and wide eaves, is very popular because it embodies economy of space, good appearence and maximum comfort. Side walls are of stucco. The porch columns rest on foundations of cement block which harmonize perfectly with the stucco walls."

-*1927 Wardway Homes*

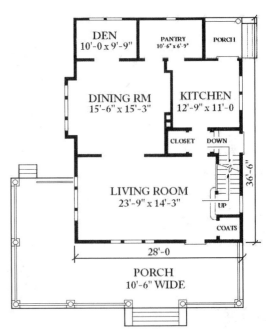

Model #161 - Renamed Indiana in 1917
(1912-1921 Not Ready-Cut)

1912 ($1205 NRC), 1913 (NRC), 1914 ($1090 NRC), 1915 ($1311 NRC), 1916 ($1311), 1917 ($1493 NRC), 1918 ($1987 NRC), 1919 ($2477 NRC), 1920 ($2405 NRC), 1921 ($2405 NRC)

"The Indiana has been designed for those who wish a square type house, with plenty of porch room and all modern conveniences. The Indiana porch is large, wide, roomy - a big, comfortable porch. By extending on two sides there will always be a shady spot. In the interior arrangement, you will note in place of the bedroom usually found on the first floor a larger pantry and a den or sewing room." -*1918 Wardway Homes*

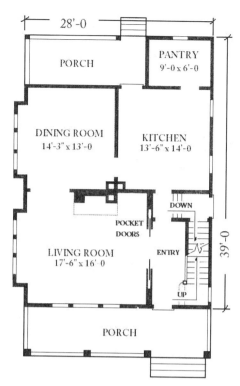

PORCH

PANTRY
9'-0 x 6'-0

DINING ROOM
14'-3" x 13'-0

KITCHEN
13'-6" x 14'-0

28'-0

39'-0

POCKET DOORS

DOWN

ENTRY

LIVING ROOM
17'-6" x 16'-0

UP

PORCH

#160 (1912-1916 Not Ready Cut)

1912 ($1199 NRC), 1913 (NRC), 1914 ($1198 NRC),
1915 ($1208 NRC), 1916 ($1266 NRC)

"For a square house, isn't this about the finest you have ever seen for anywhere near the price? Our architect has certainly surpassed himself. Note the large veranda with its large colonial columns, porch rail and one-inch square balusters. This house also has a large and convenient rear porch."

- *1912 Building Plans of Modern Homes*

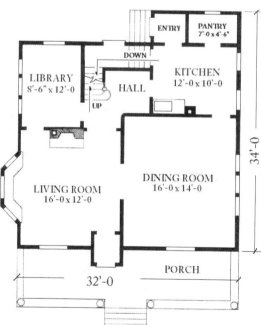

ENTRY

PANTRY
7'-0 x 4'-6"

DOWN

LIBRARY
8'-6" x 12'-0

HALL

KITCHEN
12'-0 x 10'-0

UP

LIVING ROOM
16'-0 x 12'-0

DINING ROOM
16'-0 x 14'-0

34'-0

PORCH

32'-0

#163 - Renamed Jefferson in 1917
(1912-1917 Not Ready Cut)

1912 ($1205 NRC), 1913 (NRC), 1914 ($1245 NRC),
1915 ($1285 NRC), 1916 ($1314 NRC), 1917 ($1425 NRC)

"For the home of a prosperous farmer, or the head of a large household, the Jefferson needs no word of endorsement. Stability, completeness and convenience, are exemplified in every part. A large kitchen with pantry, large well lighted dining room, sleeping room on the first floor, outside entrance to basement, four well lighted sleeping rooms on the second floor, bath, and an abundance of closet rooms - all speak in no uncertain terms of abundance, property and convenience."

1917 Book of Homes

Four Square / Hip Porch

Searcy (1922-1925 Ready-Cut)

Gordon-VanTine Design

1922 ($2975), 1923 ($2834), 1924 ($2648), 1925 ($2648)

"The strong, simple lines of this home bespeak solid, substantial worth. The broad porch with its overhanging roof, the massive columns and newels, combine to give the impression of prosperity and warm hospitality that one who passes must instinctively feel. Comfort and plenty of room was the goal of the designer of the Searcy"

-1923 Wardway Homes

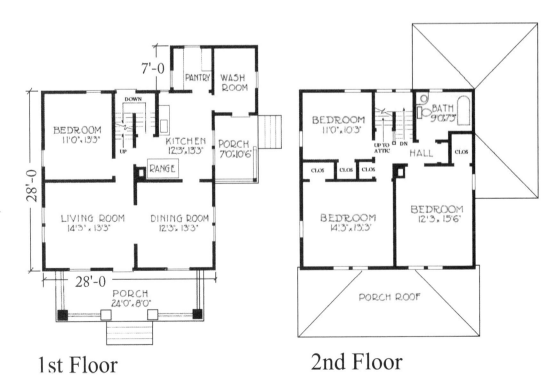

1st Floor   2nd Floor

The McKnight residence in Quinter, Kansas was a Wardway *Searcy* built in 1926. The picture of the house (lower) was taken in 1928. The current owners are Eric and Michele Roesch-Johnson. (photograph by Rose Thornton).

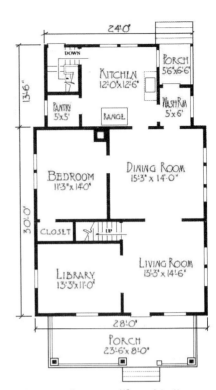

Malverne (1922-1925 Ready-Cut)

Gordon-VanTine Design

1922 ($3042), 1923 ($2988), 1924 ($2756), 1925 ($2745)

"Good planning for the farm home is even more important than for the town house, for it is "lived in" more - to a greater extent it is the center of things. Then, too, the farm home is more a workshop than the city house -espically the kitchen. One cannot send the work out or call in help or feed the threshers at the hotel. So our farm homes are really specially planned. These problems are considered and solutions found."

-1923 Wardway Homes

Montpelier (1922-1925 Ready-Cut)

Gordon-VanTine Design

1922 ($2238), 1923 ($2199), 1924 ($2026), 1925 ($1995)

"The universal appeal of this Wardway home is in its simple, straight lines plus abundant room and real economy of construction. It typifies the value, good taste and all-time satisfaction the big square home always brings to its owner. Consider the details of the exterior of the Montpelier for a moment. Notice the fine balance and correct proportions given by the wide, closed cornice and the generous sized dormer. The large front porch with its sturdy round columns lends an air of strength and dignity."

-1923 Wardway Homes

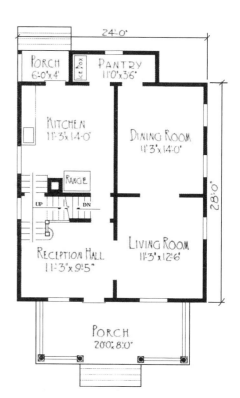

Porch 6'-0"x 4'
Pantry 11'0"x3'6"
Kitchen 11'3"x14'0"
Dining Room 11'3"x14'0"
Range
UP DN
Reception Hall 11'3"x9'5"
Living Room 11'3"x12'6"
24'-0"
28'-0"
Porch 20'0"x8'0"

Camilla (1922-1923 Ready-Cut)

Gordon-VanTine Design
1922 ($2248), 1923 ($2185)

"Because of its dignified, substantial outward appearance, spacious comfort within and economical construction, the square house is a great favorite for town or country. The broad, massive porch, the well proportioned dormer and the wide closed cornice around the entire house, preclude any possibility of monotony and stamp the Camilla as the properly designed home."
                    -1923 Wardway Homes

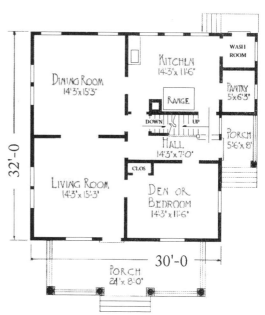

Wash Room
Dining Room 14'3"x15'3"
Kitchen 14'3"x11'6"
Pantry 5'x6'3"
Range
DOWN UP
Hall 14'3"x7'0"
Porch 5'6"x8'
Living Room 14'3"x15'3"
CLOS
Den or Bedroom 14'3"x11'6"
32'-0"
30'-0"
Porch 24'x 8'0"

Miami (1922-1927 Ready-Cut)

Gordon-VanTine Design
1922 ($3135), 1923 ($3067), 1924 ($2828), 1925 ($2775), 1926 ($2775), 1927 ($2888)

"This home represents a combination of all those features desired by most farm folks. The large living room is a feature which everyone wants. You will notice the dining room also is large - in fact, unusually so. This is to accommodate the frequent farm guests and the threshing crew in the summer. The extra room for den, bedroom or farm office is a necessity for the farm home."

                    -1923 Wardway Homes

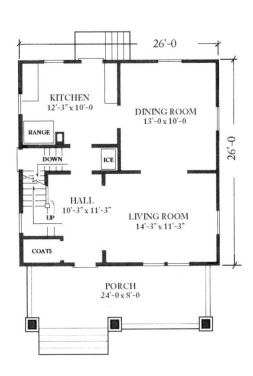

KITCHEN
12'-3" x 10'-0

DINING ROOM
13'-0 x 10'-0

RANGE

DOWN

ICE

HALL
10'-3" x 11'-3"

UP

LIVING ROOM
14'-3" x 11'-3"

COATS

PORCH
24'-0 x 8'-0

26'-0

26'-0

Stanton (1925-1928 Ready-Cut)

Gordon-VanTine Design

1925 ($1960), 1926 ($1960), 1927 ($1993), 1928 ($2055)

"This large, comfortable home gives the greatest possible value for your money. The square house is always economical to building. Although unusually roomy, this house is compact, convenient and easy to heat. It is so well planned that it has none of the plain characteristics of the square house. A well porportioned dormer breaks the otherwise plain roof line, and a substantial eight foot porch extends the full width of the house."
-1927 Wardway Homes

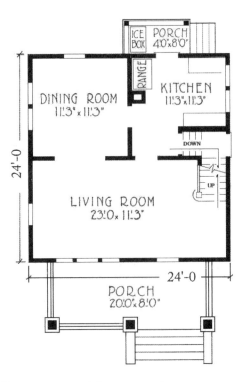

ICE BOX

PORCH
4'0"x8'0"

RANGE

DINING ROOM
11'3" x 11'3"

KITCHEN
11'3"x 11'3"

DOWN

UP

LIVING ROOM
23'0 x 11'3"

24'-0

24'-0

PORCH
20'0 x 8'0"

Colby (1926 Ready-Cut)

Gordon-VanTine Design

1926 ($1773)

Simlar to Sears *Fullerton*

"This stately square home is an exceptional value. Its large pleasant living room with open staircase at one end is indeed delightful and provides plenty of space for a big family. Opening from the living room through a wide arch is a bright well-lighted dining room with its three big windows and swinging door leading to the kitchen. Notice how well the kitchen is planned. It is flooded with light through the twin windows and glass in the rear door."
-1926 Wardway Homes

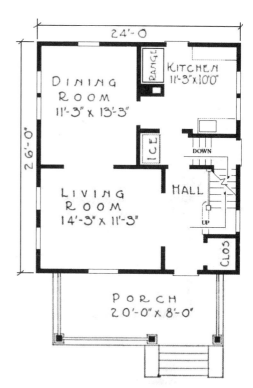

Marley (1925-1926 Ready-Cut)

Gordon-VanTine Design
1925 ($1878), 1926 ($1878)

"A well proportioned, attractive appearing, hip roof home of the square type - a design that is sure to appeal to the builder who is interested in getting the most for his money. The large roomy front porch, the wide eaves, the well-balanced dormer, and the contrasting stuccoed walls above the belt course give a pleasing exterior."

-1925 Wardway Homes

A Wardway *Marley* in Colonial Heights, Virginia (photograph by Rose Thornton).

Masonry, Plumbing, Heating and Electrical Systems Not Included?

The homes that Montgomery Ward shipped (both un-cut and ready-cut), did not include plumbing, heating and electrical fixtures or masonry. Theses items were purchased separately and shipped with the kit home.

The weight and bulk of concrete block and brick made shipping impractical. Most cities had a least one brick or concrete block plant, so financially, it was not practical to ship these materials.

The plumbing, heating and electrical fixtures offered similar challenges. Some of these "modern homes" wcrc more modern than the communities into which they were sold! In the early years of the 20th Century, not every city could boast of municipal water, waste, gas or electrical systems.

Before World War One, plumbing, electrical and heating systems were typically installed by the home owner. Most houses had a handful of electrical outlets, a few light fixtures, and a 30-amp fuse panel. Plumbing was limited to the kitchen sink and maybe a small toilet room. Homes were heated by wood, coal or kerosene stoves. By the 1920s, even modest homes were becoming more modern and increasingly complex with multiple bathrooms, modern appliances, and central heating systems. Contractors and subcontractors with their unique areas of expertise were typically employed. As houses became more complex so did building codes and each municipality had its own unique set of rules regarding installation.

A homeowner in Wisconsin would require a very different heating system than one in Florida. And there were personal options to consider, too. Did the owner prefer a coal-fired steam boiler, a hot water heating system, or perhaps a gravity-fed hot-air furnace?

Given the uniqueness of every lot, the desires of the home owner, the skills of the contractor, and the influence of local ordinances, kit home companies such as Montgomery Ward did not include plumbing, heating or electrical fixtures with their houses.

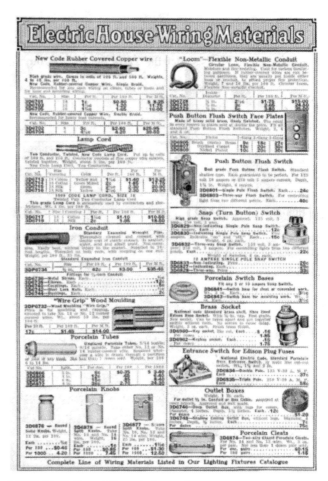

1918 *Building Material* catalog

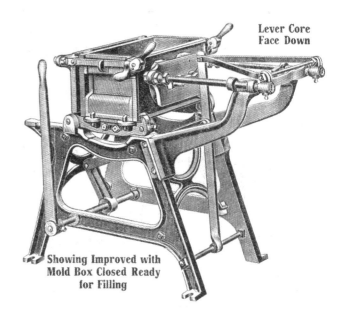

Many thrifty home builders purchased machines from Montgomery Ward and made their own concrete blocks, one at a time. (1918 *Building Materials* catalog.)

"A great many of our customers prefer Warm Air Furnances for the purpose of heating their homes. Warm Air is a moderate priced, quick, satisfactory and economical method of heating" (1923 *Wardway Homes* catalog).

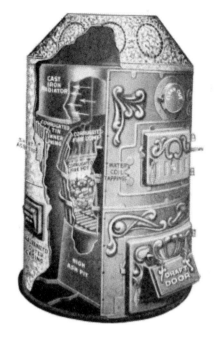

$37⁴⁰ Colonial BATH ROOM Outfit

THIS IS A VERY POPULAR COMBINATION—A HIGH GRADE OUTFIT IN EVERY RESPECT

"We are able to furnish you everything required to complete the entire installation of your plumbing system in your new home, even to the very last detail. Our line of plumbing material is complete. We furnish full plan and instructions, showing how all the different fixtures are connected" (1916 *Book of Homes*).

In rural locations without electrical service, "modern" homes would have their own gas plant to provide for lighting. There was "positively no chance for an explosion of any kind. The generator is removed far from buildings, and the construction made so simple and fool proof that nether carelessness nor ignorance could cause any danger whatever" (1914 *Building Plans of Modern Homes*).

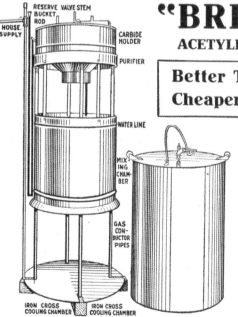

"BRITELITE"
ACETYLENE GAS PLANTS

Better Than Electricity
Cheaper Than Kerosene

There isn't a reason in the world why you should not have all the convenience and satisfaction of a perfect, safe, and sanitary lighting system in your home, and in all the buildings on your premises. You need not envy the homes where electric lighting makes the rooms so bright and cheerful. You can have a light fully as clear, clean and luminous, and actually at less cost than Kerosene. You can combine the excellence of electric light and the cheapness of coal oil, without the high cost of the first and the disagreeable odor of the latter.

A still greater argument for "Britelite" gas outfits is the absolute safety of their operation. There is positively no chance for an explosion of any kind. The generator is removed far from your buildings, and the construction made so simple and fool proof that neither carelessness nor ignorance could cause any danger whatever.

There is no waste of gas, because the plant generates the gas as it is used. There is no accumulated gas stored up, with chances of leakage and loss. Only 20 gallons of water are used for 100 lbs. of carbide; others use 100 gallons for the same quantity.

#116 (1909-1914 Not Ready-Cut)

1909 (Blueprints), 1910 ($720 NRC), 1911 ($634 NRC),
1912 ($711 NRC), 1913 (NRC), 1914 ($673 NRC)

"Commodius eight-room concrete block house, with a large
veranda, the roof of which is supported by concrete block
columns. The house has a cottage roof, and the windows
are of the eastern or Queen Anne - that is, top sash divided
into small lights. The first floor has reception hall, living
room, dining room, kitchen and pantry. The living room has
a mantel. The second floor is reached by an open stairway
leading from the recption hall. This floor has four bedrooms, bathroom and five closets.

The interior finish is of yellow pine, with western pine
doors. Many of our customers finish the hall, living roon
and dining room in oak, and if you wish it this way, write
and state so, and we will quote a price deliverd to your
station. The material for this house can all be shipped in
one car from factory in Northern Illinois. To those of our
customers who live in the far west, we can ship direct from
coast factory, all lumber and millwork."

- 1914 Building Plans of Modern Homes

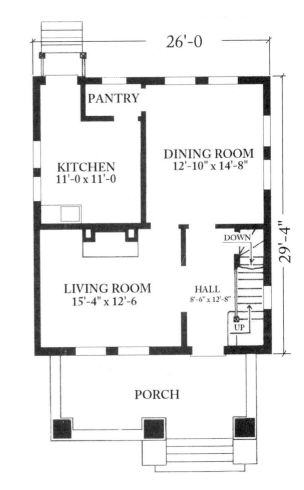

A Wardway *#116* in DesPlains, Illinois that was razed several years ago (photographs by Rebecca Hunter).

Congress - Renamed Argenta 1922 (1917-1927 Ready-Cut)
Gordon-VanTine Design

1917 ($1178), 1918 ($1473), 1919 ($1585), 1920 ($1539), 1921 ($1539), 1922 ($2095), 1923 ($1945), 1924 ($1858), 1925 ($1858), 1926 ($1858), 1927 ($1947)

"The object of the designer of the Congress establishes a departure from the general run of square type houses. To this end he has adapted an attractive gable roofed porch with wide spreading eaves in conformity with the house proper. The front elevation with massive porch piers, large triple window and attractive front door asume a dignity and individuality seldom found in a home of this type."

- 1918 Wardway Homes

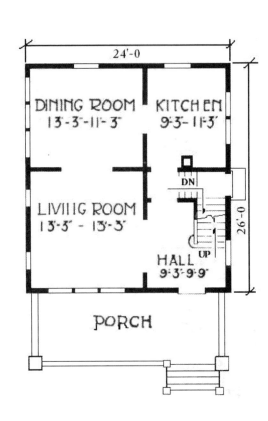

The *Congress* as featured in the 1917 catalog

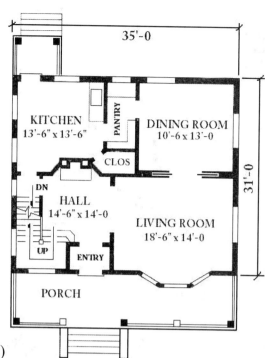

Circle label: Four Square / Concrete Block

#117 (1909-1915 Not Ready Cut)
Radford Design
1909 (Blueprints), 1910 ($968 NRC), 1911 ($908 NRC),
1912 ($960 NRC), 1913 (NRC), 1914 ($992 NRC), 1915 ($998 NRC)

Floor plan labels: 35'-0, 31'-0, KITCHEN 13'-6" x 13'-6", PANTRY, DINING ROOM 10'-6 x 13'-0, CLOS, DN, HALL 14'-6" x 14'-0, LIVING ROOM 18'-6" x 14'-0, UP, EN'TRY, PORCH

"A concrete block house that gives a more graceful appearance than is usual with this type of construction. Concrete block houses are cheaper than stone, and if properly built to form a dead air space between walls and plaster, will be dry and healthful. This design gives a great deal of value for the money."

- 1915 Book of Homes

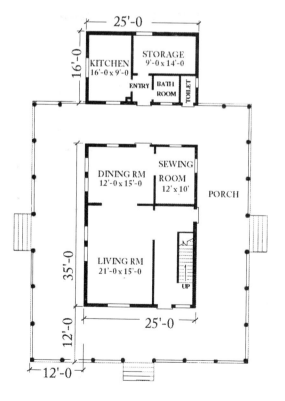

Circle label: Four Square / Concrete Block

#154 (1911-1914 Not Ready Cut)
1911 ($1408 NRC), 1912 ($1483 NRC),
1913 (NRC), 1914 ($1347 NRC)

Floor plan labels: 25'-0, 16'-0, KITCHEN 16'-0 x 9'-0, STORAGE 9'-0 x 14'-0, ENTRY, BATH ROOM, TOILET, DINING RM 12'-0 x 15'-0, SEWING ROOM 12' x 10', PORCH, LIVING RM 21'-0 x 15'-0, UP, 35'-0, 25'-0, 12'-0, 12'-0

"This house was designed especially for a tropical or semi-tropical country. You will note the detached kitchen, which is customary where one does not wish any servant except the serving maid in the house proper. The house has a very fine buffet in the dining room, a nice cabinet in the sewing room, and a very attractive book case in the study. The finish is of yellow pine, except doors, which are of western pine."

-1914 Building Plans of Modern Homes

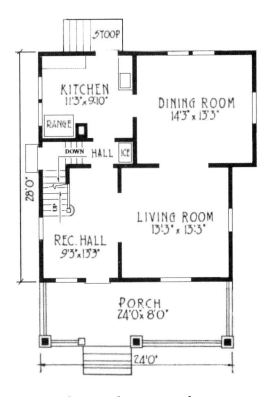

#148 (1911-1914 Not Ready Cut)
1911 ($1328 NRC), 1912 ($1394 NRC),
1913 (NRC), 1914 ($1448 NRC)

"Customers' requirements are especially taken care of in this large, plain house, with no waste of room, and no extra expense on the exterior. Were it not for the especially large porch the house would be plain, but this porch makes of it a very neat appearing house, a house that anyone might be proud to own."

-1912 Building Plans of Modern Homes

Monticello (1922-1923 Ready-Cut)
Gordon-VanTine Design
1922 ($2265), 1923 ($2143)

"This large, square house, dignified and well built, appeals to the conservative buyer who wants a house emphasizing comfort. The simpler designs, which owe their good looks to their fine lines and proportions rather than their decorations, usually are the most enduring types. Such a home as this always will be in good taste - never out of style. The Monticello is the kind of home that wears well."   *-1923 Wardway Homes*

"The Lexington" – Material Supplied Not Ready-Cut Only

FIRST FLOOR PLAN

Size of House
30 feet wide by
22 feet long

SECOND

A Charming Dutch Colonial Home

HOW often we have admired the dignified simplicity and the generous hospitality in every line of the homes of long ago. "The Lexington" with its true Dutch Colonial gambrel roof, shingled walls, shuttered windows and latticed porch retains all the beauty of the rich olden with necessary modern conveniences added. The flower boxes, trellised entrance and porch are touches which add to the charm and comfort within.

Entering, you pass through a vestibule, which has a large coat closet, into a hall. Before you is a beautiful open stairway; to the right the splendid fireplace on the opposite side of the living room meets your eye. Entering the living room you are immediately impressed by its size and the beauty of the French doors leading to the porch. Three other large Colonial windows give an abundance of light and air. The position of the porch at the side gives a greater degree of privacy than one otherwise located.

The dining room is commodious, well lighted and cheery. It offers an excellent location for a buffet along the sidewall between the two windows.

The kitchen is compact and most conveniently arranged and includes our special built-in kitchen case No. 860 as well as a built-in broom closet. The combined rear and grade entrance door is down three steps in an entry in which the refrigerator may be handily reached from the kitchen or iced from outside.

Upstairs are three bedrooms, a bath and a hallway that is well lighted by a twin window in the rear former. The largest bedroom has two closets, while each of the other rooms and the bath has one. An abundance of closet room, as you see. One of the deep shelved linen closets is located in the hall just outside the bathroom door, convenient to all bedrooms.

A feature of this house is that the four walls are at the front and rear, absolute assurance that your neighbors cannot build close enough to darken your rooms.

A basement under this house will give ample room for furnace, fruit cellar and laundry if desired. We furnish our plans so as to give proper

Gambrel Dutch Colonial

Harvard - Renamed Cornell 1930 (1917-1931 Ready-Cut)

1917 ($1271), 1918 ($1478), 1919 ($1709), 1920 ($1659), 1921 ($1659), 1922 ($1842), 1923 ($1970), 1924 ($1875), 1925 ($1875), 1926 ($1875), 1927 ($1969), 1928 ($2030), 1929 ($2179), 1930 ($2179), 1931 ($2496)

"The Harvard offers a wonderful living room. Big and spacious, extending the entire depth of the house. Windows on three sides keep it bright and cheery. The handsome Colonial fireplace makes the room even more inviting. The Harvard is big and roomy throughout – an excellent home for the larger family – yet it is priced so low and Ward's payments are so easy that the family of moderate income and average circumstances can easily arrange to build. Wherever you build this home, it will be the outstanding house on the street. The true colonial design is always in style – always distinctive, always imposing. You will be surprised at the greater social activity your family will enjoy when you live in the aristocratic Harvard. Don't put off the wonderful experience of building this home of your own another month.

Every room – every detail was designed just the way you would probably plan it yourself. There are no odd, space-wasting corners. The distinctive entrance with its quaint dutch seats leads into a convenient vestibule. The dining room is to the left of the roomy center reception hall. The living room is to the right and the colonial staircase with a handy closet beside directly ahead. The ever popular sun porch leads from the dining room. We predict the big bright kitchen which you will want to equip in the new color in vogue will be the handsomest, most pleasant "workshop" in your neighborhood! Four bedrooms, a bath and center hall presents the most convenient, most private arrangement of rooms you can imagine. Every bedroom is bright and airy having cross ventilation and an outlook on two sides. The centrally located bath will be a beautiful room when you have decorated it in pure white or in one of the new color combinations so popular today."

- 1929 Wardway Homes

A Racine, Wisconsin *Harvard* (photograph by Rebecca Hunter and Dale Wolicki).

The *Harvard* was among Montgomery Ward's most popular models but is difficult to identify given the abundance of Dutch Colonial style residences. The hooded entrance porch with its seats has frequently been altered and the six/six sash windows may have been replaced. The second floor dormer is perhaps the one feature that remains intact, its side walls pulled inward from the floor below. The *Harvard* is similar to the *Cambridge*, both measuring 32' x 22'.

1st Floor

2nd Floor

Cambridge (1927-1931 Ready-Cut)

1927 ($2144), 1928 ($2210), 1929 ($2377),
1930 ($2489), 1931 ($2398)

*"The Cambridge faithfully conforms to that old
delightfully Dutch Colonial architecture that so
characterized the early Knickerbocker residences in
Pennsylvania and New York. In this design, Wardway
architects have maintained every modern comfort
and convenience demanded by people of today. You
will enjoy the charm and character of this home - the
low sweep of the gambrel roof - the massive fireplace
chimney - the cozy sun parlor - the shuttered windows
- and the hospitable hooded entrance."*

- 1931 Wardway Homes

The *Cambridge* and the *Harvard* are similar in appearence and both measure 32' x 22' but the *Cambridge* features a semi-circular entrance hood and
paired 4/4 swinging window sash in the upper floor
bathroom.

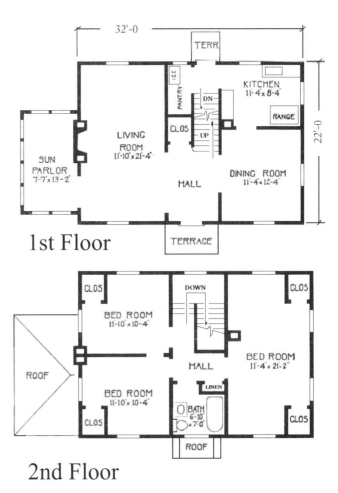

1st Floor

2nd Floor

A 1928 *Cambridge* in East Lansing, Michigan (photograph by Dale Wolicki).

This *Cambridge* in Park Ridge, Illinois was the residence of J.A. Webb, Manager of Wardway Homes. The original hood above the entrance was replaced some years ago (photograph by Dale Wolicki).

Dutch
Colonial
Side Gable

Lexington - Renamed Sovereign in 1929 (1922-1930 Ready-Cut)

Gordon-VanTine Design

1922 ($2625), 1923 ($2663), 1924 ($2375), 1925 ($2375), 1926 ($2375),
1927 ($2464), 1928 ($2540), 1929 ($3100), 1930 ($3100)

The *Lexington* and the *Sylvan* are identical in appearence but the *Lexington* measures 22' x 36' and has a slightly different floor plan.

"How often we have admired the dignified simplicity and the generous hospitality in every line of the homes of long ago. The Lexington with its true Dutch Colonial gambrel roof, shingled walls, shuttered windows and latticed porch retains all the beauty of the early home with necessary modern conveniences which radiate the cheer and comfort within. Entering, you pass through a vestibule - which has a large coat closet - into a hall. Before you is a beautiful open stairway; to the right the splendid fireplace on the opposite side of the living room greets your eye. Entering the living room you are impressed by the size and beauty of the French doors leading to the porch. Three other Colonial windows give an abundance of light and air. The position of the porch at the side gives a greater degree of privacy than one otherwise located."   - 1924 Wardway Homes

1st Floor

2nd Floor

A Wardway *Lexington* in Irwin, Pennsylvania (photograph by Dale Wolicki).

Dutch Colonial Side Gable

Sylvan (1917 Not Ready-Cut)
1917 ($1261 NRC)

"Artistic? Who would say it is not artistic? Not a harsh line in its entire designing. Note how pleasingly the dormer lines are combined with the broken roof lines ... the graceful curve of the portico roof ... the overhanging cornice ... the square type lattice panels of the sun porch."
— *1917 Book of Homes*

The *Sylvan* and the *Lexington* are identical in appearence but the Sylvan is smaller measuring 24' x 30' and has a slightly different floor plan. It appears the *Lexington*, introduced in 1922, was a revision of the earlier *Sylvan* but given the four year gap these houses are considered seperate models.

Larchmont (1931 Ready-Cut)
1931 ($3196)

In 1931 the *Lexington/Sovereign* was redesigned and renamed the *Larchmont*, the latter have significant differences so that it is considered a differnt model.

"Destined to be the Aristocat of any neighborhood - architecturally beautiful and impressive. Exactly the kind of home you've always pictured as fulfilling all the joys of living. Of Dutch Colonial heritage, the Larchmont is considered by many to be our finest home. The beautiful treatment accorded the roof in this Dutch Colonial is really the key to its genuinely comfortable appearance. Note how the eaves swing outward - how that portion of the roof extending over the sun porch blends perfectly into the lines of the main roof; making it inseperable, harmonious part of the whole."

- 1931 Wardway Homes

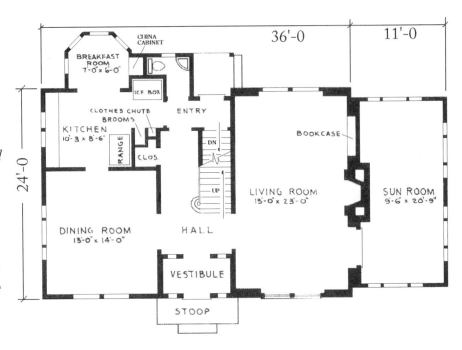

Princeton-1st - Renamed Elizabeth 1929 (1926-1931 Ready-Cut)
Gordon-VanTine Design
926 ($2348), 1927 ($2329), 1928 ($2398), 1929 ($2632), 1930 ($2578), 1931 ($2440)
Similar to Sears *Oak Park*

"To live in the Elizabeth brings happiness, comfort, and the respect and esteem of others. Study the picture – close your eyes – imagine the Elizabeth built on your own lot. You can own it! Ward's Easy Payment Plan makes that possible. A lot and a few hundred dollars – that's all you need. And in a few weeks you can move into this home of your own. Striking, distinctive – the low gambrel roof, wide dormers, quaint slatted blinds, wide bevel siding and delightful hooded entrance make it so. The Elizabeth adds dignity to any neighborhood. You enter through a vestibule into a large, pleasant hall. Convenient clothes closet, living room, kitchen, and colonial staircase are reached from this hall. On the right side of the hall is a wide cased opening, the entrance to the long pleasant living room. In cool weather one of the greatest charms will be the cheerful, open Colonial fireplace. Terrace door at one end leads to cool porch, which will be most popular all summer long."
                        - 1929 Wardway Homes

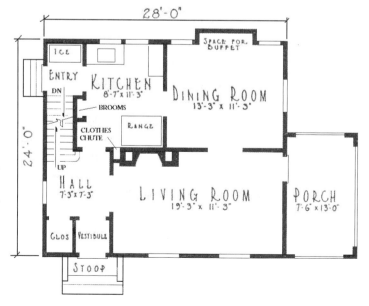

Cranford (1929-1931 Ready-Cut)
1929 ($1728), 1930 ($1875), 1931 ($1855)

The *Cranford* is a distinctive design easily identifed by the large faux front gable that disguises the gambrel roof. Although the model house featured a stucco exterior accentauted by half-timbering, shingles and wood siding were alo popular. The living room can have four narrow double-hung sash windows or three standard size double-hung sash windows.

"It is astonishing how much space can be tucked away under a gambrel roof. The Crandford is the ideal home for a narrow or shallow lot. For it is only 24 wide and 22 feet deep, yet it has six rooms unusually big and pleasent. The English half timbered style is always distinctive. Here it is carried out in stucco with gable beams in dark weathered brown. The steep gable, hooded entrance with its timbered door and the casement window above are distinguishing details seldom found in a house which can be built for so little. "

— *1930 Wardway Homes*

This *Cranford* in Charleston, West Virginia is a perfect example with stucco exterior accentua ted by half-timbering, four narrow living room windows, and timber door (photograph by Rose Thornton).

A Valpariso, Indiana *Cranford* (photograph by Dale Wolicki).

A Western Springs, Illinois *Cranford* used for advertising in 1931 (photograph by Rebecca Hunter).

A two-story side-gable Wardway *Cranford* in Hinsdale, Illinois (photograph by Rebecca Hunter).

An unaltered Wardway *Cranford* In Lansing, Michigan (photograph by Dale Wolicki).

A Wardway *Cranford* in Berkley, Michigan (photograph by Dale Wolicki and Rose Thornton).

Salem (1928-1931 Ready-Cut)
1928 ($2096), 1929 ($2237), 1930 ($2296), 1931 ($2238)

Although it was offered for only a few years the *Salem,* Montgomery Ward's version of Sears *Puritan* (1922-1929) was very popular. They arc identical in appearance, size and floor plan. The two features that distinguish between the Salem and the Puritan: the first floor windows aside the entrance of the *Salem* features six-over-one sash windows while the *Puritan* features eight-over-one sash windows; the attic gable of the *Salem* has a fan-light window while the *Puritan* has a larger round top window.

The Sears *Puritan* as featured in the 1926 catalog.

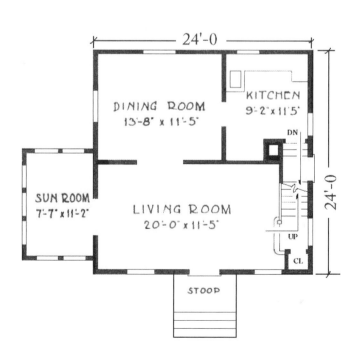

A Wardway *Salem* in Glen Ellyn, Illinois (photograph by Rebecca Hunter).

A Wardway *Salem* in Lansing, Michigan (photograph by Dale Wolicki).

20'-0

28'-0

KITCHEN
7'-6" 12'-0

DINING RM
11'-0 x 15'-6"

PANTRY

DN

LIVING ROOM
19'-0 x 10'-0

UP

PORCH

Model #155 - Renamed Maine in 1917
(1911-1916 Not Ready-Cut)

1911 ($525 NRC), 1912 ($560 NRC), 1913 (NRC), 1914 ($587 NRC),
1915 ($604 NRC), 1916 ($624 NRC), 1917 ($693 NRC)

"Home #155 presents a pleasing variation of home #129 while giving the same exceptional value for the money. The gambrel roof is very popular from the standpoint of both appearance and practicability and by extending the second story over the porch it is possible to add a bathroom." — *1915 Book of Homes*

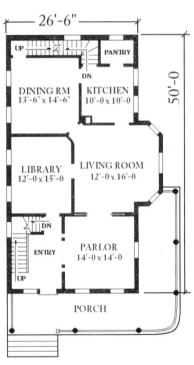

26'-6"

50'-0

UP

PANTRY

DN

DINING RM
13'-6" x 14'-6"

KITCHEN
10'-0 x 10'-0

LIBRARY
12'-0 x 15'-0

LIVING ROOM
12'-0 x 16'-0

DN

ENTRY

PARLOR
14'-0 x 14'-0

UP

PORCH

Model #153 (1911-1914 Not Ready-Cut)

1911 ($1183 NRC), 1912 ($1245 NRC), 1913 (NRC), 1914 ($1260 NRC)

"Concrete block houses have become quite common within the last three or four years time. This is due to the fact, no doubt, that they can be constructed much more cheaply than brick or stone ... We believe you will agree with us that this is the most attractive concrete block house you have ever seen."

-1915 Building Plans of Modern Homes

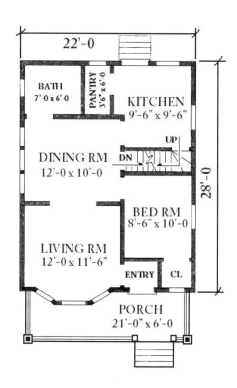

Dutch
Colonial
Front
Gable

22'-0

BATH
7'-0 x 6'-0

PANTRY
3'-6 x 6'-0

KITCHEN
9'-6" x 9'-6"

DINING RM
12'-0 x 10'-0

UP
DN

BED RM
8'-6" x 10'-0

28'-0

LIVING RM
12'-0 x 11'-6"

ENTRY   CL

PORCH
21'-0" x 6'-0

Gary "B" (1917 Ready-Cut)
1917 ($866)

"Three of our very popular homes are shown in the Gary A, B and C. You will notice the same floor plan is used in each, but the roof and porch plans vary to avoid any tendency to monotony should a contractor desire to build several of these homes on adjacent lots."

- 1917 Book of Homes

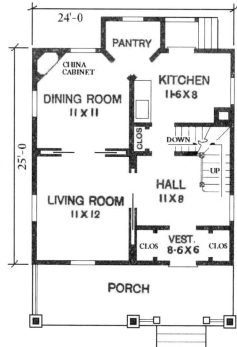

Dutch
Colonial
Cross
Gable

24'-0

PANTRY

CHINA
CABINET

KITCHEN
11-6 X 8

DINING ROOM
11 X 11

CLOS

DOWN

UP

25'-0

LIVING ROOM
11 X 12

HALL
11 X 8

CLOS

VEST.
8-6 X 6

CLOS

PORCH

Model #115 (1909-1916 Not Ready-Cut)
1909 ($773 NRC), 1910 ($773 NRC), 1911 (NRC), 1912 ($750 NRC), 1913 (NRC), 1914 ($762 NRC), 1915 ($898 (NRC), 1916 ($958 NRC)

"For $898.00 we will furnish the materials required to build this home, consisting of all lumber, lath, shingles, trim, medicine cabinet, hardware, sash weights, pipe and gutter, and painting material. We absolutely guarantee the material we furnish to be sufficient to build the house according to our plans and specifications."

- 1915 Book of Homes

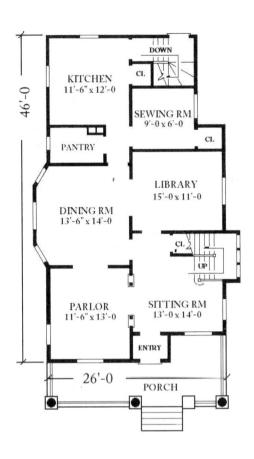

Model #176 (1914-1916 Not Ready-Cut)
1914 ($1097 NRC), 1915 ($1267 NRC)

"For $1267.00 we will furnish the material to build this ten room house, consisting of all lumber, lath, shingles, flooring, finishing lumber, doors, windows, frames, trim, colonnade, china closet, medicine case, sash weights, hardware, pipe and gutter, building paper, and painting material."

- 1915 Book of Homes

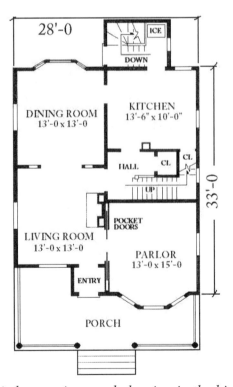

175 (1914-1916 Not Ready-Cut)
1914 ($1206 NRC), 1915 ($1195 NRC), 1916 ($1275 NRC)

"The gambrel roof is the distinctive feature, setting off an exterior that is harmonious and pleasing in the highest degree, while permitting an unusually good arrangement of room and closets on the second floor. Likewise it is an economical form of construction because the roof virtually forms the second floor. Notice the straight lines of the porch roof, carried unbroken around the entire house"

-1915 Book of Homes

The
New York
$2043
Not Ready-Cut

A Duplex
Building
of
Moderate
Price

24 feet wide by 42 feet deep

The above price is for the material un-cut. Ready-cut price is - - - $2194

Here's an investment worth while. Did you ever stop to consider the financial return on an investment of this kind? There are many families today owning a duplex house who have made their payments from the regular income obtained from renting either the upper or lower floor, while making the other floor their home. The proportionally greater cost over the single house or bungalow is insignificant when compared with net profit.

To a person considering a purchase of this kind, the New York should certainly appeal. The usual unwieldy and cumbersome appearance of the duplex house has been overcome in this design. Many single houses cannot boast of such good proportion.

The front entrance is common to both first and second floors. This feature alone tends to conceal the duplex type.

The arrangement is practically identical on both floors. A large living room with prominent bay, a well proportioned dining room and convenient kitchen, all well lighted, comprise the living apartments. Two bedrooms, with a closet opening off each, a bath, sleeping porch and back porch complete the arrangement. How seldom do you find a duplex house with a sleeping porch.

Take another look at the picture, then at the floor plans and compare the price with similar houses and you will realize the saving you will make by purchasing the New York.

New York Specifications

Material list for this home follows the general specifications as given on pages 4 to 7.

Porch, 24 feet 6 inches x 8 feet. Center sill, 6x8 inches. Wall plates, 2x6 inches. Floor joists, 2x8 inches. Studding and rafters, 2x4 inches. Ceiling joists, 2x6 inches. Hip rafters, 2x6 inches. Attic floored through center. Height of ceiling, 9 feet each floor.

Front door, first floor, 3x7 feet. Whittier design, bevel plate glass with side lights. [...] vestibule first floor. Whittier d[...]
floor. Back doo[...]
Inside doors, 5-cros[...]
Casement window[...]

So many
families that [...]
making no change [...]
omit attic floor and [...]

Multiple Family

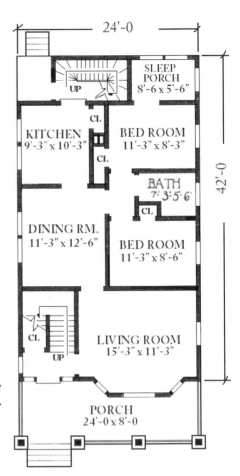

New York Duplex (1917-1921 Ready-Cut)

1917 ($1998), 1918 ($2194), 1919 ($2587), 1920 ($2346), 1921 ($2346)

"Did you ever stop to consider the financial return on an investment of this kind? There are many families today owning a duplex house who have made their payments from the regular income obtained from renting either the upper or lower floor, while making the other floor their home."

- 1918 Wardway Homes

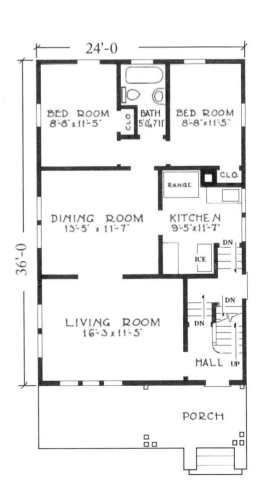

Ferndale Duplex (1928-1931 Ready-Cut)

Similar to Sears *LaSalle*

1928 ($2265), 1929 ($2456), 1930 ($2526), 1931 ($2526)

The Ferndale was offered as a Duplex but some examples have been converted into single-family residences.

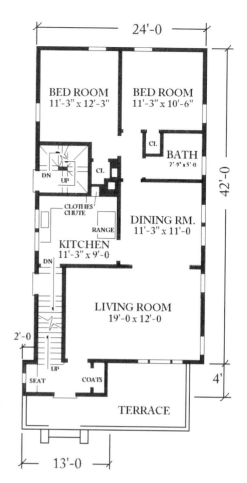

Parkside Duplex (1930-1931)
1930 ($3143), 1931 ($3143)

"You can build and live in this beautiful home, and let your tenant help pay for it. Brick veneer front with stucco and half-timbered front gables; sides and back stucco as pictured and priced. May also be built with all stucco gables, shingle or bevel siding if you prefer."

- 1930 Wardway Homes

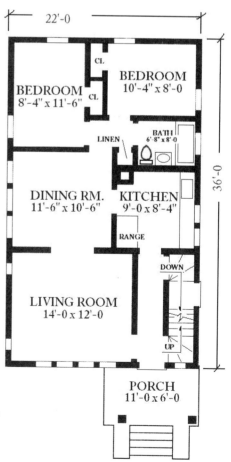

Cortland Duplex (1930-1931 Ready-Cut)
1930 ($2687), 1931 ($2497)

"The Cortland offers convincing proof that two families can live in a home of unusual beauty and comfort for the amount of rent usually paid by one. If you are the owner of this fine duplex, you can collect rent, make it meet your payments and in a short time own the home outright. Wide bungalow siding combined with stucco gables, with English half timbering of unusual beauty, give this home the dignity and charm of an Old Country Manor."

- 1930 Wardway Homes

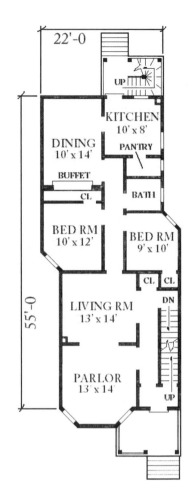

#145 Duplex (1911-1914 Not Ready-Cut)
1911 ($1389 NRC), 1912 ($1464 NRC), 1913 (NRC), 1914 ($1471 NRC)

"A two-flat building designed so it can be built on a 25 foot lot. Oak interior finish, hardwood floors, and oak veneered doors, with six rooms and bath on the first floor, and seven rooms and bath on the second. We show this with frame construction, but if you so desire, we will quote on construction of brick, brick veneer, or concrete blocks."

- 1914 Building Plans of Modern Homes

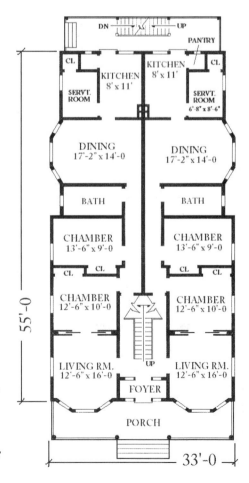

#169 Four-Flat (1914 Not Ready-Cut)
1914 ($2853 NRC)

"This illustration is from an actual photograph, showing a most attractive four-flat building. The appearance is that of a double house, rather than an apartment building. Note the wide, roomy veranda and balcony, extending across the full front of the house. Each apartment has six rooms and bath."

- 1914 Building Plans of Modern Homes

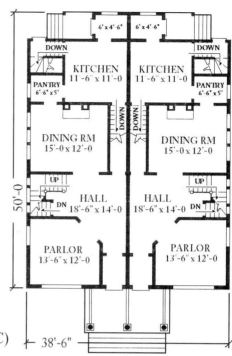

#111 Duplex (1909-1915 Not Ready-Cut)

1909 ($1824 NRC), 1910 ($1824 NRC), 1911 ($1952 NRC),
1912 ($2050 NRC), 1913 (NRC), 1914 ($2007 (NRC), 1915 ($2087 NRC)

"Where one has sufficient ground room, it is a good idea to erect a double house, for you can build at much less expense than for two single houses. This house has a sloping roof from the ridge to the front, with a dormer in the center; a veranda with one roof but divided in the center by porch rail, making each porch seperate from the other."

- 1914 Building Plans of Modern Homes

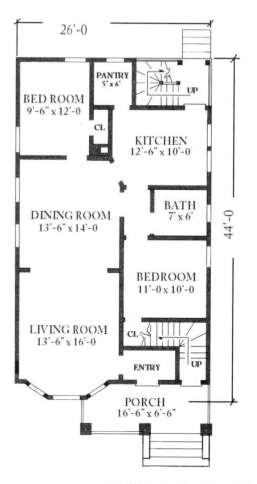

#194 - Renamed Richmond in 1917
(1916-1921 Not Ready-Cut)

1916 ($1178 NRC), 1917 ($1479 NRC), 1918 ($2031 NRC),
1919 ($2269 NRC), 1920 ($2223 NRC), 1921 ($2223 NRC)

"Here is another duplex house, somewhat different ... yet perhaps with just as many commendable features. It is, indeed a worthy rival"

- 1917 Wardway Homes

Bibliography

Aladdin Homes; Various catalogs from collection of authors.

American Builder and Building Age;
  How General Motors Builds Homes; March 1928
  Mail-Order Competition Bringing Dealers and Builders Together: Pfund; June 1931

Architects' Small House Service Bureau; *How to Plan, Finance and Build Your Home*; Denver; 1922.

Asher, Louis E. & Edith Heal. *Send No Money*. Chicago, IL: Argus Books, 1942.

Bennett Homes; Various catalogs from collection of authors.

Bruce, Alfred and Sandbank, Harold, *A History of Prefabrication*, Raritan, NJ: The John B. Pierce Foundation Housing Research Division, 1945.

Building Age; *Sears, Roebuck turns Builder*; April 1930; National Trade Journals, Inc.; New York City.

Business Week;
  We Start to Manufacture Homes; March 2, 1930
  Quantity Production Reaches the Home Builder; March 26, 1930

Chicago Daily Tribune; April 5, 1931; *Sell More Ward Homes in 1931 Last Year*

Columbus (Ohio) Dispatch; *Retail Resurrection -Montgomery Ward name is back as an Online Catalog*: January 15, 2008

Emmet, Boris & Jeuck, John. Catalogues and Counters, *A History of Sears Roebuck and Company*. Chicago, IL: The University of Chicago Press, 1950.

Fortune; April 1933; *Mass-produced Houses in Review*; Time, Inc.; Chicago, Illinois

Gordon-VanTine Homes; Various catalogs from collection of authors.

Halliday Homes; Various catalogs from collection of authors.

Harris Homes; Various catalogs from collection of authors.

Henry, Les; *Catalogue Houses, Eaton's and Others*; Henry Perspectives; Saskatoon, Canada; 2001.

Hoge, Cecil, C.; *The First Hundred Years Are The Toughest: What We Can Learn From the Century of Competition Between Sears and Wards*. Berkeley: Ten Speed Press, 1988.

Hunter, Rebecca; Montgomery-Ward Blueprints for Model #185

Lewis-Liberty Homes; Various catalogs from collection of authors.

Montgomery-Ward catalogs, collection of authors
     1909 *Book of Building Plans*
     1910 *Book of Building Plans*
     1910 *Building Materials*
     1911 *Building Plans of Modern Homes*
     1912 *Building Plans of Modern Homes*
     1914 *Building Plans of Modern Homes*
     1915 *Book of Homes*
     1915 *Building Materials*
     1916 *Book of Homes*
     1917 *Book of Homes*
     1918 *Wardway Homes*
     1918 *Building Materials*
     1919 *Wardway Homes*
     1920 *Wardway Homes*
     1921 *Wardway Homes*
     1922 *Wardway Homes*
     1922 *Home Heating*
     1923 *Wardway Homes*
     1924 *Wardway Homes*
     1925 *Wardway Homes*
     1925 *Building Materials*
     1926 *Wardway Homes*
     1927 *Wardway Homes*
     1928 *Wardway Homes*
     1929 *Beautiful Wardway Homes*
     1930 *Beautiful Wardway Homes*
     1930 *Building Materials*
     1931 *Beautiful Wardway Homes*
     1931 *Building Materials*
     1931 *Wherever You Go! Montgomery Ward & Company, Wardway Homes*

Montgomery Ward & Co; *The History and Progress of Montgomery Ward & Co*: Chicago, IL: Montgomery Ward & Co. 1925.

Nye, David E. *Electrifying America: Social Meanings of a New Technology*, Cambridge, Massachusetts: The MIT Press, 1990.

Pacific Homes; Various catalogs from collection of authors.

Radford, William; *Radford American Homes*; Chicago; 1903

Scott County, Kentucky; Trust Deed for J.A. and Eva Tolman. Book 46 Page 277.

Sears, Roebuck and Company Homes; Various catalogs from collection of authors.

Southern Pine Association; *Homes for Workmen*; New Orleans, 1921.

Sterling Homes; Various catalogs from collection of authors.

Thornton, Rose;
   The Houses That Sears Built; Gentle Beam Publications; Alton, Illinois; 2002
   Finding the Houses That Sears Built; Gentle Beam Publications; Alton, Illinois; 2004

Thornton, Rose & Wolicki, Dale; *California Kit Homes – A Reprint of the 1925 Pacific Ready Cut Homes Catalog*; Gentle Beam Publications; Alton, Illinois; 2004

Wolicki, Dale & Todd Dore; *Aladdin Homes: Comfortable, Convenient and Cozy*; American Bungalow; Summer 2003.

Wolicki, Dale; *The Historic Architecture of Bay City, Michigan*; Bay County Historical Society; Bay City, Michigan; 1998

To re-order

Montgomery Ward's Mail-Order Homes

Please send $34.95 + $5 shipping and handling, to:

Gentle Beam Publications
P. O. Box 3472
Portsmouth, Virginia 23701

This book can also be ordered online at
www.wardwayhomes.com

This book is available at quantity discounts for bulk purchases.